Nexus Analysis

Nexus Analysis introduces a new and exciting theory by two of the leading names in discourse analysis and provides a practical fieldguide to its application.

People, places, discourses, and objects form the key elements of social action. 'Nexus analysis' allows participants to explore these elements and trace their historical trajectories towards actions, in order to anticipate their outcomes.

Using as a study their own experience of pioneering computer-mediated communication in Alaska in the late 1970s and early 1980s, the authors conduct a 'nexus analysis' of those events and discourses. As email and audio/video conferencing technologies expanded the possibilities for education and social interaction, the authors played an active role in shaping and analyzing their use. Looking back on that early formative period and assessing its impact on the present world, the authors evaluate moments of social importance in order to examine the linkages among social practices, Alaskan peoples, and technologies. They consider the power of communication media to cause and ramify change.

In this intellectually captivating yet accessible book, Ron Scollon and Suzie Wong Scollon provide the reader with a working example of a new theory in action, as well as a personal and engaging snapshot of a key moment in the history of communication technology, as Internet technology transformed Alaskan life.

Ron Scollon is Professor of Linguistics at Georgetown University, USA and is Editor of *Visual Communication*. **Suzie Wong Scollon** is Network Coordinator, Associated Sociocultural Research Projects, Georgetown University, USA. Their book: *Discourses in Place: Language in the Material World*, was published in 2003 by Routledge.

Nexus Analysis

Discourse and the emerging Internet

Ron Scollon and
Suzie Wong Scollon

Routledge
Taylor & Francis Group

LONDON AND NEW YORK

First published 2004 in the USA and Canada by Routledge
29 West 35th Street, New York, NY 10001

Simultaneously published in the UK by Routledge
11 New Fetter Lane, London EC4P 4EE

Routledge is an imprint of the Taylor & Francis Group

© 2004 Ron Scollon and Suzie Wong Scollon

Typeset in 11/13pt Perpetua by Graphicraft Limited, Hong Kong
Printed and bound in Great Britain by MPG Books Ltd, Bodmin

Every effort has been made to ensure that the advice and information in this
book is true and accurate at the time of going to press. However, neither the
publisher nor the authors can accept any legal responsibility or liability for
any errors or omissions that may be made. In the case of drug
administration, any medical procedure or the use of technical equipment
mentioned within this book, you are strongly advised to consult the
manufacturer's guidelines.

Library of Congress Cataloging in Publication Data
A catalog record for this book has been requested

British Library Cataloguing in Publication Data
A catalogue record for this book is available from the British Library

ISBN 0-415-32062-3 (hbk)
ISBN 0-415-32063-1 (pbk)

Contents

Preface

On a dark December day in 1980 when the temperature was nearly 40 degrees below zero and the valley in which Fairbanks, Alaska, lies was filled with choking ice fog that glittered brilliantly in the campus lights, Suzie Scollon proposed an idea to Ron Scollon that radically changed our lives. Five years before the invention of the Internet she proposed that we use the internal electronic mail system of the University of Alaska Computer Network (UACN) to teach university classes, to communicate among faculty, and to communicate between faculty and students who lived across the 1280-mile span of Alaska where there were UACN facilities – from Kotzebue on the Arctic Coast to Ketchikan in the Tongass rain forest of southeast Alaska, a distance about the same as the distance from Dublin to Budapest.

At the Center for Cross-Cultural Studies in the School of Education of the University of Alaska in Fairbanks Suzie was teaching students in remote villages of Alaska in the Cross-cultural Educational Development program. This partial distance education program used a complex system of plane travel for teachers and students, mailed correspondence, and the very new university audio conferencing network. Ron was teaching graduate students in education on campus in Fairbanks. Suzie had learned of the university's existing electronic mail system (UACN) which was present through network terminals in most offices of the university. This system was built on the ARPANET structure and was among the very first non-military email networks. Suzie's proposal was that we should first learn how to use this forbidding system to talk among colleagues who were spread throughout a state that was an expanse of mountains, rivers, glaciers, and forest and of vast tundra plains. Then if we could do that we should try it with students.

A month later in January 1981 we began to use email conferencing to teach the graduate education course 'Language, Literacy, and Learning'. We believe that this was the first time this medium was used in the US in credit-bearing university instruction. This was a face-to-face course taught on campus which we augmented by requiring each student to engage with the class discussions via an email conference. We followed in September of 1981 with a course delivered statewide via email and audio conferencing with the title, 'The Social Impact of Instructional Telecommunications'.

At the same time that we were doing these courses Suzie held an evaluation contract with the University of Alaska Instructional Telecommunications Consortium to investigate and evaluate television, electronic mail, audio and video conferencing media in the distance delivery of all university services and administrative work. Ron conducted projects with the National Endowment for the Humanities and the Alaska State Department of Education. Together we organized a professional development seminar under a grant from the Andrew Mellon Foundation to examine common traditional classroom teaching practices to contrast those practices as they are restructured through the use of new media.

All of these projects were directed toward one fundamental issue: Improving the access of Alaska Native people to public institutions – educational, medical, legal, and economic – from which they were being systematically excluded, largely on the basis of communicative technologies and practices.

We use the term 'nexus analysis' to cover this wide range of projects. The original meaning of the word 'nexus' is a link between two different ideas or objects which links them in a series or network. So in the simplest meaning a 'nexus analysis' is the study of the ways in which ideas or objects are linked together. For some analysts who have an interest in business or economics, a nexus analysis is usually the preliminary study you would make before you opened a business in a new location, a new city, or even a new country. You'd want to know about the power and water supplies, the socio-political structure, patterns of taxation, and the availability of materials and of labor. Our interest as ethnographers is in social action and so for us a nexus analysis is the mapping of semiotic cycles of people, discourses, places, and mediational means involved in the social actions we are studying. We will use the term 'nexus of practice' to focus on the point at which historical trajectories of people, places, discourses, ideas, and objects come together to enable some action which in itself alters those historical trajectories in some way as those trajectories emanate from this moment of social action.

Another way to put this is to say simply that nothing happens in a social and political vacuum. Thirteen years before we began the projects that we describe in this book, in 1968, huge oil deposits were discovered at Prudhoe Bay on the Arctic coast of Alaska. With so much money in oil sales and resource development at stake it was a nerve-wracking thought that nobody really knew to whom this oil belonged. A suit was brought by Alaska Natives against the US government claiming ownership not just of that land but all of present-day Alaska. After very difficult negotiations the Alaska Native Claims Settlement Act of December 18, 1971, was passed by Congress. This act extinguished claims to the lands of Alaska by Alaska Native people in exchange for a cash settlement, the title to large portions of land, and other health and human services. These settlements were located in thirteen new Alaska Native regional corporations. In this way the world oil trade and the legal claims of Alaska Native people formed two cycles in the nexus we were involved in.

In 1972 the Alaska Native Language Center was formed by the government of Alaska with the mandate to provide research and materials development to enable the use and preservation of Alaska Native languages. Thus pressures to finalize the legal relationship of Alaska Natives to the US Federal Government were coupled with state legal pressures to support and maintain the cultural and linguistic independence of Alaska Natives within these new socio-political structures.

Yet another theme which constituted this nexus was that two years later in 1974 the US Supreme Court in the Lau vs. Nichols decision mandated that all children who spoke languages other than English should be given education in bilingual education programs. In Alaska this created a tremendous pressure both on the schools themselves to deliver these mandated educational services and on the university, particularly such entities as the Alaska Native Language Center, to conduct the research, materials development, and training that it would take to respond to these legal requirements. And in 1976, just two years later, the so-called 'Molly Hootch' case was settled. This was a class action suit against the State of Alaska the result of which was to require 126 villages across the state to build, staff, and maintain high schools for children in those villages rather than sending those children away from their homes to boarding schools one or two thousand miles away as had happened in the past.

In the broadest cycle of this nexus, the world system, all of this was occurring at the height of Cold War tensions between the US and the Soviet Union. The longest border the US shares with another country is neither the Mexican border to the south nor the two Canadian borders, but the border with Russia (the former Soviet Union). Interestingly, as we note in Chapter 4, the exact length of this border is either not known or not disclosed by either of the relevant nations, Russia and the United States. Because these two superpowers were only two and one-half miles apart at the closest point, these Cold War dynamics were always present in the rest of the socio-political issues of the time.

This was the environment in Alaska into which we arrived in 1978 when Ron took up a position at the Alaska Native Language Center. Within this nexus we will discuss in this book there were huge problems to be solved and significant state and federal legal mandates to adhere to as Alaska Native people began to form the world's largest land corporations and health and social services corporations while at the same time they were struggling to regain control of their own languages and education. The work of linguists and educators was at the very center of this maelstrom of social, cultural, political, legal, and economic activity.

In the pages of this book, then, you will read of two things. In the first place we will give what can be really only a very brief view of our activities as linguistic anthropologists who, in becoming embroiled in the hectic pace of social change in Alaska in those few years, played some role in developing modes of communicating that were then almost unknown outside of Alaska but are now quite common in daily life, principally email communications. Our intention was mainly focused on educational and organizational life. Our interest in that aspect of this work is to analyze with some care the ways in which practices of discourse form linkages with the affordances and constraints of technological modes of communication.

The second, and for us the most important, part of this work, is to delineate through using it a way of doing ethnographic discourse analysis which we are calling *nexus analysis*, the study of the semiotic cycles of people, objects, and discourses in and through moments of socio-cultural importance. 'Nexus analysis' may be a new term within the domain of discourse analysis; for us, however, it picks up a theme which we began to develop before going to take up our work in Alaska. In two working papers written in 1977 we tried to apply the concept of the dissipative structure to socio-cultural structures – languages, speech communities, idiolects, and phonological systems. In our work in Alaska this very new model which had been put forward by Ilya Prigogine and others informed our interest in finding and working within the complex nexus of practice that we have described just above.

Ultimately in a firestorm of activity during the period between 1978 and 1983, our work was carried out across a wide range of organizations in the State of Alaska, the Yukon Territory, and British Columbia as well as in what are called 'the Lower 48 States' from California and Idaho to Washington, DC. Because of our consultation, teaching, and training activities throughout the tertiary education system in Alaska, fifteen units of the University of Alaska spread across some 1280 miles were observed, including all three main campuses (Fairbanks, Anchorage, and Juneau), several community colleges (Nome, Bethel, Sitka, Tanana Valley, Kodiak, and Ketchikan), and several rural regional centers (Dillingham, Fort Yukon, McGrath, Nome, and Tok). We also worked on projects directly for the statewide university administration in their Fairbanks office and for the University of Alaska Instructional Telecommunications Consortium in Anchorage. Besides these we worked with the other two tertiary institutions in Alaska, Alaska Pacific University and Sheldon Jackson College, as well as with Yukon College in Yukon, Canada.

In addition to these tertiary education organizations we did projects and workshops in and for seventeen or more public schools in ten school districts centered in Dillingham, Anchorage, Fairbanks, McGrath, Tanana, Juneau, Ketchikan, Tok, Glennallen and Fort Yukon. In the Iditarod School District we did training in seven schools (Holy Cross, Grayling, Shageluk, Nikolai, Telida, McGrath, and Anvik). For the State of Alaska we did training and projects for more than half a dozen agencies including the Legislative Teleconferencing Network, the Judicial Council, the Department of Fish and Game, the State Troopers' Academy, Fairbanks Memorial Hospital, and the Bethel Regional Health Service. Other Alaskan non-federal agencies included the Tanana Chiefs Conference, the Western Regional Resource Center, the Interior Villages Association, the Fairbanks Association for the Education of Young Children, the Fairbanks Emergency Services Center (911 call center), and the Alaska Resource Managers Training Center. US Federal agencies for which we did projects and in which we were able to make observations that are used in this research include the National Endowment for the Humanities – both the nationwide programs and the Alaska Humanities Forum. We also conducted training in interethnic communication for the National Interagency Fire Center.

The reader might wonder why we are only now writing about these projects and activities that took place some twenty years ago. There are two answers to that question. In the first place, we did write a good bit about that work at the time, but what we wrote was sharply focused on just specific projects and topics. We ourselves did not have the time or the perspective to step back and gain a view of the fuller nexus of practice in which we were working then. In a few words we were just too busy to get the whole picture at that time. Each project led to the next, often before there was any time to stop and produce a written report for circulation outside of the nexus of practice in which we were engaged.

But there is another reason as well. We did actually produce a compilation of published papers, conference papers, and internal reports, particularly focusing on our work in developing the use of telecommunications in distance delivery of educational and administrative programs. We showed that to publishers in 1984. They rejected it saying that there would be no audience interested in such marginal educational experiments as using telecommunications to conduct university classes or for communication among university administrators. We need to remember that it was still a year after that, in 1985, that most historians of the Internet give as the beginning of the true Internet when the US National Science Foundation issued the grant to establish the NSFNET. When we were doing these projects and writing about them it was simply impossible for most publishers and for most of the public to imagine the way in which computer communications would develop over these next twenty years. We had a book then but no audience.

Our purpose in writing now is to return to this set of action and research projects we did in Alaska between the years of 1978 and about 1983 and to set out formally the dimensions of an action research strategy based on ethnographic discourse analysis as applied by participants in a social network. As in any case of an open-ended self-organizing system, what Alaskan social and communicative life has become in the twenty years since we did this work can never be imagined to be a linear outcome of the work or actions of any one or two people or entity or relationship, and certainly there were and are people who were working in Alaska before us and who have remained and have continued working as actively as we were working then. Thus we make no claims other than to say that, when it comes to using new media technology in organizational and educational communication, we were there very near the beginning. Further, we did engage in a large number of comparative activities across many organizations in which we took both active agent-of-change roles and observational-analytical roles.

It is this small latter claim that is the basis of our writing now. Our experiences and the data we collected and reported on at that time give us a framework for analyzing both the constellations of social practices that make up such entities often called 'institutional discourse', 'Alaska Native communicative style', 'academic discourse', or 'professional presentation' and the like. In the two decades that have passed since then together with colleagues in several fields we have developed an analytical framework that allows us to analyze the affordances and constraints of communicative media as mediational means in social actions. Taken together, then, this book analyzes the nexus which links socio-cultural communicative practices or events on the one hand and technological media of communication on the other. It provides an analytical framework that encourages the reader to engage in nexus analysis as an active participant toward the end of social change.

The projects and activities that we describe in this book depended entirely on the support and assistance of many people and many agencies. It is daunting to even try to remember now twenty years later how very many people were involved and it is humbling to realize just how much whatever we did depended upon their prior work, their support, and their encouragement.

During our work at the University of Alaska we held academic, research, or consultation positions with the Alaska Native Language Center, the Center for Cross-cultural Studies, the Alaska Native Studies program, the University of Alaska Instructional Telecommunications Consortium, and the Cross-cultural Educational Development program. While the directors, heads, and coordinators of these programs did not always agree with the results of our work they were, to a person, always supportive well beyond any requirements of either their positions or of ours. And so we wish to express our gratitude to Mike Krauss and Irene Reed of the Alaska Native Language Center, Ray Barnhardt of the Center for Cross-cultural Studies, Mike Gaffney of the Alaska Native Studies program, Jane Demmert of the University of Alaska Instructional Telecommunications Consortium, and Pat Dubbs of the Cross-cultural Educational Development program.

Former University of Alaska, Fairbanks, Chancellor, Howard Cutler, maintained an interest in our work and was very helpful in providing both materials and feedback on several of our reports. The subsequent Chancellor, Pat O'Rourke, is one of the few higher-level university administrators we know of with a vision not only of the degree of restructuring required of modern universities but also of the ways in which that restructuring might be accomplished. We wish to thank him for his support through his Computer Awareness Program which Ron Scollon directed for the Academic Year 1982/3.

The Professional Development Seminar was generously supported by a professional development grant from the Andrew Mellon Foundation. We wish to thank former Vice Chancellor F. Lawrence Bennett for providing us with support for that seminar and Cecilia Martz who participated as a research assistant on that project.

Our research on telecommunications was supported by a contract to Suzie Scollon from the University of Alaska Instructional Telecommunications Consortium. We wish to thank the Director, Jane Demmert, for her support of this research.

The National Institute of Education supported part of this research through their Grant No. G-80-0185 to Ron Scollon for the period October 1980 to December 1981. We wish to thank NIE for this support as well as to say that the National Institute of Education is in no way implicated in the findings of our research.

For the period of February 1981 to May 1981, Nita Towarak and Dawn Weyiouanna worked as graduate assistants on this research. As students they were able to conduct interviews of both faculty and students from a point of view impossible for faculty researchers to encompass. As students they also suffered the considerable anxiety of being caught 'in between' us and our 'subjects'. The quality of data achieved in non-focused research such as this is achieved at the cost of fairly high levels of personal stress. Vickie Shine was our research assistant from September 1981 to January 1982. We wish to thank these graduate assistants for bearing up under much more stress and for providing a much higher level of insight than they got paid for.

Students in many of our courses granted their permission to participate in these studies. Many participated substantially in the Professional Development

Seminar by agreeing to discuss the teaching and videotapes with both the research assistant and the faculty member from whom they took the course. It is out of concern for confidentiality that we do not thank them by name but our appreciation for them is immense.

The research group studying rhythm consisted of the authors, Ron and Suzie Scollon, as well as Carol Barnhardt, Bob Maguire, Meryl Siegel, and Cecilia Martz. Frederick Erickson participated during the summer of 1981. We wish to thank them all for much fruitful discussion.

Many faculty members of the University of Alaska, Fairbanks, provided specific comments on a preliminary paper and report which was disseminated in the Spring of 1981. Gerald McBeath, Judy Kleinfeld, Robert Smith, Joe Gross, Chris Lambert, and Sue McHenry provided many important insights and critical commentary.

Much of our thinking has been formulated in discussions with people at the Laboratory of Comparative Human Cognition at the University of California, San Diego. We wish to thank Jim Levin for a constant flow of ideas and questioning via electronic mail as well as in person both in Fairbanks and in San Diego. We also want to thank Mike Cole, Peg Griffin, Luis Moll, Esteban Diaz, Lonnie Anderson, and Robert Rueda for many discussions of literacy, electronic information technology, institutions, and the impacts of these on members of ethnic minorities, which we were able to pursue as Visiting Scholars at the Lab in the Spring of 1982.

Throughout our time at the University of Alaska we enjoyed Friday evening chats with Dennis Demmert, Howie Van Ness, Mike Gaffney, and Russ Currier. Much of the pleasure of doing such work lies in the long and informal discussions of the institution which take place in such events.

In March of 1982 under the Chancellor's Computer Awareness Program Ron Scollon was able to invite Bertram C. Bruce and Andee Rubin, then of Bolt, Beranek, and Newman to Alaska to introduce their QUILL project, a project funded by the US Department of Education which used microcomputers in writing classrooms. Carol Barnhardt and Bonnie Bless-Boenish, both of whom had been students in the first of these electronic networks emerged to take on the establishment of the Alaska QUILL project. While our own involvement was by then minimal, we wish to express our appreciation for the energy and insight with which they picked up this important thread of the discourse and carried it forward.

Gary Holthaus, Executive Director of the Alaska Humanities forum, and Richard Dauenhauer and Nora Dauenhauer of the Sealaska Heritage Foundation were constant and mostly unfunded research companions in the development of these projects, as were Courtney Cazden, John Gumperz, and Susan U. Philips with whom we were able to have extended discussions of our work on their visits to our projects in Alaska.

Two institutions which were also very important were Alaska Pacific University in Anchorage and Sheldon Jackson College in Sitka. While we did not conduct formal research in these two institutions, our other consultation work during these years provided a continuous source of comparative insight. We wish to express our appreciation to our colleagues in those institutions for many thoughtful discussions on the nature of the contemporary university.

Rachel Scollon and Tommy Scollon were among the first of the world's children to see the university invade the privacy of their home in the form of their parents' email conferencing. It would be impossible to express how much we learned then and continue to learn from their reflections on our own social interactions as well as from their own beginning uses of this new communication technology.

Coming forward to the present, our thinking about nexus analysis was first presented in the Martin Spector Lecture in Applied Linguistics at Pennsylvania State University in October of 2002. We wish to thank James P. Lantolf, Director of the Center for Language Acquisition for inviting Ron to give this lecture and for interesting discussion during our visit to State College. Preliminary versions of the Fieldguide (Appendix) were used at the seminar on Mediated Discourse Analysis at the University of Aalborg, Denmark, in November of 2002. We wish to thank the participants in that workshop as well as Paul McIlvenny and Pirkko Raudaskoski, the organizers, for much stimulating discussion and very useful feedback on our still fledgling rethinking of our earlier work. A visit to Marilyn Whalen's Knowledge, Interaction, and Practice Area of the Palo Alto Research Center to present at the PARC Forum allowed us to think through some of these ideas within a corporate research environment which gave us very important feedback on how to conceptualize our work and we wish to thank Marilyn Whalen and the other members of her group as well as Jack Whalen for important critical discussion.

Students in Georgetown University's sociolinguistics program who took 'Mediated Discourse Analysis' in the Fall of 2002 and 'The Ethnography of Communication' in the Spring of 2003 used the Fieldguide and provided important responses to these materials from which this book has benefited greatly and we wish to thank them for their patience in working with ideas that were still in the process of formulation. In writing we have benefited from research assistance from Peter Vail for which we are very grateful.

Finally, we are grateful to a number of readers of this book in manuscript form who have made very useful suggestions for reorganization or re-emphasis. These readers include Mike Gaffney and Helen Frost, who were involved in these projects from the beginning. Their perspectives on these events across two decades have been most helpful. We have also profited from readings of the whole manuscript by Sigrid Norris, Rodney Jones, Andy Jocuns, Ruth Wodak and Rachel Scollon. We only wish that we could find the time and the words to make the book address all of their interests and concerns.

1 Discourse analysis and social action

The president of an organization stretched across the span of Alaska with main offices in Anchorage, Fairbanks, and Juneau and six subsidiaries decides to save time and travel costs by using video conferencing to conduct routine monthly meetings with his vice-presidents in those other sites. After three months he decides that they will return to face-to-face meetings rotating among the three main offices. He has become uncomfortable with the quick rise in power within the group of one of his vice-presidents. The vice-president's easy video style coupled with a carefully placed background design for the video conferences has quickly, if subtly, begun to undermine the older president's well-practiced rough and ready ability to control the flow of discussions and the decision-making processes of face-to-face meetings.

A traditional university graduate seminar adds an email list discussion to the normal in-class discussions of readings and topics in the third week of class. A student who has not yet spoken in class sends a message that evokes a strong and interested response from many of the other students. In the energetic discourse which follows this student writes, 'This is the first time in my life twelve people are paying attention to me at once. I feel like I am speaking for the first time.'

A legislative hearing is being held by audio conference. Legislators in the State Capitol, Juneau, are hearing from citizens as far away as two days' air travel in the Aleutian Islands on current pending legislation having to do with changes in the delivery and accessibility of health services. A woman in Unalaska makes an impassioned plea not to cut the services of traveling doctors and nurses. As she makes her plea the only legislator remaining in the room stands up and leaves the room. Her plea is not recorded nor is it heard by anyone in Juneau other than the researchers who are present in the audience seating portion of the room.

Discourse and technology

The events in these three stories happened between 1978 and 1983. We were observers of these events in each case. In each case the events took place in English and in each case a form of social interaction – a business meeting, a university seminar, and a legislative hearing with regular and well-understood and well-habituated practices – was restructured through good intentions and for good purposes by using the very new technologies of the video conference, email, and the audio conference. In each case the social relationships, forms of power, and accessibility of some individuals was significantly altered in relationship to others within the same situation. While the business meetings using video were quite useful for the rising vice-president they were at the point of becoming disastrous for the president. A student who had interesting ideas found that he could express them to his classmates and the teacher for the first time. Conversely, of course, other students who were accustomed to holding the attention of the seminar group in face-to-face classes were somewhat sidelined. Perhaps legislators are quite accustomed to ignoring the representations given in public hearings, but rarely do they feel they may simply walk out of the room. Common face-to-face politeness practices tend to hold them to their seats and to hold a listening posture on their bodies. Freed from these restrictions by the audio conference, they were able to simply leave the room to do other things.

Discourse and technology are intimately related to each other, but in order to highlight this point we need first to clarify what we mean by the term 'discourse'. In the simplest and most common sense we take discourse to mean the use of language in social interaction. We would refer to a 'good morning' greeting, a conversation, a telephone call, a personal letter from a friend, or an email message as discourse. But we would also include a municipal ordinance, a state law, a text assigned as a university reading, a memo from the Chief Justice of the State Supreme Court to the Judicial Council, or a report on sentencing patterns based on ethnicity to be discourse as well. All of these entail the use of language to accomplish some action in the social world.

We will argue that for each of these forms of discourse and for all others we have not mentioned there is a supportive or enabling technology. When we think of technology perhaps it is most common to think of the video conferencing cameras and display screens (as well as the very complex and extended system of studios, satellite up- and down-linking equipment, and the satellites themselves) or the similar audio conferencing or email systems we now so often use to communicate. It is important for us to remind ourselves that all discourses are based on technologies, though some of them are considerably simpler and much older and more naturalized in our practice than others.

All of the texts in our lives are based on a very long tradition of printing technology. This technology of the printed text is so old that what Bourdieu might have called 'phylogenesis amnesia' has set in. He used the term 'genesis amnesia' to refer to an individual's erasure of the memory of having learned a practice. We were not born reading, but for most of us there is very little memory left of the process of learning this rather complex technology of moving from printed codes on paper or now computer screens to meanings. We have so deeply naturalized the processes of using this technology that it is all but invisible to us. We just use it as part of 'ourselves'. We might think, then, of 'phylogenesis amnesia' as the process by which we have collectively lost our memory of when and how these technologies were first invented, implemented, and became embedded in the social matrix of our societies.

One reason the newer media technologies remain so visible in our lives and in television, magazine, and newspaper accounts is just because they are still so very new. They have not yet sunk into invisibility through genesis amnesia. Most of us have not yet fully naturalized our use of new media technology. Further, these technologies are still changing so rapidly that it is almost a liability to sink our ability to use them into patterns of habit as those habits will only need to be disrupted again in a short time when the new models come out running on different software and performing functions that are as yet almost unimaginable.

Even more fundamental than print technologies are the technologies of face-to-face social interactions that we recognize simply as 'meetings', 'classes', 'clinical consultations', 'public hearings', 'arrests', 'court trials', and the rest. We engage in these as common events and most researchers would likely refer to them as small group organizations, speech events, or genres of discourse. Here we are interested, however, in calling attention to the technological under-pinnings of these speech events or common action genres. Why is it difficult to hold a clinical consultation in a classroom? Why would a seminar be difficult to hold in a courtroom? Why is it a problem to try to hold a business meeting of several participants in an airport lounge? Each of these and the other genres of social interaction we could name works best (not exclusively, of course) when it is supported by very specific requirements for the structure of the spaces in which it occurs as well as the material mediational means that are available for the participants to use in conducting their activities.

A face-to-face meeting must be supported by quite definable material requirements. If the meeting is among hearing participants they must be within hearing distance of each other. If they are not hearing participants but sighted ones, they must have line-of-sight contact. This, in turn, places a restriction on how many people can be participants on an equal basis within a specific-sized physical space. Because eye-gaze is so crucial for the sighted in managing turn exchanges and the social structures of showing attention, participants who are given open access to the gazes of others are positioned as more active and engaged participants. Conversely, control of interaction can be technologized as it is in a court room by building separate physical spaces for each interactive role – the judge, the jury, witnesses, and the like. In a medical clinic or in a hospital spaces and structures are supplied on which the patient can be examined, for example, in a supine position, with the examiner's medical instruments within easy reach. Typical lecture rooms are designed so that one person, the lecturer, may roam throughout as much as one-third of the total space in the room while listeners are confined in small chairs aligned in rows oriented panopticon-style (see Chapter 3) with a view only toward the lecturer.

Discourse, when we take it in the meaning defined above ('the ways in which people engage each other in communication'), is technologized through a very wide range of material supports and extensions from the structure of the built environment and its furniture to the media by which communication may be moved across the distances of time and space such as printed texts, pictures, microphones, telephones, video and audio conferencing systems, and email or other digital-electronic systems.

But we have also said that we will use the term 'discourse' in a second level of meaning. James Paul Gee has defined a higher level of meaning for the term discourse which he refers to as 'Discourse with a capital "D"' (1999). For him this is:

> different ways in which we humans integrate language with non-language 'stuff,' such as different ways of thinking, acting, interacting, valuing, feeling, believing, and using symbols, tools, and objects in the right places and at the right times so as to enact and recognize different identities and activities, give the material world certain meanings, distribute social goods in a certain way, make certain sorts of meaningful connections in our experience, and privilege certain symbol systems and ways of knowing over others.
>
> (Gee 1999: 13)

We are much in sympathy with Gee's concept and his definition and will use it throughout this book, but we feel that there is rarely any confusion between the two levels of discourse and so hereafter will dispense with the use of a capital 'D' in writing of discourse in this broader sense.

Jan Blommaert gives us what is perhaps a more useful definition of discourse in that it is more concise than that of Gee. For Blommaert, discourse 'comprises all forms of meaningful semiotic human activity seen in connection with social, cultural and historical patterns and developments of use' (forthcoming: 6). Like Blommaert, many authors would prefer to use the more general term, semiotics, to take in this broader concept of discourse. In Chapters 2 and 5 where we talk about 'discourse cycles' we will also use the term 'semiotic cycles' because there is much more than language involved in producing these discourses.

In this broader sense of discourse there are several different discourses involved in the three examples we gave at the outset of this chapter. In the first we see a good example of what we might call 'management discourse'. This is the way managers or administrators talk (as well as dress, move, and act) in and among themselves in carrying out their day-to-day work. And here it is important to note in Gee's definition that a central piece of this discourse, like all discourses, is producing and maintaining certain identities and power relations. In this vignette it was the shifting of these identities and power relations that led the president to abandon the video conferencing technology in conducting his monthly meetings.

Management discourse is sharply different from the 'academic discourse' we find in university classrooms. In the university seminar room one signals a positive identity through such means as displaying comfort and control with the assigned readings and their often new vocabulary and technical definitions. One of the central goals of this discourse which is expressed by university faculty is to bring students into membership in the academic and disciplinary community as we shall see in Chapter 6. What students say and how students talk is a crucial part of this socialization. As we shall also see, this is not the view taken by many students. Whereas faculty tend to see academic discourse as a means to make students more like faculty, particularly in their own discipline, students tend to see the university on analogy to a supermarket – a place where one goes to shop for ideas, concepts, and tools that will be useful for them to meet their own and different goals.

In the third example we saw a kind of 'public discourse' in which elected officials and citizens communicate toward the ostensible goal of improving governance and social life within the political jurisdiction. Again, this is a rather different discourse in Gee's broad sense. Roles and responsibilities are distributed differently – the citizen's role is to inform, plead with, or persuade the elected official. The legislator's role is to act on behalf of citizens within a highly complex discourse called the legislative process. Unlike management discourse in which an elite in-group of managers works to manage and control a complex system of employees and production processes, or academic discourse in which the goal of faculty is to bring apprentice outsiders into full membership on the basis of their ways of thinking, acting, talking, and writing, this public discourse requires a somewhat paradoxical role on the part of legislators. On the one hand they must be seen to be providing services and representation for citizens – often through giving the appearance of co-membership with them in the community – on the other hand, they must manipulate their continued rise in power within the political and legislative process both on behalf of those citizens and as a careful manipulation of those citizens. Put quite simply, a legislator who is seen as unable to be manipulative *on behalf of* his or her constituency would not be likely to be re-elected, but at the same time that legislator must never be seen to be manipulating that same constituency.

The technologies that underwrite these different discourses are as closely interwoven with them as the technologies that support discourse at the simpler level and in some cases they are the same. In one sense the talk exchanged between managers at a meeting, a citizen and a legislator, or a teacher and a student are organized in about the same ways. There are regular practices for the exchange of turns, the introduction of new topics, repairing misunderstandings, making hedges, stating imperatives, or asking questions. Whether it is a management meeting, a class, or a public hearing, introducing audio conferencing technology cuts out the possibility of using eye-gaze to manage who has the next turn to speak. At this 'language-in-use' level of discourse, there is one set of relationships between the discourse and the technologies that support it.

But at the broad level at which Gee or Blommaert define discourse there are also integral relationships between the discourse of management and technology, between academic discourse and technology, or public discourse and technology as we shall discuss throughout this book. Perhaps the clearest and longest established relationship of this kind is the use of the book, the text, as the foundation of academic discourse. While it would be exaggerated to say so, one could characterize academic discourse as consisting of texts and discussions of texts. In a sense all of the other genres of discourse (notes, letters, conversations, curricula vitae, syllabuses, lectures, and the rest) are supplementary to the core technology of the book. Similarly, as we have seen in the critical discourse research of the past two decades or so, public discourse is very deeply embedded in the texts of laws (and policies and positions) and the journalistic texts of newspapers and now primarily television news texts. Management discourse, of course, characterizes itself by a concern for 'the bottom line'. That is, management discourse is undergirded by a large technological apparatus of accounting and data processing.

Much of the conflict that we observed in our research between and among these different discourses occurred at this higher level of discourse. Computing resources entered the organizations we researched as technologies of management. They were technologies for handling personnel data such as salaries of employees or data processing of the organization's 'productive' processes such as managing student enrollment information from tuition payments to grades and final credentials. Academic uses of these computing resources, in particular the messaging systems, were thought of as frivolous distractions at best and a serious drain on expensive resources at worst.

Discourse and technology are inseparable; yet to argue this is not the central purpose of the book. The ethnographic case studies we present in this book argue that any change in the technologies of discourse is inherently and necessarily a change in the discourse itself. We will take the term 'discourse' at two levels in this book, but at either level we argue that there are close ties between discourse and technology and that a change of one entails a change in the other. Our central purpose, however, is to use these ethnographic studies which we conducted in the early 1980s to extract a more general ethnographic theory and methodology which can be used to analyze the relationships between discourse and technology but also to place this analysis in the broader context of the social, political, and cultural issues of any particular time. We want to use discourse analysis to engage in social action. We call this approach to discourse analysis 'nexus analysis'.

In a sense we are arguing a commonplace as old as the *Federalist Papers* in which James Madison argued that there was an inherent and inevitable relationship between the size of a republic, its form of government, and the means of communication, including transportation used to organize its functions. Alaska in the late 1970s and early 1980s had become a communications technological leader in the world as well as the site of unheralded contradictions that would challenge Hamilton, Madison, and Jay's conception of how tightly and thinly socio-political organization could be stretched given new media technologies.

Villages of thirty people who continued to live in cabins built of logs and heated with wood fires sent their children to schools in which they watched *Sesame Street* by popping a video into a Betamax player or ran 'Little Brickout' on their Apple computers. A woman on the Arctic coast living less than 100 miles from the Soviet border drove a snowmobile for an hour through the dark winter snows to get to the nearest combination of a telephone, Apple computer, and power supply to participate in our graduate university course centered in Fairbanks more than 500 miles away to the southeast.

The historical colonization and the mid-twentieth-century institutionalization of Alaska within American socio-political and cultural discourses produced juxtapositions of cultures, technologies, and social organization that massively restructured concepts of law, of schooling, of the provision of medical services, and economic relations that stretched *a priori* assumptions about these concepts to the breaking point. The new media technologies were introduced partly for national security motives and partly because money was so abundant because of the discovery and production of the enormous North Slope oil resources. These communication technologies not only reconnected these networks but began to restructure the nature of the discourses that would be and could be carried out within them.

Our approach in this book begins (in Chapter 3) with a close focus on a rather specific and common communicative event, a traditional university classroom. Our interest, however, is in showing how what happens in that classroom occurs at a nexus or conjoining of many different trajectories – the life trajectories of each of the individual participants taken separately, the institutional trajectory of that particular university and that particular program, that physical space and many other trajectories of multiple discourses. A nexus analysis entails not only a close, empirical examination of the moment under analysis but also an historical analysis of these trajectories or discourse cycles that intersect in that moment as well as an analysis of the anticipations that are opened up by the social actions taken in that moment. Thus our nexus analysis moves from the close examination of particular classrooms to the analysis of several other points in a widening ethnographic circumference which comes to include medical interviews, judicial hearings and presentencing reports, the production of elementary pedagogical materials, and the organizational structure of a university. As we write we shall extract from our own research projects the general principles of a nexus analysis. These principles which are extracted from the main text are then gathered together in a Fieldguide (Appendix) which the reader can use to develop his or her own nexus analysis.

Discourse analysis as social action

The term 'discourse' might refer to the ways in which people engage each other in communication at the face-to-face level or it might refer to the much broader set of concerns signaled with such terms as 'public discourse', 'academic discourse', 'legal discourse', or 'medical discourse'. As a consequence, discourse analysis as a field of study might either be the micro-analysis of unfolding moments of social interaction or a much broader socio-political-cultural analysis of the relationships among social groups and power interests in the society. A nexus analysis is a way to strategize unifying these two different levels of analysis. We believe that the broader social issues are ultimately grounded in the micro-actions of social interaction and, conversely, the most mundane of micro-actions are nexus through which the largest cycles of social organization and activity circulate.

In this way we argue that discourse analysis is a powerful tool for understanding social life both at the interpersonal and at the organizational and institutional levels of social analysis. Of course discourse analysis may, in fact it often does, take a distancing and 'objective' (if not objectivizing) stance. To the extent discourse analysis distances itself from the social processes of power and change we feel it is of limited use in trying to understand social action as process. Here in this book we take an engaged stance; how things are talked about is one of the major processes by which our worlds are constructed, legitimated, ratified, contested. Therefore, the analysis itself is a form of action in that world. The fact that discourse analysis as done by academics has often been rather ineffectual is not to attest to the weakness of discourse analysts as agents of social change; it is to attest that discourse analysts in many cases have been networked in nexus of practice so distant from the worlds under examination that their analyses are not in any way part of the discourses which are constructing those worlds.

A nexus analysis is centered on three main tasks or activities:

- engaging the nexus of practice
- navigating the nexus of practice
- changing the nexus of practice.

As we develop the idea here, a nexus analysis is an ethnographic methodological strategy which begins by placing the discourse analyst within what we might call, following Kenneth Burke's *Rhetoric of motives* (1950), a zone of identification. Where and when the analysts are themselves part of the nexus of practice under study, the analysis is in itself transformative of the nexus of practice. In this way we conceive of discourse analysis itself to be a form of social action. We refer to this opening task of a nexus analysis as *engaging the nexus of practice*.

The second task of a nexus analysis we call *navigating the nexus of practice* since the analyst works his or her way through the trajectories of participants, places, and situations both back in time historically and forward through actions and anticipations to see if crucial discourse cycles or semiotic cycles can be identified. This activity is the main body of work of a nexus analysis and might take months or years depending on the *circumferencing* that is set in the analysis. As the analyst maps these semiotic cycles of people, places, and things we encourage him or her to continue opening up the circumference of the analysis, hence the term 'circumferencing' which, for us, means simply making sure that the study does not become obsessively narrowed to single moments, speech acts or events, or participants without seeing how these connect to other moments, acts, events, and participants which make up the full nexus.

Finally, the nexus analysis is through and through both a discourse analysis and a motive analysis which seeks to *change the nexus of practice*. Perhaps it is obvious that these three tasks or activities do not necessarily occur in this sequence. From the start of establishing a *zone of identification* the nexus analyst is engaged in both discourse and motive analysis. We know where we are and with whom we are dealing and what the main issues are largely through what people say about these things. To understand even the opening task requires a discourse analysis. But not only that, anything said is said from a point of view or a motive. Therefore, from the beginning a nexus analysis undertakes a close analysis of not only *what* is said (ethnographic content) but *how* (discourse analysis) and *why* (motive analysis). We place these as the third task, however, because this is the point at which sufficient materials will have been collected to enable a truly broad perspective on the project.

Our theoretical vocabulary

Throughout this book you will encounter a few terms which we hope are intuitively clear as we introduce and use them but which are drawn from an extended analytical literature including especially Burke's critical theory and what is often called socio-cultural theory, mediated action theory, and mediated discourse analysis. In the references section we show where you can find fuller treatments of the basic concepts and terms we are using, but here we want to open up our discussion of nexus analysis by introducing the key terms which we will be using throughout the remainder of the book.

We have just introduced the three main activities of a nexus analysis: *Engaging the nexus of practice*, *navigating the nexus of practice*, and *changing the nexus of practice* (conducting a discourse and motive analysis). The terms given below elaborate these main tasks and will be used throughout the book as well as given more detail in the Fieldguide (Appendix). What follow are some basic definitions.

Circumference, circumferencing

First of all there are the terms having to do with Burke's dramatistic theory or his grammar of motives which lays out ways of talking about language as symbolic action: If someone is writing on a piece of paper you might just say she is writing, but one would want to know what she is writing for whom and why. One person might say she is practicing to become a novelist, another might say she is wasting paper. A teacher would want to know how long she has been writing in order to evaluate her ability and encourage her in her endeavors. A mother might say she is just shirking her chores. In order to get a perspective on the simple observable action we need to expand the *circumference* of the analysis to ask about its origins in the past, its direction in the future, and the expanding circles of engagement with others near and far. We need to know on what timescales, from minute to millenial, the action depends, as well as in what layers of geopolitical discourses it is embedded. *Circumferencing* is the analytical act of opening up the angle of observation to take into consideration these broader discourses in which the action operates.

Motive analysis

Any description of an action is from a point of view or a position which carries with it an attitude or motive of the describer toward the action. The action of writing would be described in different ways depending on the motive of the describer. Or, to be more careful in our statement, no matter what might be the 'true' (or introspective) motive of the describer, the description itself inevitably must take a position. A *motive analysis* is a form of discourse analysis that focuses its attention on the motives which are embedded in linguistic descriptions whether these are explicit or implicit. One might say a student is simply doing a homework assignment. This places the motive partly outside the student; she is doing an assignment. We follow Burke in calling this a 'scenic' motive because the cause or motive of the action is placed outside the social actor in her environment. The same writer might say she is doing the assignment because she enjoys that kind of study. This would be, in Burke's terms, an 'agent' motive because she is claiming that the cause or motive lies internally with herself as the agent of the action. Our goal in nexus analysis is never to try to discover the 'true' motives of any action. On the contrary, it is to recognize that no statement of motive for any action can be the single and only possible discursive construction of that action. Differences in motive statements are fruitful places to search in a discourse analysis for ways in which to influence the nexus of practice.

Zone of identification

In order to do a nexus analysis you must establish a *zone of identification* with a nexus of practice. That is, you must find a nexus in which you have or can take a place as an accepted legitimate participant. Within this zone of identification you can begin to analyze the social practices of the nexus not in a distant or objective fashion but in order to change the nexus of practice.

Social action

This is any action taken by an individual with reference to a social network, also called a mediated action. Here it is important to note that we do not use the term *social action* as it is used by some scholars to mean a collective mobilization taken by a social group (or class) toward the end of bringing about a change in society. We take our perspective in this case from socio-cultural psychology and emphasize that any action is inherently social – it is only action to the extent it is perceived by others as action – and that any action is carried out via material and symbolic mediational means (cultural or psychological tools); hence the term 'mediated action'.

Mediational means (cultural tools); resources

Whether a person throws a ball with hand and arm or performs a simulated action by means of a joystick, or even writes about that action in the letters of the English alphabet, any action is accomplished with semiotic tools or resources. We prefer the very general terms *mediational means*, *resources*, or *semiotic resources*.

Site of engagement

Building on the notion of the mediated action, we situate action in a unique historical moment and material space when separate practices such as sitting at a table, writing on paper with a pencil, handing the paper to a waiter, come together in real time to form an action such as paying for a meal at a restaurant. *Site of engagement* makes reference to a single token of the type.

Nexus of practice

When a *site of engagement* is repeated regularly we refer to that as a *nexus of practice*. In the sentence, 'She just paid the waiter and left' we are focusing attention on a *site of engagement*. In the sentence, 'Paying the bill with a credit card is quite convenient,' we are making reference to a *nexus of practice*. The term makes reference to a type of action, not a specific token. But we need to be careful in that we cannot use the phrase 'paid the waiter' (the token) without implying the type, that is without making reference to a nexus of practice in which the reader would be assumed to know the whole set of practices entailed in what it means to pay a waiter.

Social practice

A *social action* taken repeatedly is considered a *social practice*. Writing in a diary is a daily practice for some people. While the idea of practice is used quite variably in the research literature to mean either very broad practices such as 'the practice of medicine' or 'academic lecturing practice', we prefer to use it in the narrowest sense of a single, recognizable, repeatable action such as the practice of handing an object, filling in a form, switching on a computer, or answering a direct question in an interview.

Ethnography/ethnographic

Ethnography is, for us, an extended study of action(s) undertaken by people in the course of living their lives. Doing ethnography requires active participation in the lives and actions with the people in which one is interested and seeks to enlist their interest and involvement in the collaborative analysis of the issues being studied. Ethnography is not simply a methodology for getting rich data for objective analysis but a theoretical position that takes it that it is important for the analyst to be identified within the nexus of practice under study. A nexus analysis is a form of ethnography that takes social action as the theoretical center of study, not any *a priori* social group, class, tribe, or culture. In this it departs to a considerable extent from traditional ethnography in anthropology or sociology.

Historical body

Different people play the same role differently depending on their history of personal experience inscribed in what the philosopher Nishida calls the *historical body*. A lifetime of personal habits come to feel so natural that one's body carries out actions seemingly without being told. Bourdieu referred to this phenomenon as *habitus* but we prefer *historical body* because it situates bodily memories more precisely in the individual body.

Interaction order

Actors on the stage of human life appear singly, in pairs or trios or crowds, with different roles and role expectations depending on their relationships. We make use of Erving Goffman's general term *interaction order* to talk about any of the many possible social arrangements by which we form relationships in social interactions. Our interest in the interaction order grows out of the fact that people behave differently depending in part on whether they are alone when they act or if they are acting together in consort with other people as they might in having a conversation between friends, taking a university class, or consulting with a lawyer or a medical doctor.

Discourses in place

All social action is accomplished at some real, material place in the world. This is true by definition because all social actions are carried out by human social actors. All places in the world are complex aggregates (or nexus) of many discourses which circulate through them. Some of these circulate on slow time cycles like the aging of the built or architectural environment of a shopping mall made of stones, wood, plastics, metals, and concrete. Some of these discourses circulate more rapidly like the conversational topics among three friends walking through the same shopping mall. Some of these discourses are very distant and of little direct relevance to particular social actions occurring in that place such as the design specifications of the table at which two friends are having coffee. Some of these discourses are directly relevant such as the menu from which the snack selection is made. We use the term *discourses in place* to call attention to all of these discourses and to call attention to the need to study empirically which discourses are relevant or foregrounded and which discourses are irrelevant (for the moment at least) or backgrounded for the social action(s) in which we are interested.

Discourse cycle

The vignettes with which we began this chapter all mention the use of a particular technology, persons taking action in the presence of others with yet others whose presence is mediated by a form of technology which we treat as a resource or mediational means. We regard the persons we focus on as social actors taking action with the aid of these mediational means. Each actor is observed at a site of engagement which is a particular moment of time in a particular place with particular others present in a characteristic interaction order with characteristic discourses in place. When the social action is routinely taken at a recognizable time and place we call it a nexus of practice.

   Thus, the organization president taking the social action of conducting routine meetings modified the nexus of practice of meetings by changing the site of engagement to video sites in multiple locations rather than gathering all participants into his presence at his centrally located office. The result was that one vice-president took advantage of the mediational means of video conferencing to dominate the meetings. The historical body of the president was so attuned to the face-to-face meeting that he was unable to adjust to the new format, while the historical body of one of the vice-presidents, modifying the discourses in place, took advantage of the new interaction order to gain influence.

In the second vignette, a student did not take the social action of speaking to the class until the nexus of practice was modified with the addition of email discussion as mediational means. Again the same historical body, with the addition of mediational means which modifies the interaction order and thus the nexus of practice, is able to take a social action that he had not taken before.

In order to understand how these small changes came about, we need to expand the circumference of our analysis in time and space from the current situation by looking at the discourses present and how they relate to past discourses and discourses which anticipate the future and to extend geographically beyond the site of the current engagement, at the historical bodies of the social actors with their past experience and future aspirations, and at the social arrangements of the interaction order with and without the mediational means of new technology. Each of these forms a cycle of discourse which circulates through the action upon which we are focused and which a nexus analysis studies backward and forward through time.

Plan of the book

Chapter 2 opens the main discussion by introducing the central theoretical ideas of nexus analysis which center on cycles of discourse. Our interest in this chapter is to outline the ways in which discourse becomes action and then, again, action becomes discourse to produce a cycle not unlike the well-known water cycle. A cycle of discourse itself interacts with other such cycles to form larger semiotic ecosystems. These concepts will be the foundation on which the following illustrative chapters of the book are organized.

In order to develop the argument that discourse analysis is itself a form of social action, we need to show how discourse (in both the sense of language in use and the sense of the broader social discourses) is integrated within the actions of people in the ordinary conduct of their lives. In Chapter 3, *From essay to email: New media technology and social change*, we begin with the analysis of two university classes, one a traditional teacher-centered face-to-face class (the panopticon class) which is centered on the reading and the production of essays, and the other a class which is mediated by the new technological means of email and audio conferencing (the technologically mediated class). We focus on the social actions involved when teachers and students do a class.

This analysis of the two very different classrooms helps us to show how the use of technology as a mediational means for conducting social actions redistributes the interaction order, brings some new discourses into play while setting other ones into the background, and is differentially established in the historical bodies of the participants. The net result is that the technologically mediated class fosters new forms of communication while simultaneously restricting or inhibiting habitual and well-practiced 'traditional' forms of university class inter-actions. In this way 'access' to university instruction is redistributed in ways that come to serve different social goals, purposes, and groups.

Whereas Chapter 3 focuses quite narrowly on the contrast between two rather different educational nexus, a traditional university class and a tech-nologically mediated class, Chapter 4, *Engaging the nexus of practice: Oil, the Cold War, and social change in Alaska in the 1980s*, opens up the lens to show the broad range of organizations, projects, and research questions which were the context or the first circumference in which we began to engage in these experiments with electronic mail and other media of communication. The argument we make is quite simple in a way: Any researcher is already located within a complex nexus of practice, he or she is already part of many complex cycles of discourse and so the first task of a nexus analysis is simply to examine and recognize where one is located. That time and that place, Alaska in the 1980s, were particularly complex examples of what Dittmar calls times of radical social change (RSC). Whether the researcher is working in such a situation or at such times, the first task of a nexus analysis is to locate oneself quite explicitly within the nexus of practice one is engaging to study.

Chapter 4 concludes by extracting some of the main principles by which a nexus analysis may be conducted by summarizing our own trajectories through these various research projects. These principles are further developed as general heuristic field questions in the Fieldguide (Appendix).

In Chapter 5, *Navigating the nexus of practice: Mapping the circumferences and timescales of human action*, we turn to the analysis of a very different type of social interaction. When an offender is convicted of certain crimes in an Alaskan court, before a sentence is given, a probation officer prepares a presentencing report. This report is based on an interview between the probation officer and the offender. Because these reports were found to be a crucial moment in a process that was resulting in longer jail sentences for Alaska Natives than for the non-native population, we examined the patterns of social interaction between the participants in these interviews. This is the first example in Chapter 5 and it moves us beyond the simpler discourse cycles to consider complex interactions among multiple cycles – the semiotic ecosystems in which multiple cycles of discourse interact with each other. In this case, although there are always many other cycles involved, the crucial two cycles are the historical bodies of the offender and of the probation officer.

Following this analysis of the presentencing report we move to our main example in Chapter 5, which is developed around a very different situation in which we were asked to assist in the production of a bilingual education booklet on beadwork. We show that the pattern of indirectly developing the context in which an action makes sense is consistent with the ways Alaska Natives respond to non-natives whether that is in a presentencing interview, a university classroom, or a medical consultation. We also suggest that one of the reasons asynchronous computer-mediated communication as we discussed it in Chapter 3 works well for some students is that it resonates well with the characteristic communication style or historical body of those students; conversely the panopticon-style classroom resonates with the life experiences of many others including many non-native students and faculty in the university.

In Chapter 6, *Navigating the nexus of practice: Discourse analysis and institutional power*, we open the circumference of our nexus analysis yet wider to examine the ways in which discourse and motives work to produce a much more complex semiotic ecosystem, the one often referred to in the research literature as the 'gatekeeping encounter'. We found that in a large institution such as a university, the 'gates' which control access (or exit) are not located in single, concrete moments but are often distributed as interactions among multiple cycles of discourse. The student's selection of a dorm room is an interaction among that student's own life experience or academic career, the university's housing practices and policies, the university's admissions practices and policies, and the hiring, employment, and vacation practices of rural school districts. Each of these operates as a nearly independent discourse cycle, yet together their interaction constructs a finite decision – the assignment of an undesirable room to a university student from a rural school.

In order to see how such a complex semiotic ecosystem works, we argue in Chapter 6 that we need to look at the ways discourse is used in each of these various discourse cycles and particularly at how these different cycles result in the ascription of different motives to the participants in those cycles. In this way, Chapter 6 shows how navigating the nexus of practice brings us to the third stage of a nexus analysis, changing the nexus of practice.

Chapter 7, *Changing the nexus of practice: Technology, Social change, and activist discourse analysis*, focuses directly on the question of discourse analysis and engages in an examination of our own motives in conducting the research we have reported in this book. We argue that a nexus analysis inherently requires a close study of the researcher's own activities as part of the nexus of practice within which change is being produced. We conclude by saying that we believe that any research project is more effectively evaluated by the questions it produces than by the answers it purports to give.

2   Cycles of discourse

Tommy sits on the floor playing with the Apple II+ which is connected to a television set. He turns the knob, changing the channel to a broadcast network, and tries to affect the broadcast show by programing in BASIC. It doesn't work, he complains.

Rachel comes home from the babysitter all excited about a show, 'The Electric Company', she assumes she can't watch at home, where the television set is used primarily as a monitor for the Apple II+ and occasionally for playing videotaped movies but not so far for broadcast television.

A Russian musician on tour in the United States in 2003 visits with his hosts in Haines, Alaska, where the Moscow Chamber Orchestra plays two concerts before going on to Carnegie Hall. In a discussion of technology, he asks how the Alaskans could have prevented their children from watching television during the 1980s while allowing them to use computers. His own children could not live without television, but he does not allow them to use computers.

Social action: The historical body, the interaction order, and discourses in place

The first two of these incidents took place at our home in Fairbanks on the University of Alaska campus in the Summer of 1981. That Spring we had purchased the television set to use as a monitor for the new Apple II+, after which we also bought a Betamax video recorder with which we recorded broadcast programs for viewing at our convenience and using for our students on campus and scattered in villages across the tundra and subarctic taiga. The television was used most often as a computer monitor, with which Tommy learned to program first in BASIC and then in LOGO.

The third story links to the present through friends whose children watched television at the homes of friends including ourselves though they were free to use the Kaypro computer at home. These children differed from those of the Russian musician in having bodies with different experiences in different cycles of discourse. Though the interaction order of children at home with or without parents and friends may have been similar, the discourses in place were separated not only by thousands of miles but by twenty years during which the Cold War ended and travel between Russia and Alaska again became possible.

None of the children was present in the recent conversation between Russian and Alaskan musicians and music lovers. They entered the discourse through their use or prohibited use of different objects of technology which had different relations to the discourses in place in Moscow today as compared to those in place in Alaska two decades before, when there was no World Wide Web and violence or pornography were problems associated with television but not on the graphics-primitive stand-alone computers.

At the time we first used a computer in our home we worked very hard to get it to talk to the University of Alaska Computer Network, enlisting a colleague at the University of San Diego when the software we purchased turned out to be ineffectual. Now children gain easy access to violence or pornography by just turning on a computer or even a television set in a motel with High-speed Internet Access. Television sets and computers enter homes in different stages of different discourse cycles for parents in Alaska and Russia. The action of a parent protecting a child from unwanted audiovisual input is shaped by different cycles of discourse. The meanings of objects such as computers or television sets cannot be understood independently of an analysis of both where in a cycle of discourse the object is encountered and also what other cycles are in place in that moment.

A nexus analysis can be a challenging enterprise because in some real sense just about everything we might know about can circulate through any particular moment of human action. The methodological trick is to try to identify just the most significant elements for further analysis. We try to hone our ability to focus on important elements by seeing a social action at the intersection of three main elements. A social action takes place as an intersection or nexus of some aggregate of discourses (educational talk, for example) — the *discourses in place*, some social arrangement by which people come together in social groups (a meeting, a conversation, a chance contact, a queue) — *the interaction order*, and the life experiences of the individual social actors — *the historical body*. A solid nexus analysis would need to take all three of these elements into consideration rather

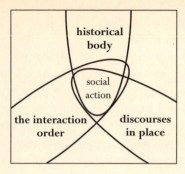

2.1

than focus exclusively on any one of them. These three elements of social action are set out in Figure 2.1.

We will begin, in Chapter 3, to show the way we are using these terms in this book by using examples from a traditional university classroom. This is because this setting is likely to be familiar to most readers. The fact that you are reading this book means that you are probably well-schooled in the practices of traditional teaching and learning, so much of what we say should be quite common experience.

Then we will draw a comparison on the basis of several computer-mediated classes which we taught in Alaska in the 1980s. We have used computer-mediated teaching for twenty years and continue to use the constantly changing and improving media as a major aspect of our teaching and research now. The reader might wonder why we focus on this research of some twenty years ago. We use our research from the 1980s in this comparison for two reasons: First, we actually did those projects as research projects and so have quite extensive data which we have triangulated in several ways including through many conference presentations and publications. Thus we have much greater confidence in the accuracy of our analysis for those first materials than we have for the anecdotes we might give based on our teaching and research today.

The second reason, however, may be more important. The use of new technologies now as then is replete with what we came to call 'potential talk' back in the 1980s. There is often a quick slippage away from describing what is actually occurring in the use of a technology to talking about the potential which is as yet unrealized. We have watched the constant recycling of talk about the potential of technological media of communication for well over twenty years and yet we see almost daily that some things which were exciting potentials in 1980 remain purely potential – for twenty years they have seemed to be just around the corner – and other things that seemed very powerful potentials have actually come and gone in that period. Still other things have become commonplace.

As just a brief example of these cycles of potential we could look at the development of computer communication itself. When we first conducted these classes in 1980 and 1981, most email – it was not yet called email very often – was in what is now commonly called 'chat' format. You signed onto the system, checked to see who was currently signed on, and you talked with them. Often people would arrange first by telephone to go to their terminals to talk. We did have the asynchronous capacity to store messages to be read when the mailbox was opened, but what we did not have was the capacity to use the system without all of the other users being able to check if you were currently online and so to interrupt your messages with an onscreen message saying you were currently being summoned by another user.

Of course as the number of users increased – in the month before we began our classes online the University of Alaska Computer Network had had just fifty-seven messages sent – and as we began to use it much more frequently than the administrators for whom it was first designed, new message software was developed to block the 'chat' capacity. Then, in due time as the use of email became a commercial success, yet newer software was written to produce the 'chat' function as a 'new' option for email users.

To avoid lapsing into simply projecting future potentials, we have chosen instead to focus on the research and data we developed in those first years, in the early 1980s. By focusing on our actual data, we believe we can produce a solid analysis while at the same time providing a kind of baseline against which we and you can measure just how far we have come (or not) in the intervening twenty-some years.

In our own ethnographic research, we feel it is important to keep the main focus of our attention on social action. That is, our main interest is to try to understand how people take actions of various kinds and what are the constraints or the affordances of the mediational means (language, technologies, etc.) by which they act. For example, in our book *Discourses in place: Language in the material world* (Scollon and Scollon 2003) we talk about how a person does something as simple as crossing the street at the corner of a busy intersection in a city. In the first place, the person is motivated by his or her reasons for being there at that corner and wanting to be across on the other side. Perhaps the pedestrian is on a shopping trip and she wants to go to the store which is across the street from where she is standing. When she comes to the corner she will check such things as the traffic lights, the traffic itself, and what other people in the vicinity are doing. Then, normally we might say, if the traffic lights and traffic allow her to cross, she walks across and goes on her way.

In this very simple line of action there are three main considerations: This pedestrian's historical body (that is her own goals and purposes and her life experience in crossing the street at urban intersections, but also her physical health and stamina), other people in the world around her (the interaction order), and the discourses in place at that intersection. For example, she is likely to pay attention to the pedestrian traffic lights and to the pedestrian walkways among the discourses in that place but to completely ignore the numbers on the electricity boxes or labels the city authorities have put on the covers to the water mains. In other words, she selects among all of the discourses in that place – regulatory ones, commercial ones, infrastructural ones, and even transgressive ones such as graffiti – the ones that are relevant to the action she is taking and uses just those in carrying out this action of crossing the street. So there is an interaction between her historical body (her purposes, goals, and life experience) and the discourses in place (the signs, pedestrian crossing markings, and lights) that she uses to carry out her action of crossing the street.

What this pedestrian does and how she crosses the street will be altered, however, by the interaction order. Goffman (1983) has suggested that there are really two main distinctions to be made among the other people who are present with us at a moment of action. There are those who are engaged together with us in taking that action and there are those who are simply present but not part of our own immediate social group. For example, if this woman is alone and there are large crowds crossing the street at the same time, she is likely to go along with what the crowd does. If she is reluctant, because of her historical body, to cross against a red signal but the crowd is just surging ahead to cross, she is likely to go against her own feelings of what is right to do and to cross. Or if she is alone and there is nobody anywhere in sight and no traffic, again, she might cross against a red light as there is neither a danger from traffic nor a danger of receiving a citation for a pedestrian traffic violation.

If the woman is together with a friend and the two of them are shopping together, they would form what Goffman calls a 'with' – a small group of two or more people who are socially together, who have special rights to each other's attention and who also have special rights to ignore and be ignored by others in their vicinity. In our research we have seen that often people who are together with others will behave in ways that they might not behave when they are alone. This woman might, for example, hesitate to cross against a red light when she is alone, but if her friend just sets out across the street, she might go with her to avoid breaking off the thread of their conversation.

From our perspective, then, we focus on action rather than language, people, groups or technologies alone. In this case it means our focus is on such broad actions as the teaching and learning that occur in a class. Those actions, of course, are constituted of sequences of more concrete actions as we shall see in

Chapter 3. We see these actions in light of three main factors – the historical body of the individual social actors, the discourses in place at the time of action, and the interaction order (the social groupings) within which they occur.

Practice, discourse, and historical body: Cycles of discourse

Many of the practices by which the traditional or what we might call the 'panopticon classroom' is constructed have been learned very early in life and, furthermore, it has largely been forgotten that they have been learned. They seem entirely 'natural' to the person in whose historical body they reside. This is particularly true of the panopticon classroom where the construction of the whole activity depends on such unconscious practices as responding when your name is called, lifting and stretching our your hand to receive something when someone appears to be giving you something, sitting together with other students in a small space, giving over your (apparently) undivided attention to the teacher.

The electronic or what we will call the technologically or technology-mediated classroom, because it was so new at the time of our research, gave us many opportunities to observe how discourses become submerged into the historical body as practice through action. Now because nexus analysis is, in effect, a study of such histories and futures of discourse – cycles of discourse – we want to give a few examples by way of illustration before we go on to define the term 'cycle of discourse'.

In the first example we have a case of an email message from the technology-mediated classroom which we discuss in Chapter 3. This message, quite typic-ally, has a multiple topical thread. FTCA comments on the class topic (literacy) but within that makes a comment on the task of using the email system. FFRT follows this by first commenting on how to make corrections, either one letter at a time or one line at a time (the only means of correction available to us at that time). (See p. 54 for an explanation of the user names.) In the examples we give we have preserved all of the original misspellings and typos as a reminder of what it was to use such systems before our present text-editing capacities had evolved. Users who were accustomed to producing clear, correctly spelled and proofed text found it very frustrating to have their texts go out in such a poorly edited form. Younger users and non-academics, however, were not intimidated by such literate imperfections and tended to gain fluency much more quickly in this new, flawed medium.

FTCA Mon Feb 09 15:58 (4)

IT SEEMS TO ME THAT COMMUNICATION . . . I MEANT TO SAY 'COMMUNICATING', BUT I DON'T KNOW HOW TO MAKE CORRECTIONS ON THIS TERMINAL . . . IS A VERY LITERATE ACTIVITY. WHY DO WE EXPECT THAT IT WILL BE SO WIDELY ACCEPTED AND USED IN RURAL ALASKA??? (I WONDER HOW HOW UNDERLINE SOMETHING ON HERE)

FFRT Mon Feb 09 16:14 (8)

THERE ARE TWO WAYS TO MAKE CORRECTIONS THAT I KNOW OF. —NE THING YOU CAN DO IS TO TUSE THE 'AT' SIGN TO CORRECT THE LAST CHARACTER. ANOTHER THING YOU CAN DO IS TO DELETE THE LAST LINE BY USING CONTROL X.

THIS IS PRETTY LITERATE BUT MAYBE A VERY DIFFERENT KIND OF LITERACY. MAYBE THIS WILL HELP US SORT OUT WHAT ASPECTS OF LITERACY HAVE TO DO WITH A SYSTEM OF REPRESENTATION AND WHAT ASPECTS HAVE TO DO WITH THE SOCIAL (AND OTHER) CONTEXTS IN WHICH INFORMATION EXCHANGE TAKES PLACE.

If we focus just on the problem of the correction of typing errors, we have these texts:

- FFCA: I don't know how to make corrections on this terminal.
- FFRT: There are two ways to make corrections that I know of. —ne thing you can do is to use the 'at' sign to correct the last character. Another thing you can do is to delete the last line by using control X.

By using lower case here we have already transformed the originals in a small way. Of course we are ignoring many other transformations that have occurred since we printed out those messages on heat-sensitive paper back in the early 1980s, including typing them up as Apple II+ files, printing them out on an Epson MX-80 printer, later on scanning that printout to make Word-compatible files a few years ago, photocopying those printouts, and now typing them here again. And, of course, by the time you read them they will have gone through yet another sequence of transformation into printed book text. So you are seeing this message at a certain point in its historical cycle which has already entailed many changes.

All discourses go through these cycles or transformations. Maybe the most interesting transformations, though, were the 'post-it' notes we all made of such directions. Ron had one that was like this (but of course in handwriting):

one character @
one line <CTRL X>

Ron made that note from a mimeographed booklet of instructions for using the University of Alaska Computer Network email system and tacked it up on the terminal in his office. This note was one of a forest of notes on how to use the system that sprouted around the edges of all of our screens. As he began to use the system more and more, he looked at these notes from time to time as he needed them, but progressively began to internalize them simply as things he knew how to do. By the time he externalized this instruction in a message to FFCA the original mimeographed notes had been lost and the post-it had fallen from the edge of his terminal. This is one very short cycle within which a bit of action, making the corrections, had been made explicit as a set of procedures (in the mimeo sheets), had been transformed into another form of discourse (as the post-its), been further transformed into the historical body as a practice, been re-externalized as a message to FFCA who then went through the same cycle from discourse to repeated actions to practice.

When we examine the action of handing a student's paper back in Chapter 3 which is very common in the traditional or panopticon classroom, we will see that one of the preceding actions was reading out the student's name. For most of us the ability to read is learned early and through genesis amnesia it is mostly forgotten how and when we learned. We did catch a moment of this process in the life of our own daughter, however, when she went to kindergarten. She already knew how to write the letters of the alphabet but when she came home after the first day, she was all excited and wanted to tell us what she had learned. She said that she had learned how to write the letter 'a'. This was a bit surprising, but we asked her to show us how she writes it. She showed us (left side of Figure 2.2), but then quickly rushed ahead to say, 'And do you know how

 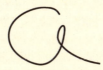

2.2

we'll write it next year?' and wrote it as it is written in the right side of Figure 2.2. Here we have a case of an interesting cycle. Before going to school Rachel had learned and practiced the 'cursive' way of writing the letter 'a'. At school she, along with the rest of the students, had been shown how they would write that letter as kindergarten students. Somehow, and she didn't say how, she had also learned that her way of writing it would become appropriate in another year when she graduated to the first grade. What we see is the anticipatory side of a cycle of discourse, action, and practice. She is looking ahead from today's action toward an action that will be accomplished appropriately in due time. In this we see that even a young child has some quite acute awareness of cycles of action, discourse, and practice as well as an awareness that social competence is often tied to placing oneself at the right place (that is the expected place) on that cycle of 'development'.

One final example of the cycle of discourse and action will help forestall the idea that it is always discourse that leads to action and thence to practice. It may just as often revolve through a different arc of the cycle. We have written elsewhere (S. Scollon and R. Scollon 1984) about how our son, Tommy, learned to run simple programs on our first Apple II+ computer when he was just four years old or so – just at the time we were doing the research we describe here. There were two programs that he particularly liked at that time, one called 'Trilogy' and the other 'Kaleidoscope'. He was able to run both of these programs by engaging the action sequence of typing 'R', 'U', 'N', <space>, 'T', 'R', 'I', 'L', 'O', 'G', 'Y'. That is, he typed these letters one at a time and in this order. He was also able to type RUN KALEIDOSCOPE to run that program.

There was no way, however, that we could say that he could 'spell' these words. He could not say the letters in this sequence, though he could easily say the words 'trilogy' and 'kaleidoscope' and tell you those were his favorite programs. He made no connection between those sounds and the programs he could run. He could not tell someone else how to do it. He could only sit in front of the keyboard and make those movements until the program came on the screen. If he made a 'spelling mistake' he made no attempt to correct the spelling; he just started over again on the next line to repeat the sequence of actions.

Some months later we were in a bookstore and Tommy saw a novel with the title TRILOGY on the spine. He pointed to it and asked his father, 'What's that?' Ron said, 'I think you know.' Tommy looked at the book spine, at Ron, back at the book spine and then his face brightened up and he whispered triumphantly, 'Trilogy!' We believe it was only then, months after making these 'spelling' actions, that he had made this connection among the physical hand sequences on the keyboard, the sounds of the words 'Trilogy' and 'Kaleidoscope', and the symbols used to represent those letters.

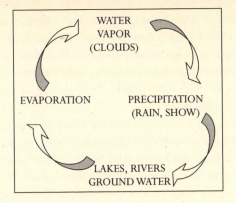

2.3

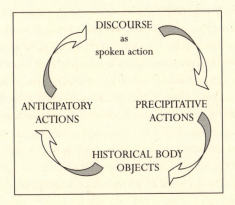

2.4

We refer to these cycles of history and of anticipation as 'the discourse cycle'. We are doing this on analogy with the very familiar water cycle. H_2O, more commonly thought of as water, takes many forms. In the air it is water vapor or clouds. When this becomes heavy enough by attaching to dust particles it falls in the form of rain or snow depending on the temperature. On the ground it may soak into the earth or form as lakes, rivers, or ponds, or, if it's cold enough, it may form the ice rocks we know as glaciers. Then again, with enough heat from the sun, the 'engine' which drives this cycle, and dryness in the air, it becomes transformed again through evaporation into water vapor and clouds. This cycle is shown in Figure 2.3, 'The water cycle'. The way discourse, action, and practice work is quite similar to this water cycle in many ways as shown in Figure 2.4, 'The discourse cycle'. Discourse in the form of spoken discourse or any form of language being used, whether it is written or spoken, becomes more 'solid' through some transformations. What was said may be written down or what was written may be transformed through actions into objects. For example, the spoken phrase 'use the @ key to erase a single character' might be 'solidified' as a post-it note and then become even more permanent as the historical body of a person who uses that computer system frequently. Similarly, spoken instructions or discussions can become designs and blueprints which are then used to guide actions in making furniture or in building homes.

But then, in turn, these objects in the world and the historical body of people can be used to form the basis of further discourse. If the teacher uses a sequence of discourse and actions to hand a paper back to a student, that set of actions might be transformed into discourse when a student tells another on: 'You know, Dr Scollon always hands us our papers back personally.' That spoken discourse might again become transformed into historical body when that student becomes a teacher and begins teaching her own classes and adopts this practice with her students (or equally if she avoids doing that because of this example).

An action such as using the '@' key to backspace and erase a spelling error or calling out a student's name before handing back an assignment in class, or any of the other thousands of actions involved in conducting a traditional panopticon university class or a technologically mediated university class occurs at the intersection of many cycles of discourse, action, and practice. We refer to this intersection as the 'site of engagement' – that moment when all those practices – calling a person's name, stepping into personal space, handing an assignment, and so forth – come together to form an action in real time. When such a site of engagement is repeated regularly we refer to that as a 'nexus of practice'. We have tried to represent the intersecting cycles of discourse of a nexus analysis graphically in Figure 2.5.

2.5 Nexus analysis.

The point at which these cycles intersect is the moment the teacher hands an assignment back to the student, for example. The large circle might represent the cycle of handing which was learned by both the teacher and the student very early in life and which has been practiced many times over the years. The oval at the top might represent the student's practice of sitting together with other students in class which has been practiced since he or she began to attend school. The smaller, thicker circle to the left might represent a less deeply learned practice such as wearing a heavy parka to class which would be the case for a student who came from California to study the anthropology of education at the University of Alaska. The small, dark circle might represent the particular synopsis of the reading which was a type of essay this same student has just begun to learn to write in this class. All of these cycles of discourse come together at this moment to enable the teacher and student to succeed in the action of handing and receiving the assignment.

Each of the moments we will discuss in Chapter 3 in the extended comparison of the panopticon class and the technologically mediated class could be represented as such a nexus. In each case some of the cycles would remain the same and some would change. The work of a nexus analysis is to find out which are the crucial cycles for any moment of human action, to navigate those cycles as a way of seeing how those moments are constituted out of past practices and how they in turn lead into new forms of action, and to discover where points of change and transformation can be found that will allow new and more effective nexus of practice.

Of the three main stages, engaging the nexus of practice, navigating the nexus of practice, and changing the nexus of practice, what we will describe in Chapter 3 are the two end points of a nexus analysis. We show in detail how our work in the 1980s engaged a particular nexus of practice – the traditional panopticon university class – and we discuss how we changed that nexus of practice. Ron was a teacher of on-campus classes of this traditional kind and Suzie was a teacher of distance-delivered university classes. By using the new communication technologies we changed the nexus of practice of both on- and off-campus classes and what resulted was a rather new and exciting set of phenomena. These new classes restructured the interaction order both among students and between students and the teacher, they required the development of new historical body for all participants while inhibiting or disabling old classroom practices, and they evolved into the new kinds of discourse we are now becoming familiar with in web and email discursive exchanges.

To put it in a few words, then, *nexus analysis* is the systematic and ethnographic study of the many cycles of discourse that come together to form a nexus of practice. In the chapters which follow we will begin to work our way through the analysis of the cycles of discourse that came together to form events such as the university classes we will describe in Chapter 3. To do that we will need to follow the cycles of discourse through other kinds of classes from elementary to graduate school and in other schools and universities. But this is not enough to see the full extent of these cycles of discourse; we will also look at how these cycles of discourse led our research through other stages in their cycle such as medical interviews in the public health service hospital in Bethel, through the presentencing reports in courts in the State of Alaska, and through a number of other situations in which differences in historical body, the interaction order, and the discourses in place were mutually constructing social situations of discrimination against Alaska Native people.

The semiotic ecosystem: The spruce budworm and the spruce-fir forests of eastern Canada

Our final theoretical consideration is to define a *semiotic ecosystem*. Many cycles of discourses come together at any point of social action. Their coming together is never purely accidental, however, even though there are often what may be thought of as accidental co-occurrences of discourse cycles. A teacher may have forgotten to mail his or her monthly electric bill payment and so have it in an envelope in the textbook being used to teach a class. From the point of view of the action of teaching a class, that electric bill and the check used to pay it are irrelevant. They would most likely be backgrounded by all of the participants even if they were visible to them. But there is no means of deciding *a priori* that these are *not* relevant. That is an empirical question that must be taken up in a nexus analysis.

In most cases, the relevant discourse cycles that circulate in a particular action are, in fact, linked together in much more complex semiotic ecosystems. The discourse cycle within which a textbook is conceived, written, published, bought, and read is linked to the discourse cycle in which a student enrolls in a degree program, takes courses, reads textbooks, takes exams, and is finally granted a degree by a university. Those cycles are also closely linked to economic cycles of prosperity and recession such that it is well known by university management that enrollments tend to rise as national economies recede and vice versa. Those cycles are also tied to personal or individual life cycles of elementary, secondary, and tertiary school attendance, credentialization and adult employment. We use the term 'semiotic ecosystem' to think about the ways in which several or many cycles of discourse are linked, extending the term from the use of the idea of the ecosystem in biological research.

As an example of how one of these ecosystems has been discussed in biological research we can look briefly at the outbreak of budworm infestations in the forests of eastern Canada. The forests we are concerned with consist principally of balsam firs, spruces, and birches. The firs are of commercial value as pulp wood and lumber. There have been six outbreaks of budworms since the 1700s which kill off all of the mature balsam firs. When the firs are killed off, the budworm population loses its food source and also collapses until the time of the next outbreak.

These outbreaks, however, do not much harm the spruce, which are less susceptible to the infestation. Neither do they harm the birches, which are not susceptible. When the firs are killed off it leaves the white birch and a dense young regeneration of firs and to a lesser extent of spruce. If there is no outbreak of budworms, the firs tend to reach overmaturity (which amounts to rotting and breaking) as well as to begin to crowd out the spruce and birch in a forest predominated by overmature fir trees.

To put this another way, the balance of the fir-spruce-birch forest over long cycles of hundreds of years depends on the periodic infestation by budworms. These infestations are a crucial part of the ecological stability of the forest ecosystem.

The budworm population itself depends on the fir-spruce-birch forest eco-system for its continued survival. Both in turn depend on climatic cycles of dry and wet periods. Between dry spells budworms are very rare. The female lays about 200 eggs. Like many insects, the male and female die after mating. About 19 percent of the eggs die because of parasites and from predators, leaving perhaps 162 of the original eggs. Of those 82 percent die because they are on the wrong part of the tree to be able to feed and become larvae. Of the surviving larvae, 86 percent die from parasites and predators, leaving only 2.7 percent to hatch as adults. Since 20 percent of the surviving adults die from parasites and predators this leaves basically just one male and one female to mate to relaunch the next cycle of reproduction.

In a sequence of dry years, however, the budworms increase so rapidly that they escape the capacity of the parasites and predators to control them and consequently begin their feeding on the balsam firs (and to a much smaller extent on the spruce).

Figure 2.6 shows these intersecting cycles for each of the relevant populations. This forest ecosystem has five main cycles: the birch stand, the spruce stand, the balsam fir stand, the budworm population and the climatic dry-wet cycle. The budworm and the dry-wet cycle are linked in time. The six outbreaks in the 250 or so years since the 1700s suggest a cycle with a timescale-circumference of about forty years. Because the weather-worm cycles result in the collapse of the balsam fir stand, that too has a timescale-circumference of about forty years. The white birch and spruce which are much less affected by these outbreaks have a longer cycle though that is indefinitely long. If the firs are not killed off by budworms, they have a suppressing effect on the stands of spruce and birch by

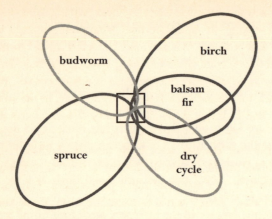

2.6 Fir-spruce-budworm ecosystem.

crowding them out. That is, those two cycles are depending upon and entrained to the budworm-weather-fir cycles.

It is important not to confuse three different kinds of cycles or systems in an ecosystem:

- the whole ecosystem within which the smaller and different species' cycles work;
- the population systems or cycles; and
- life cycles of the individuals in those populations.

The life cycle of a budworm like most northern insects is very short; it plays out in an annual cycle between spring hatching and the death or hibernation of winter. For the population cycle we have just described to exist requires the success of at least some individuals within the annual reproduction cycle. The life cycle of a tree may be forty or fifty years from seed to collapse either from maturity or from budworm infestation. Within this long life cycle, however, there are important differences between the coniferous trees which retain their leaves (needles) throughout the year and the deciduous trees which shed their leaves when the sap drops down the tree over the winter. Finally, like the interaction order we will discuss in Chapter 3, the life cycles of individual trees depend on their association in stands of like trees or in forests of different trees.

Before we take up the problem of mapping and circumferencing semiotic ecosystems, however, we need to clarify some of the problems with using the word 'cycle' in talking about either biological or conceptual systems. The word 'cycle' as it is used in talking about the water cycle means that there is a core molecule (H_2O) which remains the same whether it is liquid (water), solid (ice), or a gas (steam or water vapor). It is transformed from state to state by differences in temperature and pressure. When we use the word 'cycle' to talk about the annual cycle in the temperate zones of Spring–Summer–Winter–Fall, in this cycle there is a repetition each year but the cycle is not reversible. We do not go from Winter back to Summer; the leaves do not return to the trees without going through the bud-to-leaves stages of the cycle. When we use the word 'cycle' to talk about 'the life cycle' of a person, however, we are talking about an irreversible sequence of changes from birth through childhood and youth, then through adulthood to old age. In the life cycle there is no return from one stage to another and it is a matter of much philosophical discussion whether or not we can say exactly what it is that remains 'the same' throughout this life history of this historical body. When we talk about the reproductive cycle of a human or a plant or an animal, we are talking about yet a different kind of 'cycle'. In the reproductive cycle we mean that an organism has come to reproduce itself as another, separate, and different organism but one that grows, develops, and reproduces in much the same way as its source organism(s) and which will, itself, in turn continue to reproduce the same kind of organism.

So there are four quite different ways in which the concept of the cycle is commonly used. It is used to indicate:

- the change of state of a specific entity because of the influence of an external source of energy with changes that are fundamentally reversible (e.g. the water cycle);
- the recurring change of state of a specific entity because of either internal or external forces which, though irreversible recur in the same sequence throughout the life of the entity (e.g. the deciduous tree growing and shedding leaves, potassium secretion once in twenty-four hours by humans);
- the progression of an entity through a regular series of changes or trans-formations, each of which is irreversible, that is the entity does not and cannot return back to its initial state (the human life cycle, the budworm egg–larvae–insect cycle);
- the regular reproduction by an entity of other entities like itself and which, in turn, reproduce further instances of the entity – thus, continuity is not through the specific entity but through a class of entities reproduced by their own ancestor entities (e.g. human reproductive cycle).

Finally, we should note that our use of the term 'semiotic ecosystem' is not in our minds simply developing a metaphor for thinking about discourse or cycles of discourse. While we have not elaborated the connection, the fir-spruce-budworm is not just or only a biological ecosystem, it is also a discursive or semiotic ecosystem. The only reason we know about this cycle in this case is because of another, very complex discursive system called scientific or biological research. What was sketched out above in an objectivist way is the summary of a long cycle of scientific research involving historical documents, biological field notes, analyses, conference reports, and publications. Not only that, the central reason we have learned about this ecosystem is because of the circulation through it of the discourse of commercial lumber production. We know about these fir trees because they are or have been an economic resource. That is, a motive analysis tells us that we have this complex discourse in great part because of national economic motives. We know a great deal less about equally interesting ecological cycles that have no direct economic impact.

Conversely, we also want to emphasize that discourse cycles are not just analogies based on material cycles. Discourse cycles are all material cycles as well. In one instance the materialization of the discourse may be in the form of the movements of body parts in spoken language. In another instance these are materialized as written documents. It is the job of a nexus analysis never to presuppose the links among cycles of discourse but to seek them out for analysis.

3 From the essay to email: New media technology and social change

Now that she has got her snow machine started, Diane pulls the hood of her parka tight around her face, checks that her books and emergency gear are stowed snugly behind her, and sets out from Shishmaref across the ice and snow for the one-hour run to Kotzebue. It's a clear afternoon in late February with a bright moon and stars and it's not too cold – only about 20° below zero – so she enjoys thinking about her class while she navigates the endless hummocks and ruts of the well-worn route. She hopes there will be some messages from the class on the terminal at the university building in Kotzebue that respond to her thoughts four days ago about using computer communication for the seven Iñupiaq kids in her fourth-fifth grade class. She could worry later about how to get them all into Kotzebue and whether the university would let them use the terminal for a while for the kids. The kids would love it.

Marie doesn't bother to put her parka back on because she doesn't have to go out of the building between her two classes. She comes into the room and puts her stuff on an unused chair behind her and sits down where she usually sits between the girl from Anchorage and the guy from North Dakota who's been teaching for a few years in Tununak. When they come in they chat for a while until the teacher comes down from his office upstairs – he's not carrying a parka like everyone else, of course – and he starts to hand out their quizzes from last time and the notes for today's lecture. Marie sees that she got an A– and that's a bit better than she thought. When he goes to close the door the class gets quiet and they turn their attention to what he's starting to say – something about the quizzes he's just handed back.

The traditional and the electronic university class

The class Diane is taking is a University of Alaska graduate course in Education called 'Language, Literacy, and Learning'. The time is Spring 1981. She is a teacher in the small elementary school in Shishmaref on the Arctic Coast of northwest Alaska. She gets reading packets mailed to her at the school but to participate in the class discussions she needs to take the hour trip to Kotzebue where she can use the university's electronic mail system as well as the telephone hook-up. In Shishmaref the only telephone is in the Village Council office and it is in constant use by people in the village and cannot be tied up for the length of time it would take for the class audio conferences. She is one of the first people in the world to take a class for university credit using email and audio conferencing as the media of instruction. She is ecstatic about this because, as much as she loves Shishmaref, there is nobody in this small village to talk to about her problems teaching in the small elementary school other than her husband, and only a few people in Kotzebue, a small city.

Marie is a student taking graduate Education courses on campus at the University of Alaska in Fairbanks. The course she is taking is called 'Language, Literacy, and Learning'. The time is Fall 1980, the semester before Diane's class. It is a seminar that meets once a week for three hours and involves a lot of reading — much more than any of the classes she has taken before this and she has to keep up on it or she misses a lot in the class lectures and discussions. She lives in the dormitory, studies in Wood Center and the Library, and takes her classes in the Gruening Building. For her it is a world of people. They are everywhere. She has a roommate in the dorm and like all of them who live in the dorm can't even go to the toilet without running into people, both friends and strangers who want to talk. While at first she hated this, she has come to enjoy the group of people she takes her classes with — they are mostly the same people in all the classes — and they often study together and have potlucks together on weekends.

We start with these two contrasting experiences of a class which Ron actually taught at the University of Alaska. For confidentiality, of course, the two students are fictional composites of actual students who took these two classes, the first example, Diane, in the Spring Semester of 1981 and the second example, Marie, in the preceding Spring Semester of 1980. Other non-consequential details have been changed in the interest of confidentiality as well. These two classes are in some formal or bureaucratic sense the same class. Students taking each class received the same university graduate credit. They read many of the same academic articles and books. In both classes they discussed the ways in which our knowledge of language and discourse is constrained by our long history of literacy, especially the technology of print literacy. A central theme in which we were all interested was whether or not it was appropriate to use literacy-based strategies of teaching and learning such as reading textbooks and writing tests in the education of the children throughout Alaska who are among the first people in their cultural history to use literacy to represent their languages.

In the Spring of 1981 we wanted to run the course using the university computer system and the audio conferencing network as our media because we wanted to know the effects these new media might have on how we ourselves as university teachers or researchers and public school teachers think, talk, and exchange texts. These 'Language, Literacy, and Learning' classes were the predecessors of the class we taught the next year on 'The Social Impact of Instructional Telecommunications'. All of this thinking was directed toward our interest in providing non-discriminatory access to the educational, medical, legal, and business, and government institutions of the State of Alaska.

Here is a verbatim transcript of a television interview with Suzie in the Fall of 1981. It explains how we began this project:

I taught for XCED two years ago. That's the Cross-cultural Educational Development Program. It's a program for rural teacher training. So they do everything by correspondence, well, not everything. They have field coordinators who live in each region who tutor the students. But I was in Fairbanks and the only contact I had with my students was by mail and I found that very frustrating.

Somewhere in the middle of the semester I found out that it was possible to use the Legislative Teleconferencing Network to talk with my students. I tried that once and it was kind of nerve-racking, but still it was better. At least we got to talk a little bit.

Well, after that I was outside [Alaskan and Canadian jargon for anywhere in the world south of Alaska or northern Canada] at a seminar on research and development and I just happened to go to a bookstore in Berkeley and pick up a couple of books on computer conferencing. I'd never heard of it before. [The books were Johansen, Vallee, and Spangler's (1979) *Electronic meetings* and Hiltz and Turoff's (1978) *The network nation*.]

I read them and thought that that had a lot of possibilities.

Then I found out that the University of Alaska had its own computer network. At that time it was just Juneau, Anchorage, and Fairbanks that were hooked up. So I started learning how to use the mail system.

At that time I was negotiating a contract with UAITC [University of Alaska Instructional Telecommunications Consortium] and I communicated with their office in Anchorage using the computer. And I kind of liked that way. Both of us have never been comfortable with telephones. In twelve years we've been married we've had a TV for less than a year. We've only had a phone for a few years now. I found computer messaging a very comfortable way of communicating.

UAITC was having meetings on computer-assisted instruction and using microcomputers in schools and the biggest problem we ran into was the lack of software. So I thought that putting students into direct contact with instructors where they could interact would be more powerful than any kind of canned program where the computer is used as a teaching machine.

So I put pressure on Ron. He was teaching a course on campus, a graduate seminar in education [the 'Language, Literacy, and Learning' course] and I encouraged him to get a computer ID and to have everybody in his class get an ID and start a computer conference. That worked out pretty well. They had regular once-a-week meetings. But then in between and sometimes after class – the class met from seven in the evening to ten, people would go right from class after three hours of discussion, go to the computer and stay there until midnight and just continue.

What happened was that people who had never said anything in class in the first few weeks got on the computer and started discussing ideas that they had. And then the people who did talk in class started to notice that other people had ideas and some of them got into it too. It was a really lively discussion of issues that came up in class.

So then we got the idea of teaching this course ['The Social Impact of Instructional Telecommunications']. We wanted to do an experiment or a demonstration because UAITC was putting all this hardware in place and nobody seemed to know just exactly how it was all going to work. So we thought we'd try this.

We'd been thinking about the idea of the social impact of each different instructional telecommunications medium. So it seemed like a natural thing to teach. We thought that since there was so little known about these media, if we got in right now there wouldn't be too many people who would say we should have known more than we did. I guess we've learned a lot doing it.

We did learn a lot and made a lot of mistakes. Of course computer and other electronic communications have changed dramatically in the twenty-some years since we did these first experiments with computer-mediated communication. In the following chapters we will talk about other fields of social life in which we also did research and provided consultation at this time from the judicial system in Alaska to communication in business and government organizations. For example, we worked with Alaska state troopers and with 911 (emergency) call-center service people, with Alaska resource managers and pre-school teachers, with probation officers and with university faculty in the humanities on inter-ethnic communication, organizational communication, and the uses of the new communication technologies. Those other projects form part of the nexus of social institutions and histories that were the world in which we conducted these educational experiments.

Here in Chapter 3 we want to focus more closely on just these two classes so that we can set out a comparison to show how a nexus analysis can reveal how the use of the technologies of communication – in this case computer and audio conferencing – entailed very different social events, social relationships, and patterns of discourse. We will use the three-part framework which we set out in Chapter 2 arguing that action takes place as an intersection or nexus of three kinds of cycles – the historical bodies of the participants, the interaction order within which they establish their ongoing relationships, and the discourses in place – to develop our comparison of these two kinds of university classes, beginning with the interaction order.

The interaction order in a traditional university class

The interaction order of a traditional classroom is constructed out of two main types of interaction. One is what Goffman would call a 'platform event' and the other he might classify as a 'meeting'. A platform event is one in which one person (or several) performs as a spectacle for the observation of another group of people who observe as an audience. This would include lectures, musical and dramatic performances, political speeches, and so forth. A meeting is an event in which a group of people conduct a line of discussion with relatively equal status in their rights to take the floor and speak. We could introduce the idea that the interaction order of a traditional classroom is a 'panopticon event' as suggested by Foucault's writing because a typical class in our research data was basically organized around the talk of the teacher and, even when it became a discussion involving many students, it remained for the teacher to monitor the flow of turn exchanges.

The panopticon classroom interaction order, sometimes called the teacher-centered classroom, is one in which the teacher is at the hub of a communication wheel. The teacher speaks to everyone in the class, everyone in the class who speaks speaks either to the teacher or possibly *through* him or her. That is, when

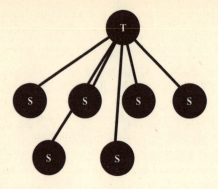

3.1

students respond to something said by one of the other students, they typically raise a hand or nod or indicate to the teacher first that they want to speak and then, when authorized by the teacher, speak to the other student. These relationships are sketched in Figure 3.1. In the great majority of university classrooms we observed in Fairbanks, Anchorage, Juneau, and Sitka (and we might add in our current home university, Georgetown University, as well as in the variety of universities we have visited and taught in during the years in between) the seating is arranged to facilitate this panopticon interaction order. The teacher is placed at the front in a large space – often as much as one-third of the total space in the room – and he or she is most often standing at a podium or behind a table which forms a symbolic bulwark or fortress to enhance his or her all-seeing, all-monitoring position in the social interaction. Students in these classrooms are seated in smaller chairs, normally arrayed in rows where the students are shoulder-to-shoulder – normally within what Edward T. Hall calls intimate space. Even where this arrangement is altered to put the chairs in a circle or to seat students and teacher around a table, the most common configuration is that there will be a gap on the two sides of the teacher so that symbolically the closest student is within the wider circle of space, personal space.

This seating arrangement places the teacher and students in an array that makes the relationships among students fall within the intimate to personal range of Hall's interpersonal distances but normally places the teacher at the still further social distance from the students. We have seen many students and teachers restructure the chairs in the rooms they are in to maintain this set of social relationships. The most common strategy is for students to take up places in the second row of seats when the first row is within the teacher's personal space.

Along with these spatial and physical arrangements, the teacher is perceived as the owner of the space. Teachers may ask students to get up and close or open the door or windows. They can walk around and make free use of the blackboard and other instructional equipment. They can ask students to come to the front to present, and, even if teachers take a seat among the students when a student is presenting, they remain in control of the social flow of activities in the classroom and may resume their place at the front at will.

Attendance in a panopticon classroom is also the teacher's prerogative, though we should be sure to point out that this is a situational ratification of a power normally held by the university. Teachers can hold students accountable for their absences from prior meetings of the class and often take roll, sometimes directly by calling names and recording them in a record book. More often roll is taken indirectly by passing out marked assignments and quizzes, or lecture notes. Many of the teachers we have observed, after they have gone through the class passing out returned assignments, will comment out loud for all to hear such things as, 'I see Maria isn't here today', or 'Does anybody know where Paul is?' In the latter case the students are interpellated or hailed into the process of accounting for each other's participation in the panopticon event.

As part of the participation control rights of the teacher, we have noted that students need to gain the teacher's permission to be absent, normally in advance, or to bring other non-registered people to the class. If someone appears in the room who is unanticipated, it is the teacher who has the right (and responsibility) to call that person to account for himself or herself and his or her presence. A person who is present in the room and is unknown to most of the participants is automatically assumed to be a guest of the teacher, not one of the other students.

A panopticon classroom is different from some platform events such as formal lectures or concert performances because in the classroom there is no MC who makes an introduction to formally bring the performer onstage. There is some variability among teachers we have observed in whether they prefer to be in the room early and wait to start the class while the students come in and get ready for class. These teachers often engage in discussions with the students about non-class matters such as the weather, sports, news, or other social events. Other teachers prefer to wait until the class is assembled and then march into class, go directly to their panopticon position, and begin speaking. This will be quite important to return to in Chapters 4 and 6 because we have found that the degree of synchrony and the ease of exchanges between teachers and students, even in the panopticon, teacher-controlled classroom, varies depending on the extent to which the teacher 'tunes-in' to the students or, conversely, expects the students to 'tune-in' to herself or himself.

The panopticon class interaction order has quite clear practices by which it is opened and closed. These include closing the room door, handing out papers, assignments, quizzes, or lecture notes, throat clearing, shifts in voice level and direction, eye-gaze, changes of posture from sitting to standing (or vice versa),

and key words or phrases that signal a boundary. There may also be technological signals such as checking microphones in large lectures or turning on slide
projectors and dimming the lights. We might add that recently we have added
shifts required for the use of presentation software.

No one of the markers we have just mentioned is sufficient by itself. None of
them is inevitably a marker of the inception or termination of the panopticon
class interaction order, but we have no cases in our data nor have we seen in the
years since any cases in which a teacher simply began speaking the first words
of a lecture without making some quite noticeable and formal signal that the
interaction order was now shifting into that of the panopticon. By far the most
common signals of the shift into the panopticon interaction order are closing the
door, handing out various papers, and taking up a physical position at the center
of the 'stage'. Almost always there is a brief utterance: 'Shall we get started?'
'I guess everyone's here now, so I'd like to start by . . .'

Likewise the panopticon interaction order is terminated by the teacher
stepping out of the panopticon role. This is usually done with an utterance such
as, 'That's all we have time for today,' or 'We'll take that up next time.' Along
with this are gestures such as assembling his or her notes, tapping them
rhythmically on end on a table or lectern to align them squarely, or putting them
away in a folder or briefcase.

These practices for opening and closing the panopticon interaction order are
crucial because the primary difference between this interaction order and what
precedes and follows it in the same room is the exclusive attention directed to
the teacher and the teacher's interests. What lies on the outside of the panopticon
interaction in time before and after are a lot of small social interactions, mostly
brief conversational encounters. These, according to Goffman and our own
observations, are 'withs which have as their main focus of attention the production and the maintenance of a state of talk among a relatively small group'
(adapted from Goffman's definition in Scollon and Scollon 2003: 209). The
panopticon event has as its main focus of attention the production of focused
talk – talk which is centered on the topical agenda which has been set by the
teacher (or perhaps the university) in the form of either a lecture or a teacher-
controlled discussion.

The room full of people before and after a traditional university class is a
congeries of little groups of two or three engaged in smalltalk along with,
perhaps, a few singles who might be reading or just putting their things in order
for the class. These small conversational encounters – and one of them often
involves the teacher – begin when the first participants arrive, are often carried
out in rather loud voices, frequently as carry-overs or continuations of conversations which have begun earlier in the hallways, and ebb and flow like the
chatter of a party. At the end of the panopticon event they immediately break

out again, including sometimes someone coming to begin a conversation with the teacher if he or she has remained for a moment in the classroom. The work of starting up, maintaining, and concluding the panopticon event is a considerable one that takes clear signals as well as long practice for all of the participants. A sure mark of the beginning teacher is his or her difficulty in both herding the participants together into the panopticon and in keeping the conversations from breaking out again whenever he or she fails to command the focused attention of everyone assembled.

We can summarize these aspects of the panopticon class interaction order as follows:

- The teacher is the hub of a communication wheel.
- The teacher controls turn exchanges (one-to-many; many-to-one).
- There are physical arrangements to map these social arrangements (teacher separated from students; students close together).
- The teacher owns the room space; has wide latitude in using front third of the space.
- The teacher controls the presence or absence of students and of guests.
- The teacher ratifies participation through direct or indirect roll taking.
- The teacher controls the practices for opening and closing the panopticon interaction order.
- Within the panopticon event attention is directed to the teacher and the teacher's interests unless these are temporarily delegated to another participant.

Discourses in place in a traditional university class

There is an entire academic discipline focused on English for Academic Purposes as well as, of course, many studies of other languages and how they are used within academic discourse. These researchers have focused their attention on the production and rhetorical structuring of academic lectures and of academic papers – in particular they have been concerned to study the writing of journal papers for publication. Here our interest is somewhat more limited. We want to summarize the main ways in which discourse is used in the panopticon traditional university classroom so that a little later we can make a comparison with how it is used in the computer-mediated classes we have observed. Thus our analysis here is limited to points which in our research were common across all of the traditional classrooms we observed which were primarily in the social sciences, the humanities, and education.

Discourse in a traditional university class is focused on topics which are pre-set in the course syllabus and which are controlled by the teacher. Sometimes, indeed, the topics have been set by the institution such as the university or program's curriculum committee, and even the teacher has little latitude in making major changes. What is important for us here is that the shift from the prior and subsequent small-group chat within the classroom into the central event, the panopticon class, is first and foremost a shift of the discourse toward focusing on a single topic, the topic defined in advance by the syllabus and the teacher and in most cases also prepared for by assigned readings from books and journals. It might be an exaggeration to put it this way, but the purpose of this discourse is to learn what the authorities have to say and these authorities are researchers or authors who have written on the subject and the teacher of the class. It may vary from class to class whether or not the teacher is assumed to be one of the authorities the students are to learn from. What is clear is that they are to learn at the very least how he or she understands the assigned readings.

The discourse is oriented on the surface toward understanding these texts but, more crucially, since this understanding is evaluated by the teacher, we can say the discourse is oriented toward a mutual agreement between the teacher and the student about what grade should be given to the student at the end of the course. Successful reading (that is, a reading that will lead to receiving a good grade in the teacher's evaluation) is displayed primarily through two means: speech in class and written assignments such as short essays, quizzes, or exams. Each of these types is evaluated by the teacher and held against each other in a kind of triangulation. We have heard teachers say, 'Herbert got a bad grade on that last quiz, but I *know* he understands the material from what he says in class, so I don't think I'll count that grade so much.' Or conversely we have heard, 'Sandra says so little in class I had no idea she had understood that article so well; but she's really aced that mid-term exam.' Also teachers say, 'Winnie really does well on her essays; on her quizzes she seems to choke up when she doesn't have time to think; in class she's mostly pretty sharp.' Students' spoken discourse in class as well as their written discourse on assignments is evaluated on how well they show that they have come to adopt the language, concepts, and arguments of the texts they have been assigned to read.

The converse side of the sharp focus on teacher and syllabus-defined topics is that all other discourses in that place are de-selected for attention. Part of the shift from the pre-event and post-event to the panopticon class event is a suppression of topics that are not relevant to the syllabus or teacher-selected topic. Often we hear what is like an enormous and extended parenthesis around the class when the teacher closes the class and someone says to a friend, 'and as I was saying, just after we got to the party . . .'

But it is important also to note just how many other discourses are present in the classroom which are being de-selected for attention. Most students are carrying books from other classes. The economics textbook is stowed away during the psychology class even though what is being learned in the psych. class might have major implications for what is being taught in the econ. class. The logos, brand names, slogans, and the rest of the cacophony of commercial discourse that is printed on our clothing, our notebooks, the instructional technology in the room, and the furniture is silenced as irrelevant. The way Bonnie chuckled a bit when Marcia answered the teacher's question remains silenced until after Bonnie and Velma are out in the hallway. The university equipment numbers stamped on or engraved in the desk, the chairs, the overhead projector remain 'invisible' in this discourse. No one discusses the fact that it is 50° below zero outside, there is ice fog choking the air, it has been dark with only a few hours of light for two months now, and the room is full of large, puffy down parkas that signal all of this. These and many other discourses are present in every classroom just as the manhole covers leading to the water mains in the street are present when we cross the street. In the classroom only the syllabus-controlled topic is given license; the rest is placed below the attentional threshold.

The focus is on written discourse which enables covert discourses to remain active, even if they are sub-rosa discourses. What Bonnie would like to say to Velma might be written on a note and passed to Velma, or, what is more likely, it might be written into Bonnie's notebook as if it were a note on the lecture and then placed so Velma might read it. What is severely limited is the spoken expression of any discourse that is not relevant to the syllabus-selected topic. In all of this, whether it is ratifiable note-taking or subversional personal commentary or even a letter to a friend written in the guise of lecture notes, the technologies of text are academic articles, student notes, teacher notes, syllabuses, or black- or whiteboard writing in which alphabetic text dominates over any form of graphic text or images. The student who draws images is thought of as 'doodling', engaged in idle hand movements while her mind is engaged elsewhere. Rarely is it imagined that these images might be the stuff of conceptual processing.

Because of the topic-dominance of this discourse, turns at speaking tend to be monologic in the sense that they tend to be extended discourses, if we may use that word now in a different sense, rather than the short exchanges that are more typical of conversational encounters. Most of the actual speaking time in the traditional class period is occupied by the teacher, this by a very large margin. But when students take (or are given) the floor (and required to take it) they are expected to produce teacher-like extended and developed responses, not short answers.

This monologic nature of the discourse replicates in the single speaker's turn at talk what is expected when multiple speakers speak (normally in a teacher-student-teacher-student pattern rather than a teacher-student-student-student pattern). The idea is that the discourse will proceed along a logically developed line of argument. References will be made back to earlier presuppositions and arguments and forward to conclusions yet to be drawn. It is skill in making this sort of linear logical argument that is being closely evaluated and all discourse, whether it is that of a single speaker or that of multiple speakers is expected to conform to this logical structure which has been called the structure of 'essayist literacy'. In many ways the classroom spoken discourse, based on texts which students and the teacher have read, all works in the service of enabling students to become proficient writers of extended argumentative text.

We can summarize the discourses in place in the traditional classroom as follows:

- Discourse is focused on syllabus-defined and teacher-controlled topics.
- Topics are organized by readings from the academic literature, normally through assigned texts.
- Displays of successful reading are shown through speech in class and through written assignments, normally in essay format or quizzes and exams.
- The semiotic focus on syllabus-defined texts and topics is maintained by the exclusion of all other discourses either present or potentially present.
- Written discourse is privileged over spoken discourse.
- Technologies of text are academic articles, student notes, teacher notes and syllabuses, black- or whiteboard writing. Alphabetic text dominates over graphic text and images.
- Speaking turns are monologic.
- Speaking turns are managed by the teacher and must show topical relevance.
- All discourse has an argument-based rhetorical structure.

Historical body of the individuals in a traditional university class

Teachers

Even on their first day of university teaching teachers come to the class with some sixteen or more years of experience in the classroom, many of those years in university classrooms exactly like the one in which they are teaching. Their historical bodies, that is their life experiences, their goals or purposes, and their unconscious ways of behaving and thinking have been formed to a large extent within schools. Many of the teachers we have interviewed, indeed most, have never in their lives been through one full year that was not geared to the academic calendar since the first year they went to school at about five years old.

The teacher is thoroughly practiced, albeit from the student side of the room, in all of the discourse and interaction order factors we have noted above. While he or she might be uncomfortable going to the lectern or front table or desk rather than taking up a student seat, he or she knows exactly where to take up the teacher's position and what to do there from long experience of watching it happen before. University teaching is one of the rare professions into which one enters with such a long and extended apprenticeship in the discourses and practices of the profession.

The teacher, even at the beginning, has had some four to ten years of experience in the discourses and interaction practices of the university. He or she has written many extended essays and in most cases a full-length doctoral dissertation as well. Teachers use these rhetorical and literate structures regularly in their own professional development in doing research and publishing in journals. They may, however, be new to preparing the syllabus for a course and in taking on the role of the leader of a discussion. This is actually rare in that most university teachers have had to prepare such agendas and lead such discussions for seminars in their own graduate work.

The teacher's goals and purposes will be many and complex, of course, but they are grounded in the fact that they are doing this teaching to receive a pay-check. These purposes will normally be oriented toward producing an extended academic career. At the same time, that career will depend much more solidly on the results of their research and publication than their teaching in most cases. Thus they may bring to the traditional classroom a minimalist goal of simply staying in control and surviving the teaching. In a sense the university teacher in the classroom has little to lose even if students do not learn very much.

At the same time university teachers are likely to have a relatively high interest in the subject matter, particularly when the course is in the area of their own specialization. As we will discuss in Chapter 5, a point that is particularly important in our studies in Alaska but which is also very relevant throughout the world where students are from cultural groups that are different from that of the teacher and the university, most university teachers outside of the classroom in their dealings with friends and families engage in regular practices of the spoken discourse structures of turn exchange and argumentation that are valued in the classroom.

Because they have chosen or ended up in an academic career it will come naturally to them to evaluate students on the basis of how well they are following in their own footsteps. As we have found in our research (see Chapter 6), most university teachers evaluate students on the basis of how well they are coming to think and speak and behave like professionals in their own field. Thus students in psychology are evaluated on how much they look and act like psychologists; students in literary analysis are evaluated on how much they begin to look like literary critics.

Students

Students come to the classroom with very different structures of historical body than their teachers. Some will have gone straight through school from kindergarten or the first grade right up to university. Others will have had periods of schooling in different systems if their parents have traveled. Still others will have had periods out of school in which they were working. Most students will have had twelve years or more in which they have internalized and practiced the student practices of the student–teacher role performance. They know the basic structures of academic discourse and of the panopticon interaction order. They know where to sit, when to talk and when not to talk. Nevertheless, students are very different in their internalization of the skills of producing extended essays and in engaging in academic discussions. Unlike their teachers, they almost never have any occasion for using or practicing these skills outside of the university classroom.

By the time they reach the university, students have had many teachers of many types and personalities and so they are skilled in 'getting around' their teachers and can predict what they are likely to do in response to their own actions. Students bring these skills to accomplishing their own goals and purposes. For most these goals and purposes are organized around receiving institutional credentials – normally a Bachelor's degree – and with the least effort while devoting much of their time to the social life of being young adults away from home and parental supervision for the first time. Their goals can mostly be achieved by receiving passable but not excellent grades in each of the classes they take.

Students often have little or no knowledge or experience of the discourse practices of the university argumentative or essayist type. They might have had some short essays to write in school prior to the university, but the majority of the students we researched at universities in Alaska in the 1980s saw the discourse structures and practices of the university classroom as somewhat esoteric abilities that had no use or function in the society outside of the university.

This perception is tied as well to the students' view of the university within a client or services model. Unlike the teachers who evaluate them on the basis of how well they are becoming socialized into academic life and discourse, students evaluate their teachers and their courses on the basis of how interesting or useful the course and its materials appear to be for a life outside of the academic world.

We can summarize the historical bodies of the teacher and students in the traditional classroom as follows:

The teacher
- The teacher has normally had sixteen or more years of performing the student face of the teacher–student role in the panopticon classroom.
- The teacher has four to ten or twelve years of performing in the extended essay and discussion genres of the university discourse; he or she uses them regularly in making professional advancement through journal publication, for example.
- On the other hand the teacher may be new in taking the teacher's panopticon role, in preparing syllabuses, and in leading discussions.
- The teacher's goals are based on institutional membership – he or she is there as part of salaried or paid work and normally expects to be retained or not, advanced or not, depending on his or her performance in taking on the panopticon expectations.
- The teacher usually has a high interest in the subject matter of the course; it is normally one of his or her career specialty areas.
- Many more teachers than not practice the turn-exchanges of argumentative discourse outside of the classroom in other social events.
- Teachers primarily evaluate students on the basis of a socialization model: How much are the students becoming like 'us'?

Students
- Students have had twelve years or more in which they have internalized at least some of the practices of the student–teacher role performance.
- Students are very different in their internalization of the skills of producing extended essays and engaging in academic discussions; they rarely have any use for these skills outside of classes.
- Students have had much practice in 'getting around' their teachers; most will have had many teachers by the time they sit in a university class.
- Students' goals are based on receiving institutional credentials, normally a Bachelor's degree. This plays out in seeking passable grades in each class.
- Students' interests may have little to do with the subject matter which may be required by curricular requirements.
- Students often have little knowledge of or practice in the turn-exchange practices of argumentative discourse outside of the university classroom.
- Students evaluate their own performance on the basis of a client for services model: How interesting or useful does the course seem to be for a life outside of the academic world?

The shifting sands of the interaction order, discourse, and historical body: The computer-mediated class

When Marie came into that class in the Gruening Building at the University of Alaska, Fairbanks, in our opening anecdote, things played out pretty much along the lines we have just described above. She took her seat in the student arena of the panopticon, engaged in small chat until the teacher formally convened the class. She sat together with the other students throughout the lecture, sometimes taking notes, sometimes responding to questions the teacher asked, and sometimes listening to what her classmates were saying. When the class ended she resumed her conversation briefly as she packed up her things and left the room. Much of what happened ran off on a time-table through an almost entirely automatic set of rehearsed practices. She was one class closer to the end of term, one class closer to finishing her Master's degree.

When Diane got on her snow machine for the trip into Kotzebue her experience with 'the same' university class could not have been much different. She came from a small home in a small village into the somewhat larger Kotzebue. After stowing her snow machine, she went into a small frame building which is the University of Alaska's regional center in Kotzebue, took off her outside gear, and made a bit of conversation with the director of the university center in Kotzebue. It was his terminal she would use to log-in to the university computer network. Except for the long snow machine trip, her experience of this computer-mediated class is not much different from that of the other students who took the course sitting at university terminals, even the ones who took it on the Fairbanks campus.

In the case of the computer-mediated class which follows we will parallel the section that preceded this on the practices of the panopticon traditional university. We will show how the interaction order is structured, how discourse is used, and how the historical body of individuals influences their participation in the actions which we call taking this university class.

The interaction order in a technology-mediated university class

The teacher organized the computer-mediated class by preparing the readings and mailing them to the registered students. Along with the mailed readings were instructions for log-in to the university computer as well as instructions for call-up for the class audio conferences. As a form of the interaction order the first concern is to understand a distinction between primary and secondary social interaction. Primary interactions take place with the participants in the same physical space where they have access to what Goffman calls the 'naked' senses of each other. That is they can see and hear (and smell, etc.) the other participants and by taking specific distances from each other, with eye-gaze, and the timing of their turn-exchanges they can display and confirm or deny each other's claims to social relationships of various kinds. For example, in the panopticon class the students and teacher mutually establish and continually ratify their relationship by maintaining the social distance between themselves, by the teacher's special rights to sit or stand or move around, and to nominate specific other participants to take the floor. Secondary, that is mediated, social interactions occur between the participants and the texts they study. For all of the participants in the panopticon class, teacher and students alike, the authors of the texts they are reading are not currently present, they participate through a distant medium — the printed word — and the teacher controls their participation in the class through selecting the class's attention to them.

The interaction order of the technology-mediated class also has a double nature of a primary set of face-to-face social interactions and secondary, mediated ones. The primary interactions in the technology-mediated class are with non-participants in the class; the social interactions with the class are secondary in that they are mediated through those primary participations. Diane uses a terminal located in the Kotzebue regional center's office and the person she sees and talks to in and among and around her computer messages, the person who hears her talk and can see her facial expressions 'in' the class in the audio conferences is this regional administrator, not the class participants. They talk and joke and laugh about the class and the weather and many other things at the same time Diane is 'participating' in the class.

This is not much different for the students who take the technology-mediated class on campus. They disperse throughout the campus to wherever terminals are available. There are one or two in the dorm; there are several in the School of Education; there are more in the Business School and the Library. At the time we first taught these classes there were no terminals located in labs or classrooms dedicated to technology-mediated classes and there were no home computers being used to dial-up the university computer ports. When they participate in the technology-mediated class they are normally seated next to administrators or administrative staff who are sending memos about university matters, not other university students and not participants in the course.

This aspect of the technology-mediated class or other computer-mediated communications did not change significantly when we were able to conduct classes and other conferences from home via modem and telephone. The primary participants changed from being university administrators and staff to being family members, of course, but they were nevertheless not ratified participants in the secondary, mediated interaction order.

So if the panopticon interaction order is characterized as a grouping where all of the participants are mutually present to each other and where the focus of attention is on a single person of greater authority, the teacher, and on his or her topics of interest, the technology-mediated class interaction order is one in which all (or most) of the primary social relationships are with non-participants in the interaction, the technology-mediated class interaction itself is secondary or embedded within those primary face-to-face relationships and there is no focused or controlled topic of interest which is managed by any of the participants whether primary or secondary. As we documented these email messages and audio conference exchanges there were three main topical strands woven into a complex thread: First and really the dominant one was the thread of the technology-mediated class itself. We constantly talked among ourselves and with the primary participants about the use of the technology and its implications, but mostly about how to actually use it successfully. Second, we carried on complex conversations among the primary participants and the technology-mediated class participants. We saw such messages as, 'My husband who is sitting right here just said . . .' and in the audio conferences we heard: 'Oh, just a minute; there's somebody knocking at the door.' The third topical thread was, of course, the course materials; but discussion of these topics and readings never rose to dominate the interaction. In short the interaction order of the technology-mediated class was never isolated as an interaction that was separate from other concurrent social interactions in which the participants were involved.

In Figure 3.2 we show how the technology-mediated class interaction order was often idealized in the research literature and continues to be idealized today. What are highlighted are the multiple interactions of all participants with all participants with no central control.

In Figure 3.3 we show how the technology-mediated class interaction order works in actual practice. The circles marked with 'P' indicate primary, face-to-face communications in the physical locations where the participants are located.

We can conclude this discussion of the technology-mediated class interaction order with a few more points which derive from this interaction order as well as

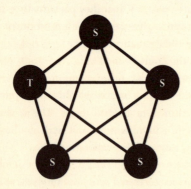

3.2

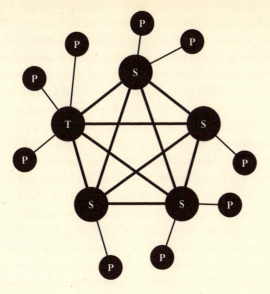

3.3

from the computer- and audio-mediated nature of this class. First of all this interaction order is very closely tied to the physical circumstances of the placement of the participants in the world. It is inherent in the technology-mediated class that the participants are not (mostly) physically present to each other. Of course we do need to comment that on occasion our students or we ourselves would find ourselves sitting next to each other in a place where there were multiple terminals talking to each other via computer as if we were at a great distance. One student commented that she had met one of the other students in the corridor; both were rushing to do something and so hadn't stopped to chat. Only a few minutes later when they both realized that they had been rushing to different terminals on campus so that they could send messages to each other did they see the absurdity of their situation.

Ownership of the spaces in which the technology-mediated class took place (both computer- and audio-mediated aspects) did not belong to either the teacher or the students; it was the university administration which was perceived as owning the spaces. Permission to use the terminals had to be sought; there were no regularly scheduled time periods in which the terminals were dedicated to the purposes of the class and not used for any other purpose.

Within the physical spaces of the computer terminal itself, there was a quickly developed sense that one should not occupy more than a screenful of visual space at a time. As we shall see when we look at the discourse more directly, there was a move toward short, multi-threaded 'utterances' instead of the long, monologic turns we observed in the panopticon classroom. Perhaps most interesting is that on the screen the account identifications made a minimal distinction among participants. 'FF' was 'Fairbanks faculty', 'FS' was 'Fairbanks undergraduate student', 'FT' was 'Fairbanks graduate student', and FA was 'Fairbanks administrator'. Thus Ron was FFRTSCOLLON; Suzie was FFSBSCOLLON; an undergraduate student was FSJP(NAMEOMITTED); a graduate student was FTDW(NAMEOMITTED), and an administrator was FAJD(NAMEOMITTED). The four-way distinction marked by the letters 'F', 'S', 'T', and 'A' are the merest reflections on the screen of the social and institutional distinctions which are marked in the panopticon classroom by control of one-third of the physical space and by constant visual orientation to the teacher occupying that space.

In the case of the panopticon classroom it is the teacher who closes the door, hands out the assignments, and who takes up a position at the head of the class to make the transition from pre-class conversational encounters to the panopticon interaction order. In the technology-mediated class it is the technicians of the University of Alaska Computer Network and the Teleconferencing Network who give account authority, identifications and passwords (USERIDS), and who manage the opening up of the interaction. In this teachers, students, and administrators are on the same footing in their social and communicative rights and obligations toward each other. Once the technology-mediated class interaction is 'opened', it remains in an open, drop-in state.

Still there is the question of roll taking, the question of ongoing ratification of the status of participants. When someone does not respond in the panopticon class we check visually to see if they are physically occupied in some other way. When someone does not respond in the technology-mediated class there is no immediate way to know if they are not responding for lack of something to say, if it is because they have located themselves elsewhere, or if the equipment is down. As the three messages below show, from time to time roll is taken. In the first message Ron is checking to see if any students had sent a message. In the second case, later in the same day as the first, a student is checking on other participants without marking just whom he is looking for. In the third case an administrator who is taking the class is checking up on the presence of the teacher.

(1) FFRTSCOLLON Fri Sep 18 10:13 (3)

HI,
ANYBODY AROUND THIS MORNING?
RON

(2) FSNS(NAMEOMITTED) Fri Sep 18 17:22 (3)

WELL, GROUP, IT LOOKS LIKE THERE'S NO MAIL
ANYMORE. I'LL JUST PUT THIS IN, FEELS KINDA EMPTY
IN THERE SO NOW WE'LL ALL HAVE A LITTLE SOME-
THING TO READ. HAVE A GOOD DAY. (NAME OMITTED)

(3) FABV(NAMEOMITTED) Wed Nov 11 18:25 (3)

RON ARE YOU OUT OF TOWN? HAVEN'T READ OF YOU
LATELY. FEEL LIKE I'VE LOST A SOUL OR SOMETHINGOR
IT SEM LIKE THERE IS AN EMPTY SPACE OUT THERE.

So now we can summarize the main characteristics of the interaction order in the
technology-mediated class as follows:

- Primary (real-time and face-to-face) social interactions are with non-
  participants in the class; secondary mediated interactions are class
  communications.
- Interest is non-focused and uncontrolled; it shifts frequently between course
  topics and the conduct of the interaction itself.
- Students and teacher communicate in a 'chain-and-wheel' model of high-
  connectedness; each-to-all and each-to-each.
- Exchanges occur as participants choose; no central or other control of who
  contacts whom.
- Physical arrangements emphasize primary interactions; screen-based class
  interactions are minimally discriminated.
- University administration owns the physical spaces and terminals; teacher
  and students are 'borrowers' of these mediational means.
- All participants equally are confined to single-screen, line-at-a time participation windows.
- The interaction remains in an 'open' state once conference is established; it
  is initially opened by computer technicians.
- University computer network controls access to participation, monitors the
  participation, and drop-in guests interrupt frequently in both primary and
  secondary interactions.
- Students and teachers mutually check on and ratify each others'
  participation.

Discourses in place in a technology-mediated university class

Much of what we have to say about discourse in the technology-mediated class follows quite directly from the characteristics of the interaction order and can be stated quite directly. The discourse is distributed among multiple participants of different statuses. Often the bulk of the discourse is among non-ratified primary participants. During an audio conference, for example, Diane and the administrator in Kotzebue chat with each other while a student from Anchorage is making a point. Perhaps Diane sees the interest in her point but the administrator who is right there doesn't and so commands Diane's attention to his topic for a moment. The audio conference convenor equipment automatically switches off any voice transmission but one and so they can chat with impunity knowing that the other participants cannot hear them.

In the computer messages, there was a quick evolution toward messages which had a maximum length of one screen. Physically scrolling up and down was rarely practiced. Participants tended to read the message as it printed on the screen, which in those days was mostly a bit slower than normal reading speed. When the message ended they simply responded as if it had been a spoken utterance. That is, they did not use characteristic literacy practices such as going back and re-reading before responding; they used the practices of oral discourse by responding when the message came to an end. This meant that the first parts of long messages were simply ignored or forgotten in the response. This soon led to message 'turns' which fell within a length that could be conveniently remembered or recalled with a quick glance back up to the top of the page.

Because a screenful of text was then about twenty lines, there was an evolution toward short, almost epigrammatic messages. Further, each message tended to contain a topical weave of the three main threads: the task of managing the conference, the social relationships among the participants, and the content of the course. It is interesting to us that in Halliday's systemic functional grammar (Halliday 1978, 1985) there are three simultaneous functions of any utterance: a texual function, an interpersonal function, and an ideational function. A point that invites further analysis is that it seems that the email messages of our technology-mediated class functionally separated these three functions to some extent.

In the excerpt below there are these multiple threads. The message opens by wondering about how the medium might be used for various forms of expression. This is a topic that is central in this course on 'Language, Literacy, and Learning' and had been discussed in the readings, though the student makes no direct mention of any texts. Then note some of the very personal, real-time comments such as 'it is too early in my day' and 'I find it ANNOYING'. Also note that she makes a comment about the physical location of her message activity: 'the first step would to replace these fluorescent lights'. Finally, she comments on the medium directly, 'why do I get this retransmit last line blurb occassionally?'

FTDM(NAMEOMITTED)   Tue Mar 03   10:36 (18)

i was wondering when people were going to start using this electronic passenger pigeon for to send of creative doodling, spontaneous thought swirls, and other interesting types of saying/not saing kinds of things. it occurred tome that this would be a great place for the unpublished and/or aspiring poet-writer to circulate his/her ideas. i'm tempted to give a for instance or two, but it is too early in my day. perhaps the evolution that i see occurring in the conten and structure of our messages has something to do with the increased familiararity that we are experiencing with the medium. also, we are probably getting more familiar and comfortable with each other. maybe if everyone could leave their favority chair or cus-hion and their most comfortable pair of sandals or slippers at the ter-minal that he/she uses most regularly, we could develop some form of ritual around the use of the system. if we were to institute a rite or ritual, the first step would to replace these flourescent lights with something that is more considerate of the human eye. anyone have any other suggestions as to how we might set up a generally conducive setting for to communicate with each other through a medium? why do i get this retransmit last line blurb occassionally? i find it ANNOYING. i find myself leaving.

In the panopticon class all forms of discourse but topic-centered, relevant points which are delivered in a style that highlights the rhetorical line of argument are excluded. One sees this shift in style at the two crucial moments at the opening and closing of the class when it shifts from the casual conversational encounters to the panopticon interaction order and back again. In the message above, there is a mix of topics and these topics are presented in a running cohesive unitary style. The message is casual and 'chatty' throughout with no stylistic separation between points which have to do with course content, points that express the writer's own personal feelings, and questions about the use of the technology. In other words, discourse cohesion is maintained across the whole weave of multiple threads of separate topics.

The participation of the teacher and students in this class is widely varied. Mostly the teacher is very active but for a week or so he was traveling and did not participate at all. Students who were on the Fairbanks campus had regular, daily, in some cases hourly contact because terminals were relatively easier to locate. A student such as Diane could participate only when the weather and her teaching and family schedule allowed her to make the snow machine trip to Kotzebue. The result is that there was a regular recycling of topics. Comments were often episodic – a person simply said what they had to say without indicating any topical relevance to what had been said before or to what might follow. Most common is that a student would drop into the conference every few days, find a long list of messages from the more active students or teacher, read them all, and then send one or two messages in response to whatever had struck his or her interest. Very rarely did anyone make any attempt to note and respond to all of the topics which had been raised.

An obvious outcome of these multi-threaded and episodic discursive practices was that the teacher had little or no control over the general topics or tenor of the discourse in this class. He did not give lectures though from time to time he mailed written notes to the students. While there was in volume much more 'talk' in this class than in a traditional panopticon class because, after all, anyone could say whatever they liked whenever they could, there was no sense of discursive cohesion toward the development of the course content.

We can summarize the main characteristics of the discourse in the technology-mediated class as follows:

- Discourse is distributed among multiple participants, some primary – physically co-present with the participant – and some secondary, who have different statuses.
- In the screen-based, mediated discourse texts are short (one screen) and multi-threaded.
- There is a topical weave among three main threads: The conduct of the class itself as a technological task, the social interactions and relationships among participants in both primary and secondary statuses, and the content topics of the course.
- Text is integrated stylistically with the casual and informal style of the social interactions and the task-management discourse dominating; thus, academic content is discussed in a chatty, informal style that is non-argumentative and operates by a non-sequential logic.
- Topical relevance is maintained among the three themes – the task of managing the class, the social relationships, and course topics. Cohesion operates across the topics of a single screenful of message more than between episodes in a single topic across multiple messages.

- Because participation is asynchronous in many cases the development of topics is episodic and recurrent; 'old' topics are repeatedly re-introduced; new ones missed.
- There are no lectures by the teacher, no evaluatable responses by students to questions posed by the teacher.

Historical body of the individuals in a technology-mediated university class

We began to develop our interest in technology-mediated classes because of a social problem. That problem was the discrimination and consequent lack of access to the educational, legal, medical, and other services to which Alaska Natives were entitled. As we will note in Chapter 4 and go into in more detail in Chapter 5, one source of this discrimination developed out of differences in habitual patterns of social interaction practiced by many Alaska Natives on the one hand and the teachers, doctors, lawyers, police, and government officials of the State of Alaska who were largely English-speaking whites from the mainland US on the other. Our research and that of many others led us to think that much of the problem had its root in simple matters of discourse – the ways in which one presented oneself to others, the way turns were exchanged in conversation, the ways topics were initiated and controlled, and an overall value placed on talking.

In the technology-mediated class the teacher had no edge over students in the use of the technology. The use of computer communication was new to everyone, teacher and students alike. At the very beginning the teacher, Ron, had the edge because he was on campus and had access to several other users of the network. He also was soon able to arrange to have a terminal installed on the desk in his office. This was, we think, the first terminal installed on a faculty desk outside of the sciences and computer sciences departments. Nevertheless, students quickly learned to use this system and within just weeks several students had emerged as the technological leaders of the class. It was to them we all went to solve problems with the technology. Thus the expert–novice aspect of the teacher–student relationship was inverted at least in the management of the class.

The majority of messages involved the discursive thread of talk about the technology. Therefore, in those messages there was at least that portion of the message in which the expert–novice relationship was inverted. To put this another way around, in the technology-mediated class the expert–novice role relationship was continually in flux throughout a single text. In one portion of a message the teacher would or could make claims to expertise concerning the course content, in another portion the students could make claims to expertise concerning management of the technology. Since the discourse was largely stylistically coherent throughout each message, this meant that this aspect of the teacher–student role was continually flip-flopping. The net result was a rapid leveling of statuses between the teacher and the student.

In the panopticon class virtually all aspects of the class except the course content are taken to be deeply submerged in historical body and practice. It is taken for granted that behind the teacher's ostensible purpose in teaching the course content is the teacher's more fundamental goal of developing a career and earning a salary. Behind the student's ostensible purpose in learning are the more fundamental goals we have mentioned such as passing just well enough to get the degree, or learning the course content but for purposes other than those of the teacher or the discipline, or in a few cases becoming a fully socialized member of the discipline.

In the technology-mediated class goals for the teacher and students were very different. As Suzie said in the television interview reproduced at the beginning of this chapter, we were looking for better ways to do distance education. We were interested in technology partly in order to accomplish that goal. We were also interested particularly in the asynchronous properties of computer-mediated communication as a way of addressing the problem of access to education and social services by Alaska Natives. We wanted to see if it would work. For their part, some students such as Diane wanted to enrich their lives and careers while remaining in remote villages, and distance education, for all its effort and difficulties, was better than having only the small population of her village and her elementary students to talk to. For all of us, teachers and students alike, these early technology-mediated classes had as a major goal simply learning to use the new technology. We all felt like we were on the cutting edge of a development that would become commonplace in our world in the near future and it was exciting to be there.

In spite of the excitement of doing these early technology-mediated classes, the cost for the teacher was very high. We estimated an average time commitment for the teacher in doing an 'equivalent' technology-mediated class and panopticon class was about 3:1. At the same time the payoff in institutional terms was very low. The university provided no compensation for the time differential. The technology-mediated class counted for faculty load the same as a traditional panopticon class. Part of that difference has been moderated in the twenty years since because now many people, many teachers and perhaps most students, come to a technology-mediated class with their skills in computer communication already deeply practiced in historical body. At the same time in most cases universities have not developed the infrastructural support equivalent to the standard panopticon classroom; both teachers and students often have to buy and use their own computers and pay for their own off-campus email accounts and service providers. This difference in infrastructural support which we observed in our projects twenty years ago is roughly equivalent to expecting teachers to buy the blackboards and chalk they use and for students to bring their own chair to class.

For students the payoff of these technology-mediated classes was high and the cost relatively low. They enjoyed the much more relaxed schedules that did not pin them to specific class hours for their courses. Mostly they found their participation in these ground-breaking classes promised to provide a payoff in their professional and career advancement.

Within the historical body of the teacher were both the social connections and the skills in dealing with other university faculty and administrators. Of course, Ron was able to get access to a terminal much more easily than students in the course who had to somehow account for their presence in the administrative spaces of university offices rather than classrooms. This also went up against other practices at that time. The university social structure allocated typing to administrative support staff. It was thought to be improper for a faculty member and certainly for an administrator to do any of his or her own typing. Teachers and administrators wrote things out on paper which were then typed by secretaries. Thus it was quite a violation of then-current practice for Ron to have a terminal installed on his desk in his office. On the one hand it violated the sense that faculty would not wish to type and on the other it also usurped the ownership of terminals and the very new stand-alone word processors by the secretarial staff.

In developing the ways of using these new media, participants in the classes 'borrowed historical body' from existing practices. Sending messages on the university computer was, for us, assimilated to playing the new computer games. In fact much of the talk in the course messages was about playing games. The texts themselves appropriated from informal registers and genres of talk – chat, conversations, jokes, and other forms of verbal play. Rarely did the participants bring into the technology-mediated class any of the styles and forms from their traditional classroom and schooling historical body.

Because of this, finally, the technology-mediated class strongly disadvantaged those participants who were skilled in the traditional patterns of academic discourse. Students who at first produced long didactic messages which laid down a line of argument were soundly criticized or ignored. Because of the difficulties of the system itself – corrections of typos and syntax were very difficult as we had only line editors, screen editors had not yet been developed – messages were filled with typos and grammatical mistakes and participants who were accustomed to careful statement and proofreading were reluctant to show their ideas to others in unedited form.

Conversely, the technology-mediated class advantaged the participants who either were practiced in asynchronous communication, in taking slower turns, or enjoyed playful or poetic or otherwise non-academic forms of discourse. Our original thoughts were that this medium might be useful in alleviating some of the ways in which access to the university (and other social agencies) was blocked through differences in communicative style. We were supported in this by these studies. We were wrong to imagine that this was simply a question of a divergence between Alaska Native people and non-natives. There was simply a massive redistribution of participation in which what we might think of as panopticon-style academic discourse was almost entirely disabled and made unusable and a host of other asynchronous, aphoristic, episodic and epigrammatic, and multi-threaded discourse were favored. Whoever had within their life experiences accumulated a historical body of essayist literacy, the panopticon style, was blocked and inhibited from practice; whoever had within their historical body an array of other communicative styles and discursive strategies was given a ground in which those styles and strategies could flower.

Now we can summarize the main characteristics of the historical body in the technology-mediated class as follows:

- The teacher had no edge over students in the use of the media; it was new to all participants; but students quickly evolved to expert status by comparison with the teacher.
- A major goal for all participants was to learn and use the new technology.
- The 'cost' to the teacher was large – about three times the average time commitment of a panopticon class; the 'payoff' was low – no compensation for time.
- The 'cost' to students was low – much more open schedule, much less academic performance required; 'payoff' was high – enjoyment, professional and career advancement in a perceived leading-edge area of expertise.
- The medium privileged those with access to terminals and, since these were under administrative control, it privileged those with social access to university administrators.
- Participants 'borrowed historical body' from computer games, informal chat, and textual play; not from 'serious' forms of discourse and activities.
- Technology-mediated classes disadvantaged those who were skilled in traditional academic patterns of discourse, advantaged non-standard forms of discourse.

A non-determinist approach to action and social change

When a teacher makes the opening moves to transform the aggregate of people in the room from a bunch of conversational encounters into the interaction order which we have called the panopticon class, he or she might do several things. As in one case we observed, he picked up the sheaf of student papers from his lectern at the front of the room, he then went through them one paper at a time and read

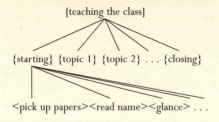

[teaching the class]

{starting} {topic 1} {topic 2} . . . {closing}

<pick up papers><read name><glance> . . .

3.4

the name of the student out loud, looked up and around to locate the student, they exchanged a glance, he stepped close enough to the student to hand her the paper, the student took the paper, the teacher went to the next student in sequence until the papers were all distributed. Then he went to the classroom door, pulled it closed, and said: 'It looks like we're all here, so why don't we get started.'

We could call this action 'starting the class' for convenience. It is the first move in a larger activity we could call [teaching the class]. That might consist of {starting the class}, {introducing the topic}, {giving the first point}, . . . {calling for questions}, {question and answer period}, {giving the next assignment}, {closing the class}. {Starting the class} is itself composed of smaller-level (or shorter-term) actions as we have seen such as <pick up batch of papers>, <read a student's name>, <exchange a confirming glance with student>, <step toward student>, <hand the paper to student>, . . . <pull the door closed>, <walk to lectern while saying . . . >. Many researchers prefer to call the actions at the lowest level 'actions'; they would call the sequences of actions 'activities' to keep from confusing a specific, concrete action with a sequence of such actions. We could sketch out this hierarchy of action and activity sequences as we have in Figure 3.4. It is important to keep this hierarchy of multiple actions and activities in mind as we analyze the differences between the panopticon class and the technology-mediated class. We will focus at first on just one action in this action sequence of {starting the class} which is, itself, part of the bigger activity of [teaching the class]. We will look at <hand the paper to student>.

The action of handing involves a minimum of two social actors, one to give and one to receive the object. It also includes the object that is handed over. The object itself is the main resource or mediational means by which this action is accomplished though certainly the hands, eyes, and body are also used. In the first place, then, handing will depend to a great extent on the physical characteristics of the object. We hand a large and firm object like a book differently from a small or delicate object. A very big object such as a package weighing several pounds will take two hands and the giver is likely to confirm with the receiver that he or she is ready to receive the weight: 'This is a bit heavy, got it?'

But before the handing can occur two other conditions have to be met. First, the two participants in this action have to come to agreement that it is going to occur, then, secondly, they must position themselves appropriately. In the first instance the action requires some kind of anticipatory discourse or communication. In this case the teacher has called out the student's name and exchanged confirming eye contact. From this point of view, then, we can see that two of the previous actions, <reading a name> and <mutual glancing>, are crucial to accomplishing the action of handing. In a way they begin to establish a commitment to this action. As we will argue below, these little practices are well established in the historical body of students from very early in life, so much so that they hardly require a moment's thought. They happen mostly invisibly. The student in a class, upon hearing the teacher call his or her name, now automatically looks up and at the teacher whatever else he or she might be doing. In kindergarten this student had to be told: 'When I call your name, you need to look at me.' Now she does it without thinking further.

We say that these actions of reading a name and mutual glancing are prior conditions to the teacher handing the papers back. We say this because there are many opportunities for failure and embarassment. A teacher may simply take a paper to a student who is engaged in conversation with another student. The student doesn't see the teacher approach or hand the paper in her direction. When she happens to turn a bit she notices and then shows acute embarassment for having left the teacher just standing there with his hand stretched out. The teacher himself is made vulnerable for embarassment in front of the other students as not commanding the immediate response of a student and therefore as someone who is in less than full control of the micro-social interactions in the class.

Secondly, once it is established that handing will occur, the participants have to position themselves at the right distance in order for the handing to take place. At the moment of transfer their hands are well within Edward T. Hall's zone of intimacy though perhaps their bodies remain just at a personal distance. Thus for the handing to occur, the teacher and the student must position themselves within the semiotic space of intimacy.

Finally, the paper itself is handed through a long and practiced set of micro-movements that are adjusted to the weight of the object and the timing of the movements of their hands toward each other. Any very small failure of this timing and of these movements and the object falls. This can easily lead again to the embarassment of either the student or the teacher having to reach down to the floor to regain control of the paper.

We have taken this very minute approach to the study of human action as the starting point for a nexus analysis because, as we have learned in our research, much of the social world that we come to take for granted is constructed out of these rather small pieces of action. In this we are simply following upon a suggestion made many years ago by the philosopher Wittgenstein. He said (Wittgenstein 1980, cited in Shotter 1993: 83):

> The *facts* of human natural history that throw light on our problem, are difficult for us to find out, for our talk *passes them by*, it is occupied with other things. (In the same way we tell someone: 'Go into the shop and buy. . . .' – not 'Put your left foot in front of your right foot etc. etc. then put coins down on the counter, etc. etc.')

We found in the Professional Development Seminar (for which more details are given in Chapter 4) that all university professors easily talk about 'starting the class' but it is very difficult for them to come to analyze it in terms of the very specific actions they take in doing this. This is important, we believe, because we found that university teachers who used this little activity sequence of handing back assignments as their strategy for starting the class were evaluated by their students as being 'more human', 'more approachable', 'more responsive' to students. Other teachers who just started in on their lectures or who handed back their papers by just handing the batch to one student and asking them to pass them around and take their own were felt to be more distant, less approachable, and not very interested in their students' needs.

This could all be rephrased as saying that teachers who used this little action sequence in starting the class were more successful in establishing the panopticon interaction order with their students. Perhaps it is not difficult to see how this works. The first move in starting the class involves individually and separately calling each student's name, mutually ratifying their agreement to do something together, moving into intimate social space with that student, and then mutually negotiating that very intricate social action of handing an object. These teachers have gone through the class one at a time to personally negotiate the agreement that (1) the teacher is in charge and at the center of social interactions, i.e., has the right to interrupt any other social interactions, (2) the student is in at least overt and physical agreement to enter into personal and even intimate social space with the teacher, and (3) they are together willing and able to integrate their social and physical movements to accomplish a joint action. When he goes to close the door, this teacher has already personally confirmed the ultimate agreement that all students will respond to his social leadership. His spoken discourse, 'I guess everyone's here now, so I'd like to start', has no main work to do in establishing his right to control the social interaction. It has the much smaller function of bringing what were separate and personalized agreements under one, blanket agreement covering the whole group.

We do not take a technological deterministic view of the differences between the panopticon classroom and the technology-mediated class. If we look at this very simple action, for example, we can open up how we think about the role of technology and other mediational means in the conduct of social interactions. In the technology-mediated class there were written assignments given, handed in, comments were made, and they were returned to the students. From the point of view of the organization of an academic class, these two classes were identical. Nevertheless, there are very important differences.

In the technology-mediated class the assignments were made through either the email system or the audio conferencing system. They were returned to the teacher by postal mail. Ron made the comments on the papers in Fairbanks and they were mailed to the distant students or put into campus mailboxes for the local students. This little practice of handing back an assignment is redistributed among other spaces, practices, and participants. In Diane's village the assignment is handed to her still in the envelope by the postmaster. To the extent two people come into intimate space for a moment and establish a moment of mutually negotiated cooperation, it is Diane and the postmaster, not Diane and her teacher. When she opens the envelope and takes out the assignment to see the comments, she is entirely alone or together with one of her children or her husband. There is nothing in this sequence that puts the student and teacher into the social and physical position of being able to use handing over of assignments to do any other work of social integration.

If we ask the question the other way around – How or when do Diane and her teacher make or establish the contact that anticipates and enables the discourses and interactions of an academic teacher–student relationship? – we see that it is very difficult to locate that moment in the long array of actions and practices that constitute logging onto the university computer network. Those contacts are simultaneously broadcast contacts among all of the other students in the class. If we seek an analogy between the technology-mediated class and the panopticon class, the technology-mediated class is like a large cocktail party of simultaneous talk in which there are both small withs in social interaction and large, party-wide utterances that are heard by everybody. The teacher who wishes to establish his or her voice in such an environment may easily be perceived as the loudmouth obnoxious partygoer who tries to dominate not just the conversation he is in but the entire discourse and mood of the gathering.

But we believe this is not directly a consequence of the use of technology as such or of the technology alone. The distribution of students far and wide across the State of Alaska preceded our technology-mediated class by many years. In a sense what our new mediational means did was to make a number of small conversations that were spread out in a very large space condense into a small room where a bit of what everyone was saying could now be heard. And, of course, it picked up the speed by which the exchanges took place over the slower system of postal mail exchanges. It was the social-political-cultural circumstances of life in Alaska that produced the distributed aggregate of students and teacher which became the class. The technologies we used made a connection among what was already distributed for other purposes. What we sought to find were the ways by which we might find new means of producing the intimate and negotiated social arrangements that enable the traditional teacher–student relationship to develop.

In our nexus analysis we do not seek to find the 'meaning' of an action in the resources or mediational means used alone or in the intentions of the social actor alone. Nor do we find the 'meaning' in any of the assumed or expressed meanings of the participants, though those are certainly relevant. Like much micro-sociological analysis, we find it important to discover how social actions, action sequences, or activities are constituted out of mediated actions, practices, and discourses to bring about particular social consequences. In this case the common academic task of returning an assignment from the teacher to a student if described in just those terms tells us very little at the level at which people act. On the other hand, a close analysis of the sequence of calling a name, exchanging mutual glances, stepping into intimate personal space, and negotiating the movements of handing show the means by which the much larger activity system of the panopticon class was constructed. And as we have seen, a disruption in these actions in any way disables this activity system, whether that is (1) having no assignments or papers to return on that day, (2) passing the papers to a single student to be distributed to the rest of the students, or (3) the technological distribution of the participants into different physical spaces.

Engaged in the nexus of practice

We started our analysis where we were located, within our zone of identification, to use Burke's concept. The social issue in which we were interested – the access or lack of access of Alaska Native people to the services of the institutions of society – was located right where we were in our classes. For Ron who was teaching on campus the opening nexus of practice was the traditional panopticon class. For Suzie who was teaching distance-delivered classes the opening nexus of practice was a relatively traditional correspondence class framework. When we conjoined these two interests through the new medium of computer and audio conferencing we found that this produced rather different accommodations of the historical bodies of the participants in the interaction order, and a different distribution of the discourses in place.

One of the principles which we developed at that time and which we have put forward here is that it is necessary to see any social action as an intersection among these three elements. Viewed from the point of view of any one of them alone the restructuring of the nexus of practice is not very visible. That narrower focus can lead to either overly deterministic accounts of the role of technology without an awareness of the importance of changes in such an element as the interaction order or, conversely a narrower focus can lead to overly conservative views that there is no real difference at all between the two types of classes.

As we began to see how the interaction among historical bodies, interaction order, and discourses was working, it became clear to us that we needed to open up the circumference of our analysis. On the one hand we felt we needed to know much more than we did about just how any social interaction works at the face-to-face level, whether that is a class, a conversation among friends, or a formal legal interview. We also felt we needed to know much more about what happens to social interactions when they take place via any other forms of technological mediation. In other words, we began to realize that we needed to study such phenomena as micro-rhythms in the integration of social interaction at the face-to-face level at one extreme and at the other we needed to study how participation in the organization of the university is structured for both students and faculty. The projects with which we began to navigate these trajectories are treated in detail in Chapter 4.

4   Engaging the nexus of practice: Oil, the Cold War, and social change in Alaska in the 1980s

A reindeer herder on the distant northwest coast of Alaska starts his single-engine plane, taxis out onto the ice which has been scraped flat as a provisional winter airfield. Taking advantage of the short hour of daylight, he takes off and circles in ever-widening circles to check on where his herd has moved during the long night. His herd is fine and the weather is good, so for a bit of fun he noses the plane around, climbs to 5000 feet and heads directly west toward the Soviet border a few miles away. Within minutes he drops down to just above the sea ice, makes a sharp turn, and heads home below the radar while fighter jets from the two Cold War nations scramble overhead, make visual contact, and return to their respective bases.

A world of contradictions and experimentation

The contradictions that were Alaska in the 1980s were the milieu in which we engaged the nexus of practice – the many nexus of practice – which we are using as the basis for our understanding of nexus analysis in this book. We began with a quite narrow circumference of attention on the conduct of university classes but as soon as we began to take into consideration the broader context of those distant university classes we were within the territory of the reindeer herder with whom we have begun this chapter. This reindeer herder not only taunted Cold War military forces in the way he flew his plane but he also showed up in Honolulu at the Pacific Telecommunications Conference among the American admirals, generals, and communications corporation CEOs, and ministers of communication from Brazil, Singapore, and Australia to talk about satellite launches and packet-switching networks. At the same time, children elsewhere in

Alaska in a village of three or four families who lived mostly by hunting moose and fishing watched *Sesame Street* on Betamax videos and played *Little Brick Out* on their Apple II+ computers in school. Alaskans were living both the newest and oldest of lifestyles with the newest and oldest of technologies – planes and computers, subsistence hunting and heating with woodstoves.

From the point of view of a nexus analysis we mostly found ourselves already located where we needed to be. A nexus analysis amounted to trying to make sense of our work and of our lives as young academics in new jobs in Alaska. We did not really need to conduct surveys and searches and preliminary pilot projects to first locate a crucial site of engagement with its pivotal mediated actions and participants and then to position ourselves within that nexus of practice. We found ourselves deeply embedded in a set of social issues that circulated through virtually every aspect of our lives.

While it is not commonly thought of outside of Alaska, the longest border the US has with another nation is the border with Russia. Oddly enough in writing this chapter we found that the exact length and exact position of that border is not known, or is not made public, by either the US government or the Russian government. From the late 1700s with the arrival of Russian fur traders through 1867 when the 'Alaska Purchase' occurred down to the present satellite, Internet, and air links with far eastern Siberian cities and settlements such as Vladivostok and Magadan, US relations with Russia have been a significant factor in the socio-political life of Alaska. When Ron first went to Alaska in December of 1963, some months before the catastrophic 1964 earthquake which destroyed so much of downtown Anchorage, the greatest safety and security concern was the Soviet military threat only a few miles from the Alaskan border. When we arrived to take up a position at the Alaska Native Language Center in 1978, still well within the shadow of the Cold War, it was natural that the University of Alaska would be linked unit-by-unit with a computer network many years ahead of universities in the rest of the world; this network had been established in part as a security measure.

If we were to map the many cycles of discourse which circulated through our lives and our work in Alaska during this time, all of them would have six major socio-political cycles as components:

1   the military security networks of satellite communications and air bases;
2   the discovery in 1968 and the rapid development of huge oil reserves at Prudhoe Bay in a strategically vulnerable position on the Arctic coast of Alaska and the subsequent building of the Alaska pipeline;
3   the Alaska Native Claims Settlement Act of 1971 which negotiated the formation by Alaska Natives of thirteen large resource corporations and a comparable number of non-profit social service corporations;

4   the establishment of the Alaska Native Language Center in 1972 mandating the production of language research and services in Alaska Native languages;

5   the 1974 Supreme Court decision in Lau vs. Nichols mandating bilingual education programs nationally; and

6   the so-called 'Molly Hootch case' mandating the building, staffing, and functioning of high schools in most rural villages throughout Alaska in 1976.

Of course we are all always embedded in such cycles of discourse, though those of today where the reader is placed might be rather different from the ones we encountered in Alaska in the early 1980s. In this chapter we will describe how our work in a variety of educational institutions – all three of the universities in Alaska and a dozen branch units of those universities as well as a dozen or more rural schools – as well as legal, government, and health service agencies engaged us in multiple and complex nexus of practice where we could observe and, through our training and consultation, begin to have an impact on the mediated actions through which discrimination against Alaska Natives was being produced.

The organizations

Our work and the activities we discuss in this book were carried out across a range of organizations in the State of Alaska, the Yukon Territory, and British Columbia as well as in what are called 'the Lower 48 States' from California and Idaho to Washington, DC, mostly during the years from 1978 to 1983, as we have noted in the Preface. Ron was first employed by the Alaska Native Language Center of the University of Alaska, Fairbanks. His main responsibilities included doing linguistic research on the Athabaskan languages of Alaska, providing consultation, teaching, and training in linguistic and educational research, and liaison with the many organizations in the state as well as throughout the US on questions of indigenous language survival and bilingual education. Suzie was first employed by the Cross-cultural Educational Development Program as a teacher and subject coordinator in cross-cultural communication and linguistics. This program provided a distance-delivered degree in education to people who lived in villages and small regional centers throughout the State of Alaska. We were both frequently called upon by other organizations to provide consultation and training in interethnic communication and, as soon as we had begun to develop our interests in the new media technologies, in the use of telecommunications in educational and government organizations.

During this period of time we traveled frequently, mostly by single-engine plane, around the villages and regional centers of Alaska. While it may seem a very large number of different organizations, many of our contacts and actual work with them were simply accidental outcomes of the difficulties of travel in

Alaska. To fly from Fairbanks to Shageluk, for example, requires a jet flight to Anchorage, a second jet flight to a regional center such as Bethel or Aniak, then a single-engine flight that might stop in one or two or three villages before reaching the final destination. A trip might take as long as a week, depending on the weather, in order to deliver a half-day workshop for teachers. Everyone then working in Alaska always carried with them multiple tasks. If one of us were going to Holy Cross to do a workshop for teachers, for example, one of the linguists at ANLC might give us a list of words to record for the dictionary he was developing. Or if the weather grounded us in Bethel, we would do an impromptu workshop in interethnic communication at the Bethel library or spend a day teaching in a colleague's class at Bethel Community College.

It was not difficult for us to become engaged in these many and complex nexus of practice. Wherever we went we visited with and lived with Alaska Native people. We saw Alaska Native people interacting with non-natives in classes, in the medical centers and hospitals, in the legal system, in hotels, in airports and on planes as pilots and passengers, in parties and social gatherings, in casual meetings in villages and in formal legislative hearings in the capital in Juneau. Because it is a large expanse of land with very few people – at that time the total population of Alaska was 464,300 people, about half of whom lived in just one city, Anchorage – we quickly came to meet 'everybody'. In the village for a workshop for teachers we met the family of a student who was taking one of our classes in Fairbanks; in a hospital in Bethel we chatted with the uncle of a new legislator in Juneau. We almost never had to work to construct a contact for research purposes because the work we were doing put us in frequent contact with most of the people we needed to meet from university students to the governor, from community college chancellors to bootleg liquor pilots, from a State Trooper on duty in the village to the US Senator returning to Alaska to chat up his constituents.

In many cases such as the time we were asked to work with a school district for several days to develop a bilingual education booklet on doing beadwork for elementary children (Chapter 5), we were working together with our own non-Alaska Native colleagues, public school teachers or administrators, and a group of Alaska Native elders, teachers, or tradition bearers. While the task was to develop the materials, the several days of working together provided abundant examples of interethnic communications that then became very fruitful data for the development of our understanding of other situations in which members of these different groups came into contact with each other for which we were not able to acquire such close and detailed data.

In most cases we worked in cycles of research and application. While we were providing consultative assistance or training in producing materials in Alaska Native languages for schools or Alaska Native corporations we were observing the micro-practices of discourse, the interaction order, and the historical body that we would then be able to analyze as sociolinguistic data. A week later we might be presenting a talk on interethnic communication for a group of resource managers and be able to use what we had learned in the task-oriented project of the week earlier to assist them in developing their own projects. The test of our research was found not so much in publications, though we did publish and present at many academic conferences, but in our ability to provide useful assistance in the tasks of constructing Alaska Native corporations, responsive bilingual education programs, high school education in the newly required schools, or effective resource management. At the same time our difficulties and problems in accomplishing these tasks which were required by our work opened up the new problems in discourse and communication that we worked on in our further research.

The projects

When we began our work in Alaska our tasks were organized around the ordinary work of being university faculty. This included teaching classes, attending faculty meetings, and doing our independent research projects. Our first interests were in coming to understand how faculty members conducted their teaching in ordinary university classrooms. When Ron moved from the Alaska Native Language Center to the Center for Cross-cultural Studies in the School of Education, we became aware of just how much research had been done on the discourse and interaction order of elementary and secondary classrooms throughout the US and the world, much of that work addressing questions of interethnic communication as well. Still, there was little research available that we could use to come to understand our most common situation, the interethnic university classroom. We began this study with a professional development seminar which was generously supported by a professional development grant from the Andrew Mellon Foundation.

The professional development seminar

During the academic year of 1980/1 five professors (including Ron), one co-ordinator (Suzie), and one graduate assistant (Cecilia Martz) met in a regular seminar to discuss our teaching. As a source of external objectivity (as well as deep embarrassment) we viewed videotapes of our own teaching for peer-group critique. In 'Professional development seminar: A model for making higher education more culturally sensitive' (Martz 1981; S. Scollon 1981) we developed the idea for what we called non-focused research by looking at our own and our colleagues' teaching strategies. Our idea was to produce a cycle of research and application that was much like the ones we had developed in our consultation and research outside of our own university teaching.

We found that there was a wide variation among the five faculty participants in this seminar on what we thought was good participation from our students in classes. We encountered significant differences between ourselves and our students in the expected logic of presentation in lectures. We found regular and significant role distancing from our roles as professors. In this seminar we began to develop the idea that there was an important contrast between what we came to call human behavior and institutional behavior which we were able to examine in more detail with a grant from the National Institute of Education (below). The contrast between institutional and human behavior suggested to us that our students felt a teacher was teaching well to the degree that he or she departed from an institutional role display. To put this in the terms we have used in Chapter 3, our students expressed strong approval of our teaching to the extent we used micro-strategies of personalizing our contacts with them and were most willing under those conditions to enter into a negotiated and mutually productive teacher–student relationship.

Telecommunications and distance-delivery university instruction

In addition to being interested in the conduct of face-to-face traditional pan-opticon university classes, we were also beginning the experimental classes using several forms of telecommunications including email, audio conferencing, and even video conferencing in a few cases. In many ways the practices out of which we construct the university classroom have changed little since the lectures of the medieval university when the professor read the text while the students copied it out. The University of Alaska Instructional Telecommunications Consortium was created in order to meet a statewide educational need for the delivery of university courses in sites which do not have regular educational facilities, that is, where there are no professors and no lectures. Suzie received an assessment and evaluation grant from the Consortium to study the effects of these rapidly developing technologies. This project gave us the institutional support we needed to begin to see the linkages between traditional technologies of communication and the rapidly developing new technologies in which we were interested.

Gatekeeping and retention

Our concern with discrimination against Alaska Native people was the origin of our interest in interethnic communication which we had studied, as we will see below, for some time before taking up this work at the University of Alaska. At that time a number of researchers, notably John Gumperz and Fred Erickson, were undertaking studies of interethnic gatekeeping encounters. In their use of the term and as we took it up, we were concerned with situations in which members of different ethnic groups came together in tightly focused situations in which an institutional member made a decision based primarily on the spoken discourse of that social interaction which had long-term consequences both for the individual who was in the applicant's position and for the institution. Many different kinds of gatekeeping encounters had been studied including job interviews and other personnel or evaluation interviews, counseling interviews, and, more and more, educational exams and classroom evaluations.

In a study funded by the National Institute of Education we were able to examine the communicative barriers to equal participation in the university by Alaska Native students (Chapter 5). This study concentrated on gatekeeping encounters, points in the system where significant decisions are being made about students' lives in brief, focused encounters. The most typical two gatekeeping encounters in education are exams and counseling sessions, but classrooms, as we have said, were more generally being talked about as gatekeeping encounters.

From the point of view of that study, we found it useful to begin to focus on very fine-grained studies of social interactions rather than on such broad activities as 'teaching a class' or 'taking a class'. As we have illustrated in Chapter 3, the micro-practice of handing an assignment back (from the point of view of the teacher) and of receiving a returned assignment (from the point of view of the student) is a very small 'gate' in which the teacher and the student make the first move in constructing the 'gates' that provide access or rejection to the student taking that day's class.

The rhythmic integration of ordinary talk

Our work with the new technologies of communication carried with it a shift in our focus from the structures of discourse and of language to an interest in media. We also moved away from an abstract and timeless analysis of the structures of codes to a concern with the role of time and rhythm in communication. We had known that squeezing an interaction into a brief time would increase the power of the participant(s) who controlled the topic, the interaction order, or the timing of the event. We had found that in computer conferencing it is the asynchrony of the message exchanges not the speed of communications that enables the diffused and distributed sorts of social interaction we described in Chapter 3. People are able to participate at times they choose, pick up themes they wish to respond to, and ignore other themes about which they have nothing to say.

At this time, then, we began a series of studies of rhythm in face-to-face conversation and in other forms of spoken discourse (R. Scollon 1981c). In these projects we worked together with Frederick Erickson (Erickson 1980), who visited our project on occasion. Our materials ranged from audiotaped recordings of radio broadcasts or of family breakfast conversation to videotaped recordings of university classes and of rural and urban elementary school classrooms. This group (Carol Barnhardt, Cecilia Martz, Bob Maguire, Meryl Siegel, and, in the summer of 1981 Frederick Erickson) found, for example, that there was an important difference between two elementary school teachers, one who was an Alaska Native and the other who was not. In the latter case we observed the teacher arrive at the classroom door, march in with a strongly tempoed walk, take up her panopticon position at the head of the class, and begin speaking in the rhythm she had established with her steps into the room. She then responded only to those students who had picked up her tempo. The Alaska Native teacher we studied came to the door of the classroom, listened for a bit to the sound of the chatter among the children in the class, moved into the room on the tempo which she had picked up from the students, went first to one small group and then another to speak with them quietly and privately, and only then moved into the panopticon position of the teacher at the head of the class. It was these studies of rhythm and tempo which led to our interest in the privatized handing back of students' assignments which we described in Chapter 3.

Videos on interethnic communication

As we became busier with our own research projects and teaching as well as with requests to provide training and consultation throughout the state and as Suzie's work with the Consortium produced pressure to provide television and other 'canned' educational and training materials, we developed the project that was known as 'Cross-talk Alaska'. This project used the same research and application cycle that we used in many other of our projects. On the one hand we had the task of producing video materials that would be useful for broadcast on the LEARN ALASKA television network throughout the rural parts of the state. At the same time we did not feel we knew what we would need to know to work outside of the fairly narrow constraints of the education and classroom research that had dominated our work at that point.

The first video we made was called 'Interethnic Communication', Number 5 in the *Talking Alaska* series made by the Alaska Native Language Center in 1979, very early in our work in Alaska. As a model we used the *Cross-talk* video which had been made by John Gumperz, Tom Jupp, and Celia Roberts in the UK for broadcast and for training in interethnic communication. 'Interethnic Communication' was a collaboration between Ron and Eliza Jones, a Koyukon linguist at the Alaska Native language Center. One of the unintended consequences of this video project was that soon, wherever Ron went in Alaska people knew who he was because they had seen the film on television. Not only that, they also immediately began to offer poignant stories about their own experiences with interethnic communication in Alaska. Thus the video elicited not data so much as corroboration that the research we had presented in that video was 'ringing a bell' with the viewers in small rural villages throughout Alaska.

The video project we did with the Consortium was begun by us as a piece of Suzie's evaluation project, but it soon took on a life of its own. As we moved on to further projects, two films were finally made by two separate groups, one headed by Carol Barnhardt of Fairbanks and the other by Cecilia Martz, now of Bethel. Critical to the idea of a nexus analysis is that we, as the researchers, do not attempt to provide any unilateral interpretation of or control of outcomes from a point of view other than our own. All of these materials are still in circulation in Alaska having effects that go on long after our original energy in these projects became re-channeled in different directions.

University Chancellor's Computer Awareness Program

Because of our work in developing the use of computer technology in the common teaching activities of the university, the Chancellor of the University appointed Ron to develop what came to be called the Computer Awareness Program. His assignment was first to survey computer use (and other computer-based technology such as music synthesis) within the faculty in the social sciences, education, and the humanities, and then to develop ways in which these new technologies could be brought into play most effectively in the functioning of the university in these areas. Of course, computers were already actively integrated into work in the sciences and engineering by the early 1980s and so the focus was just on the social sciences, education, and the humanities.

We observed as it has been observed now in many other places that there is a somewhat paradoxical dynamic operating among different kinds of technology users in an institution such as a university. We found this to be true as well, for example, in consultation that Ron did for the National Endowment for the Humanities. In the first part of this dynamic, one group of computer users is devouring computer resources with an appetite that requires ever-increasing power, speed, and memory. In our case this was in the academic disciplines of sciences and engineering as well as in the management of the university as an organization with its databases on employment, payroll management, warehousing, and maintenance. In order to get these expanded resources, computer users in these organizations are encouraging general computer awareness and computer literacy programs among faculty and students or non-technologically advanced employees such as secretarial staff. This builds the political base needed in publicly funded universities to get increased resources and in private organizations to justify the allocation of profits to these new institutional purposes.

At the same time, these additional users in primarily non-technological functions such as messaging and word processing are looked upon with scorn for their 'frivolous" uses of computer resources such as word processing and computer mail. This paradox produces a pendulum-swing dynamic. First, non-technological uses are encouraged to produce a bubble of new users which, in turn, produces the ground-swell of support for better core resources. Then, these same users are squelched because their uses of the technological resources make little use of the main powers of the technology. As part of this project we looked at the paradox, we might almost call it a schizophrenia, which is built into our thinking about computers or technological resources and about institutions. We equate bigger with better, and centralized with improved access, but at the same time we fear the monolithic, insensitive, bureaucratized, central authority over information.

Preliminary work (1976–81)

A nexus analysis arises from the values and the position of the researcher; this is the crucial starting point. Our earlier work before taking up these assignments at the University of Alaska was motivated by a concern that in the United States members of what have been called ethnic minorities were not receiving the full benefits of the society while nevertheless being required to pay the full price. While we have been ambivalent about these benefits which often seem destructive of ethnic difference we have persisted in this orientation because of our need to understand our own place in life.

As an 'interethnic' couple born and living in the United States, we and our children have been confronted daily with the dilemmas of negotiated cultural difference. Within the family we constantly confront questions of our separate individual identities, histories and futures. In contacts with the institutions of public life, schools, governments, businesses, hospitals and the rest, we are constantly reminded that our treatment by these institutions depends a great deal on how our ethnicity is perceived.

And so it was largely for personal reasons that in the early 1970s we began to use our academic training in linguistics, anthropology, and psychology to study the problems members of ethnic minorities encounter in dealing with the public institutions of American society.

Throughout America, language is used as a badge or emblem of ethnic identity and so we focused our attention on language and on the media of communication. Our training in linguistics led us to believe that the structure of the language people use in institutional settings would show us aspects of their attitudes and relationships that we would not be able to see in a more direct light. Our training in anthropology led us to identify significant points in the culture where people were practicing the discrimination we were trying to understand. This led to our study of gatekeeping situations. Our training in psychology made us nervous about assuming that ethnic characteristics were somehow 'wired in' and so we studied the ways people, both children and adults, learn how to act as members of their groups.

In an earlier set of ethnographic studies we had moved slowly from a focus on the structures of language to a focus on the ways people use language to interact with each other (R. Scollon 1976; R. Scollon and S. Scollon 1979; R. Scollon and S. Scollon 1981; S. Scollon 1982).

That research was completed before undertaking the research we discuss in this book. In Hawaii, we studied the early stages of the learning of English syntax. This study, which resulted in Ron's doctoral dissertation in 1974, led us to think that, from the very beginnings of recognizable language in a child, that language is based in human interaction. It seemed, though, before drawing any conclusions about humans in general, we would have to test our ideas against a child learning a language very different from English and in a very different place.

At the time we thought that structural differences in the languages would be the most important aspect of a child's learning of a language. We chose to study languages in the Athabaskan family because they were so markedly different in structure from English and because they were languages spoken in Alaska. What we did not expect to find was that the typical forms of interaction of the people who spoke the languages had a tremendous importance both on the structure of languages and on people's attitudes toward them. At the same time we began to find that the structure of the language itself may not be so important as whether people emphasize written or oral media for teaching and learning.

At Fort Chipewyan, Alberta, our research took a major turn from the study of languages to the study of the uses of languages in a community. We found that, over the time of several centuries, the four languages in use there – Chipewyan, Cree, French, and English – had come to approximate each other. The languages had converged in structure to a considerable extent. While looking at this convergence at Fort Chipewyan, we also observed that much of the form of an oral narrative came out of the interaction between the storyteller and his or her audience. A story told in Chipewyan was organized in four parts while the same story, told to us in English, was structured in three parts. It was the pursuit of this idea which led to our first body of research in Alaska.

At the same time that we were studying the oral narratives of elder tradition bearers, Suzie was studying the socialization of infants and young children into this predominantly oral speech community. In Alaska we extended both of these lines of research. This research became the basis for Suzie's doctoral dissertation

(1982). We found that in order to understand both the structures of traditional oral narratives and the language used by young Athabaskan children speaking in English we needed to understand the values the speech community placed on independence and personal autonomy in interpersonal, face-to-face interaction. We argued that both the language of young children and the narratives of elderly tradition bearers structurally reflected the social interactions given preference in that speech community.

In the book *Narrative, literacy and face in interethnic communication* (R. Scollon and S. Scollon 1981) we organized this research around several points. We argued that literacy in the Western world is typified by what we have called the 'essayist' style. The clear prose essay which presents ideas in a linear argument has been both the means and the goal of a Western education. We argued that this typical communicative style, which Lanham (1983) calls the C-B-S (Clarity-Brevity-Sincerity) style, reflects a typical worldview or reality set which values rationality, clarity, directness, componentiality, plurality, and above all decontextualization. The essayist text, like the modern consciousness reality set (Berger, Berger, and Kellner 1973), values the idea which is treated as independent of its context, which stands on the merits of its own argument. We also argued that in certain communities of practice within our society children are brought up from birth to participate in this reality set and this communicative style. Two or three years before the child is able to read or write, the hallmarks of this 'literate' behavior are present.

By contrast we found that there was another reality set held by many members of an Athabaskan oral speech community. We called this reality set the 'bush consciousness' because of the widespread use of the word 'bush' to refer to the northern wilderness which lies outside of the cities and regional centers. This reality set manifests a high value placed on context, individual autonomy, non-intervention in the affairs and ideas of others, and a holism in its approach to understanding. In keeping with the bush consciousness, the traditional oral narrative gives to the listener the most significant role in interpretation: the audience participates in the actual telling of the story; the listener puts things into his or her own words and concepts (R. Scollon and S. Scollon 1984b). Children in these communities are socialized from very early to pay a deep respect to the autonomy of others. They learn to avoid intervention in the ideas and affairs of others. They are expected to listen and to learn from careful attention to others and their actions, not from direct instruction (S. Scollon 1982).

These contrasts between the two reality sets, the two typifying media, and the two competing strategies of social interaction were not of merely academic concern. As we wrote about the modern consciousness and the bush consciousness, essayist literacy and oral narratives, direction and non-intervention, we were also working as teaching academics in an institution of higher education, the

University of Alaska, Fairbanks. This university, like many others, had been plagued by an apparently insoluble problem. The University of Alaska is mandated by the state legislature and by the terms of its land- and sea-grant status to serve the educational needs of all the citizens of the State of Alaska. This includes a large population of Alaska Natives, that is, indigenous Native Americans who were the first inhabitants of the land now called Alaska.

The history was clear: Alaska Natives enrolled at the various branches of the University of Alaska at a rate about equal to their percentage of the population, around 15 percent. Alaska Natives graduated at a rate that barely made 1 percent. To some eyes the attrition rate of Alaska Natives was a serious problem in discrimination against a clearly definable ethnic group (or set of subgroups – there are actually some twenty Alaska Native language groups). To others this attrition rate was clear evidence of the failure of the rural schools to prepare Alaska Natives for college-level academic work. To still others, unfortunately, this attrition rate was evidence for a fundamental incapacity of Alaska Natives to participate in the academic community.

So starting in 1978 in new positions at the University of Alaska we began to look for a way to understand the problem of the persistent failure of the bur-eaucratic institutions of the culturally dominant American society to respond to populations of clients who come to them from ethnic and cultural 'minority groups'. The projects which we have just described and to which we will return in the following chapters chart our movement through the maze of partial understandings of this problem, centering our investigations on the one institu-tion we were in the best position to observe, the University of Alaska, Fairbanks.

Strategies for beginning a nexus analysis

Taken together, the sequence of projects we have just described shows a central principle of nexus analysis: Each project leads to redefinitions of the central issues and that, in turn, leads to needing to undertake a new direction or set of projects. We had no idea when we started that we would be making video materials or working in the development of institutional structures such as the Chancellor's Computer Awareness Program. Each of these arose as more or less inevitable outcomes of earlier stages in the cycle of discourse. We were fortunate at that time to be able to make the personal and institutional changes that we needed to make to continue following out the trajectory of this nexus analysis. Put another way, the trajectory of a person through a nexus analysis may often lead to the need to move in a traversal across institutional, social, or organ-izational lines. In a few words, this is the first and perennial social change that takes place in a nexus analysis – the change of positions and identities of the researcher.

Our starting point in the nexus analysis we are describing here was a concern for discrimination against ethnic minority people, particularly Alaska Natives, in the bureaucratic institutions of the American state. Our first recognitions were focused on the use of Alaska Native languages in interpersonal gatekeeping encounters. This arose quite directly out of our own employment on the one hand (our own historical bodies), our daily work as teachers in classes and in providing consultation (the interaction orders in which we found ourselves regularly working), and the research expertise we brought to those situations in psychology and anthropological linguistics as well as the much broader social discourses of the Cold War, national bilingual education legislation, and the development of oil resources and the Alaska Native corporations (the discourses in place). In time we came to shift our primary focus to any interpersonal gatekeeping encounters, whatever language might be used. Again, in time, we came to focus on the communicative structuring of the institutions themselves.

We believe that it was important for us that we did not try to develop our original questions as analyses in any extended form. At the first stage of *engaging the nexus of practice*, the questions and problems were given to us by the people and the institutions we worked with. That was how people saw the questions and so it was most useful to begin with their own definitions of the situation. For one group 'the problem' was developing fairer access to the university for Alaska Native students. For another group 'the problem' was to develop the use of university computing resources. For still another 'the problem' was to establish and maintain a statewide computer network for national security purposes.

As we moved through our work and these projects we found that many of these definitions of the problem as well as our own identifications within them changed. Over the five or six years of these projects we moved through different networks of people, different institutional positions, and took on rather different professional identities. It would never have occurred to us at the beginning of our work at the Alaska Native Language Center that within just a few years we would be attending the Pacific Telecommunications Conference along with ministers of communication from several nations of the world from Brazil to Singapore. We could not have known that nor should we have tried. The important thing we believe was to be flexible and ready to change our own ideas about what the major issues really were or how they would be best addressed.

So our first goal was simply *recognition* and *identification*. We needed to find out what the participants and the analyst(s) believed were the significant problems and the actions and places in which they are located as well as to find a role for ourselves in these actions. While we did not use these terms then, now we would try to sort this out in the terms we have set up here, the three categories of the *historical body*, the *interaction order*, and the *discourses in place*. In a sense what you want to know is just this: Who is doing what and where are they doing it and what are the cycles of discourse which are circulating through this moment of action?

In sum, then, a nexus analysis begins with engaging the nexus of practice. This amounts in most cases to simply being explicit about how the researcher himself or herself is located in the social world and in finding or being explicit about the social issues the researcher wants to address through this research. As we suggest in the Fieldguide (Appendix) this engagement can be supplemented or developed through the use of various kinds of surveys – surveys of issues which are currently considered to be important, surveys of the participants in which you are interested, or such means as open-ended focus groups to determine where might be the best place to become concrete with specific social actions to begin the analysis. In Alaska and in our subsequent research in Hong Kong and elsewhere in the world we have used the questions you will find in the Fieldguide as ways of raising the light on the initial nexus of practice as well as to assist ourselves in engaging the nexus of practice.

If we could summarize this in just four words we could say *start where you are*. The important thing is to try to make sense of where you are and what you are in relationship to the issue you are studying. The rest of the connections will develop very soon in this process. At that point you can then move on to navigating the nexus of practice which is the main work of a nexus analysis.

5 Navigating the nexus of practice: Mapping the circumferences and timescales of human action

Rick's work day has been stressful and he has a bad headache. He has had to finish two presentencing interviews for his presentencing report for the court and one of them did not go well at all. For a probation officer these interview sessions are hard. At this stage of the legal process the defendant has been found guilty and so Rick has only thirty days in which to make his report to the court. Rick has to finish several reports of this kind every day and official records from other states usually take two months to return. This is a problem because the Judicial Council handbook clearly outlines that defendants with prior records or without any local community support network will receive longer sentences than first offenders or people who might be better off returning to their families or jobs. All he can do is try to get this information out of the convicted offenders themselves by talking to them, and a lot of them are pretty resistant, even dangerous. He has no police training and is not allowed to be armed; Rick's degree was in biology. He took the probation job because he thought he might be able to help people, but mostly he spends his time trying to trick them into saying things that he can use to incriminate them. They know better and he knows better. About all he can hope for is that he can put in his report that the offender has been cooperative with him because that will help in reducing the sentence the judge will hand down.

One of the offenders today, a guy who now lives in Anchorage but came up from California last year to work on the oil pipeline, was pretty cooperative. He'd been found guilty of selling marijuana to a couple of other pipeline workers, but he was pretty sorry to have gotten into this kind of trouble and really wanted to get this ordeal behind him, and get back to work. He and his girlfriend in town were going to get married and move back to California as soon as they'd saved enough money and, now, as soon as he could get over this conviction. Rick was pretty sure that would get him a fairly short sentence and then probation so he could get back to work. It was the other guy that was so hard to deal with.

This other offender was some kind of native guy but Rick couldn't really get him to say where he was from. He just said he was 'in town' right now. He didn't seem to have any connections in Anchorage and wouldn't say where he lived usually. Rick couldn't tell if the guy had a job or not because the guy just sat there looking down and from time to time Rick felt a bit scared that he might get violent. The offense was pretty much the same – minor sale of marijuana, but this one looked like he'd be in jail for a while because there were no mitigating factors and he was so hard to get anything out of. Somehow it didn't seem right to Rick that two guys would end up with such a different sentence for pretty much the same offense, but there was nothing Rick could do but worry about it because the guy had been so hostile to Rick.

No talk and a longer sentence

The probation officer in the opening anecdote, Rick, struggles with a kind of social interaction which we saw in many different places throughout Alaska, northern Canada, and the western US. We saw it in these probation officer interviews with convicted offenders, we saw it in elementary school classrooms, we saw it in doctor–patient consultations, and we saw it in public hearings concerning the development of oil resources.

One of the participants in the exchange, Rick in this case, is working with a very different set of expectations about how conversations, discussions, consultations or interviews work from those of the other person. Rick's life path, his historical body, carries in it certain expectations about social exchanges that include the feeling that it is good to talk to someone else you are with, you shouldn't leave long silences or fail to respond when the other has indicated he or she is finished with a turn of speaking. Rick feels you should present yourself in a positive way to others, try to show some inclusion or solidarity with them – show you have similar interests, that you have things in common. In this case where the other person is a convicted offender he is pretty sure that the natural thing the offender would do is to show that he's sorry for his offense, that he is really going to try to reform himself, and that he is especially worried about how this offense is going to affect his girlfriend, his chances of keeping or going back to his job, and their chances of getting married. In the first case the offender did just these things and Rick felt he'd behaved normally for somebody in that tough situation and he believed he would really try to reform himself. At least Rick was sure he wanted to write his report in a way that would give him the best chance of that.

It was the other offender which was the problem for Rick. We have seen this other set of expectations about conversations, interviews, or just talk in general very widely practiced among Alaska Native people. Of course there are many people who would identify themselves as Alaska Native people who would be much like the offender from California and also many Alaskans who come from 'outside' who would be much like the Alaska Native offender in this case, so we want to be certain that the reader does not feel we are speaking of any sharp distinction between ethnic or cultural groups.

This second offender was a person who carried in his historical body a practice of being very careful about what he would say, especially to strangers. He feels it is arrogant or insulting to stare at somebody's eyes when you talk and so in this case he keeps his eyes respectfully away from a direct look at Rick. He also feels, as he has been told so many times at home in the village, that he has to think carefully about his own behavior because he has to live by himself with the consequences of what he does. He has got himself in trouble now and so he doesn't want to insult his wife and mother who are living with him in Anchorage by dragging them into this mess he's gotten into. And it would be even worse for the people back home who were happy to think he was doing so well at his new job in Anchorage. For really just a few days that he slipped, he was not going to drag them all down into this trouble. He also knows that when people ask you questions, it isn't to get information; it's to tell you to think very deeply and carefully about what you have done so you won't do it again. Also, the worst danger is to try to predict and control the future. That is courting the worst kind of bad luck. So he remains silent while Rick questions him about his family and his job and his future. Every question makes him sorrier for what he did and his regret and shame make him more and more quiet.

The consequence of these very different habits of talk, these deeply practiced ways of speaking or being silent and of showing involvement or respect lead to the one who is most like Rick in his assumptions being an 'easy' case for Rick. He feels he knows just what to do and how to interpret what the man says. The other one is a difficult case, he appears unfriendly or hostile to Rick and finally just very suspicious. He seems to have no social connections in town, no concern for others, and no future. In the long run what difference does it make if he is kept off the streets for a while with a longer sentence? In any event Rick feels he did not cooperate with Rick and Rick's needs.

In this chapter we turn to a discussion of how a nexus analysis navigates the nexus of practice that is being studied. This is a very different example from the comparison of the traditional panopticon class and the technology-mediated class we discussed in Chapter 3, but in it we can begin to see some of the bigger semiotic or discourse cycles that are circulating through those two classrooms as well as through medical consultations, public hearings, job interviews, and elementary school classes in Alaska.

We want to first clarify how we are looking at the nexus of practice as a semiotic ecosystem. That is, a nexus of practice such as the panopticon class or the presentencing report interview, the legislative hearing, or the medical consultation is a system which comes together at the intersection of large cycles of discourse in the form of the historical bodies of the participants, the interaction order they establish in that system, and the discourses which circulate through that moment of human action.

. We have found it convenient to refer to navigating the nexus of practice as *mapping*. We do not really mean anything more sophisticated than that we need to get a broader understanding of the ways that times and places prior to the social action we are interested in have brought their influence into the current situation and the ways in which this social action anticipates or presupposes outcomes. Our goal in mapping is just to sketch out a map of the many semiotic or discourse cycles that are circulating through the moment of social action which we are studying. Once that rough sketch is worked out, the second step is *circumferencing*. We want to examine each of the semiotic cycles to see just what the circumference is – that is what kind of a cycle is it, how long it takes to come around full cycle, what other cycles it interacts with, and how discourses, objects, and actions are transformed, sometimes irreversibly, as these semiotic ecosystems evolve through time.

Throughout these two main activities, mapping and circumferencing, we also want to conduct an ongoing discourse analysis. That is, we will want to be looking closely at the ways discourse is used and circulates through the nexus under study, both in the narrower sense of language in use and in the broader sense of discourse systems. It is really only for ease of exposition that discourse analysis and motive analysis are not taken up until Chapters 6 and 7. Obviously, in order to see the cycles of discourse in which we are interested in our mapping and circumferencing here in Chapter 5 it is essential to look at the discourses themselves.

The ecosystem

When Rick interviewed those two offenders that afternoon in Anchorage in 1981, those interviews formed two different micro-semiotic ecosystems through which many personal, social, economic and other cycles of change were circulating. At the biggest socio-political level, the discovery and development of oil at Prudhoe Bay and the building of the Trans-Alaska Pipeline from Prudhoe Bay on the North Slope to Valdez on the Pacific Ocean in the south formed a cycle of very high-paying work, which is what brought the first offender to Alaska. The second offender was brought to Anchorage when the Alaska Native people sued the US government for rights to land, resources, and social services, won that suit, and so formed the Alaska Native Corporations to manage those new resources and services. His new job was working as a legislative liaison officer for one of those new corporations. His educational background which enabled this job originates in the cycle of change, the Molly Hootch case, which developed local high schools in rural Alaska villages. Rick came to Alaska from Michigan with an interest in Arctic biology, received his degree at the University of Alaska, Fairbanks, but in the process of going to school had come to be more concerned with social issues facing the state in this time of a boom economy.

Other cycles were circulating through those micro-semiotic ecosystems. One was the Alaska State Judicial Council's ongoing conflict with probation officers such as Rick who were threatening to strike or to quit *en masse* if they were not allowed to receive police-defensive training and to carry weapons. Some of them had been assaulted by dangerous, convicted offenders and they all felt they were being exposed to unnecessary danger in these presentence report interviews.

We have already discussed the personal, historical body cycles which were brought to these interviews by the three participants. The two from 'outside', that is Rick from Michigan and the offender who was originally from California, had very similar communicative experiences from childhood. They carried in their bodies the expectations for communications which would be open, in which turns would exchange relatively rapidly, in which both parties would engage in talk, where the offender would show deference to Rick by showing his cooperation and show deference to the legal system and penal code of Alaska by displaying his remorse and his shame and his intention to reform himself. The offender from rural Alaska carried in his historical body the expections we have already mentioned that he would show his remorse by thinking quietly himself, by not speaking or engaging in eye contact, and by not implicating other people in his shame. He would show his ability to take responsibility for his own actions in this way.

These semiotic ecosystems consist of complex interactions among broad socio-political forces and deep personal and interpersonal practices. In this book we refer to them as 'semiotic ecosystems' as a way of capturing processes which are well understood in biological studies of complex living systems but which have not often been examined with equal intensity in the study of human-social-material systems.

The nexus of practice: A semiotic ecosystem

In the two presentencing interviews we discussed between Rick and the two different offenders we said that there were several cycles of discourse which were circulating through that moment of social interaction. Now we can describe that nexus of practice – ways of asking questions, ways of responding, Judicial Council sentencing requirements, the ongoing dispute between the probation officers and the Judicial Council, the resource developments on the North Slope, the development of the Alaska Native Claims, the new rural high schools established by the Molly Hootch case and the rest which we have not mentioned – as a semiotic ecosystem. This ecosystem is a moment in the history of the world when these cycles come together to reach a culmination in human action. Like the ecosystem of the forest of eastern Canada we discussed in Chapter 2, each of these cycles is a somewhat independent system, but at the same time each depends on the other to enable the overall activity of the system.

Following the schematic representation of a biological ecosystem which we presented as Figure 2.6 in Chapter 2, we have sketched out just a few of the semiotic cycles which are circulating in the semiotic ecosystem of the presentencing report in Figure 5.1. In interpreting this figure it is important to avoid two extremes: (1) we should not exaggerate the clarity of this semiotic ecosystem. We believe this diagram and our analysis captures some of the complexity of such human actions and helps us to understand both how they have consequences and how we might try to change those outcomes, but it is still far too soon in our thinking about social interaction to rely too heavily on any analytically reduced view of social action; (2) therefore, we should not imagine that this nexus of practice can be reduced to just these few semiotic cycles. There are certainly more that are significant than we have sketched here and, until we have done a nexus analysis of the nexus of practice, we cannot be certain which of all of the semiotic cycles are the most crucial ones for us to enter into to try to bring about change.

Mapping the circumference of a discourse system

In Chapter 1 we defined two different concepts of discourse analysis. In the first case we defined discourse as 'the ways in which people engage each other

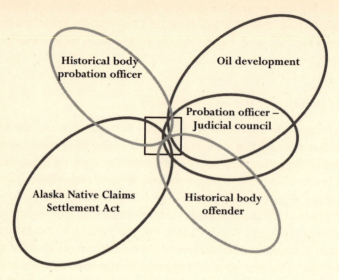

5.1 Presentence report semiotic ecosystem.

in communication'. That is, discourse in that sense has to do with the ways people speak or otherwise communicate with each other, normally in face-to-face interactions. Of course we would want to include such mediated forms of discourse as writing, telephoning, and, as we have done in Chapter 3, computer, audio, and video conferencing. The second way we defined discourse followed definitions by Gee and Blommaert and Foucault before them by focusing on larger-scale discourses such as management discourse or medical discourse. Most studies of discourse have kept their focus at one or another of these levels. They have either looked quite closely at the social interactions between two (not very often more) participants or they have looked very broadly at the large discourse-and-practice complexes that make up the powerful institutions of our society.

As we have seen in Chapter 3 in our description of the differences between the panopticon class and the technologically mediated class and at the beginning of this chapter, even when we try to focus on these broader discourses – academic discourse and legal system discourse – we find that there are very complex differences in actual practices depending on either the historical bodies which come into these interactions or the technological mediations, or, in fact both of these factors as well as many others we have not had the space to discuss.

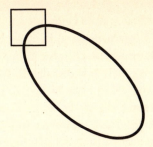

5.2 The historical body cycle of discourse.

When we talked earlier in this chapter about the differences between the urban Anchorage (Californian) offender and the rural Alaskan offender we said that each had brought to the semiotic ecosystem of the presentencing interview very different historical bodies which entailed very different assumptions about communication and communicative practices. The goal of a nexus analysis is to map and then navigate cycles which circulate through a semiotic ecosystem.

Now, to illustrate how we have done this mapping in one case, Figure 5.2, we will focus on the historical body of the rural Alaskan participant in this nexus of practice. Of course, we might have mapped out the discourses in place in a legal interview or the interaction order of a presentencing interview.

First, however, a few words about the terms we use to talk about members of different groups is necessary. There are people from many different social, ethnic, and cultural groups who live in rural Alaska with origins in Indian, Eskimo, or Aleut indigenous cultures or in Russian or other groups of European origin. Our own research as anthropological linguists has focused on study communities in which social groups who have heritage languages and practices which originate in Athabaskan languages have predominated. This is often simplified by saying we have studied 'Athabaskans'.

Because our research interest has been a concern with the discriminatory practices in the social institutions of the American state government and its attendant corporate and non-governmental agencies, and because those institutions and organizations use some form of English almost exclusively, even where the linguistic and cultural origins of the participants may vary widely, these groups are often simplified by saying they are 'English speakers'. Thus we have referred to our interests over the years as an interest in interethnic communication between 'Athabaskans' and 'English speakers' in the English-speaking social and bureaucratic institutions of the contemporary state.

We recognize the difficulties of such 'terminological screens' (as Kenneth Burke called them). We hope that in what follows it will be clear that we will speak in broad terms about 'Athabaskans' and 'English speakers' to signal this heritage group on the one hand and this social-bureaucratic complex of institutions on the other only for ease of exposition. We fully acknowledge that the bulk of the actual communication of 'Athabaskans' takes place in English and that at least some of the institutional members we classify as 'English' are, in fact, from communities of Athabaskan heritage. There seems no way out of these complexities, but, as we have argued in many places, what is important in this is the self-identifications and claims and the rights of participants to make these claims which are important. As we shall now try to illustrate, there are self-regulating and highly resistant cycles of discourse which come to be deeply embedded in the historical body on the one hand and to be the sources of overt communicative actions on the other which are also taken by participants as holding the key to these identities which we have just tried to characterize.

Athabaskan communication

Who came?

In our first project to try to understand the earliest stages of Athabaskan communication we failed miserably. Ron wanted to study the language of an Athabaskan child from one to two years of age as a comparative study of the acquisition of phonology. He had already done the research with a one-year-old child learning English in Hawai'i as his doctoral dissertation research (R. Scollon 1976). We went to Arctic Village, Alaska, in the summer of 1972 and learned two things: First, Ron's mere presence as a player in a softball game shifted the language in use from Gwich'in (Kutchin) to English; that is, by playing softball rather than just watching the game from the sidelines as he had the night before, Ron became an unwitting agent in social change, shifting the language used by dozens of people for several hours. Since we were there in Arctic Village to learn what we could about Gwich'in, our participation was having drastic effects in changing the phenomenon we were there to study. Secondly, even though there was a baby girl exactly 1 year old who might have formed a perfect comparison with the child he had studied in Hawai'i, it was socially wholly unacceptable for a male from outside the community – actually for any male but her father and the priest – to be together with her. Whenever we would arrive to discuss whether we could conduct the research, the baby would be spirited away out of sight; often right out of the cabin. In time it became clear that they were protecting the baby from his research scrutiny.

About seven years later after we had returned to Alaska from our research project at Fort Chipewyan, Alberta, in Canada, Eliza Jones, a Koyukon Athabaskan linguist of the Alaska Native Language Center who is now retired, began to teach us about how she and they view the early socialization of children. She brought a copy of *Language*, the journal of the Linguistic Society of America, into our office, outraged at what 'they' had done. She was angered by an article written by William and Theresa Labov about the early language of their child. Eliza said, 'Can you imagine they did *that* to their *own child?*' When Ron asked her to clarify she said she meant that they had closely examined their own child's speech and behavior. She said this felt to her like a form of child abuse. She noted that many people she knows in the village who have bought toys and other apparatus for the amusement of infants put tape over the mirrors so that they will not engage in self-reflection.

This discussion and many other stories and discussions with Eliza Jones sketched out a picture of an infant who is born because he or she chooses to be born. The so-called 'Mongolian blue spots' at the base of the spine that Indian and Chinese and many other children are born with and which soon fade are explained by stories not as racial characteristics as they are in Western scientific lore but as evidence that that woman has a strong child next in line to be born. Those spots are caused by that child in the other world hitting the child just born in trying to get ahead in line to be born. Dark spots indicate a strong child is next in line; faint spots indicate a weak child and that another birth might not be advised. Adults who comment on a newborn baby ask, 'Who came?' The child is thought to have an identity that is to be discovered by those in this world, not to be created or shaped by us. Thus the role of the living in respect to the newborn is to welcome this person and to seek to learn about who he or she is.

Smear Face (Nesdzeegh)

In Ron's work at the Alaska Native Language Center he did some studies of Tanacross Athabaskan narratives. That was his need. Gaither Paul was a man who wanted to have some of his stories recorded for his grandchildren who could not understand his Tanacross Athabaskan language. He told the stories and Ron recorded, transcribed, and translated them as a small publication at the Alaska Native Language Center. Some years later James Ruppert and Jack Bernet prepared a collection of Alaska Native stories (Ruppert and Bernet 2001) and asked Ron to write a brief preface to the Gaither Paul stories, and this is what he wrote:

Gaither Paul was fifty-six years of age when these stories were recorded. He was born March 18, 1923 at a caribou hunting camp between Dot Lake and the Robertson River, Alaska. Over the years he lived at Mansfield, Tanacross, and Anchorage. His father was David Paul, the first ordained Athabaskan in the Episcopal Church and his mother was Laura Luke. His father's father was Old Paul, his father's mother was Julia Paul; his mother's father was John Luke and his mother's mother was Laura Luke. Gaither Paul has eight adopted children, 14 grandchildren, and one great grandchild.

Gaither Paul is a storyteller, not a social analyst; he is a teacher, not a critic; he is a tradition bearer, not a researcher. When we met we worked together to try to accomplish three purposes. I wanted texts for linguistic analysis and from that point of view, the rhetorical or educational purposes of the texts were not my main interest. Gaither Paul and his wife, Beatrice, wanted to have his stories recorded in a form that could be passed on to his grandchildren. More powerful than either of these motives, however, was his concern to teach me through the telling of these stories.

When I approached Gaither through Beatrice, I recall that I asked in a way that I hoped was polite enough how he would evaluate himself as a storyteller. He did not directly answer my question. I was to learn this was most characteristic of his deep humility. He asked if I was ready to record. I said I was and he told me the story of *Nesdzeegh*, 'Smear Face', the man who disguised his great handsomeness and strength by distorting his face with pitch and affecting physical disability. Then, as the story unfolds, we learn that it is those who learn from Smear Face's actions of his underlying character who are rewarded with his protection. Thus, like Smear Face, Gaither Paul told me that I should look to his stories for my evaluation, not to his own comments about them. One is reminded in this of Gaither's own great concern for others; he and his wife cared over the years for over 300 foster children.

What is important for us here is that this story is very much like 'His Grand-mother Raised Him', a story known by many Chipewyan people and which was told to us by Ben Marcel in 1976 at Fort Chipewyan, Alberta, perhaps a thousand miles to the east in Canada. In both of these stories as in many others such as Frank Johnson's story in Tlingit, 'Strong Man', the central theme is that of a person who is very competent at doing something – telling stories or hunting, for example. In each case that person disguises his own ability and does not in any way show off to people who are with him. Those who learn to recognize his ability are rewarded; those who do not are neglected or even punished.

These stories of a Smear Face are so widely used that it is difficult to imagine an Athabaskan child growing up without hearing such a story many times. Not only that, as Eliza Jones has told us, just as it happened with Ron, after a child has heard a story being told he or she will be questioned later, perhaps several days later – and this is quite important in understanding the importance of asynchronous communication – about the meaning of the story. Like Ron with Gaither Paul in Alaska or with Ben Marcel at Fort Chipewyan in 1976 or Li Fang-Kuei at Fort Chipewyan in 1928, working with François Mandeville, the next stories that are told are based on how well the person has understood the importance of developing his own strength and capabilities as much as possible but at the same time never showing off those abilities.

To return just a moment to the questioning, we have been told that questions are asked mostly to encourage the child to think about his or her own behavior. A child who is misbehaving is not told what to do or what not to do. He or she is asked, 'Why are you doing that?' Or sometimes, 'Why did Smear Face punish those people who didn't recognize him?' That in itself is sufficient for the child to think through how to examine his or her own actions and to bring them in line with these quite indirect teachings of the stories.

Cooking it up and boiling it down

As we found in a project Suzie did with Virginia Juettner (Scollon and Scollon 1984b) children soon learn to tell the stories themselves. They are expected to tell them in the most succinct way possible, keeping the skeleton structure of the story together, but not to elaborate or evaluate as they tell the story. The meaning and evaluation of the story must be the one that the child or person gets for himself or herself from thinking about the story, not the meaning projected by the storyteller. One result of this is that Athabaskan children in elementary schools, when they are given standard reading and writing exercises where they are supposed to retell the story and then elaborate on its meaning, often fail in the eyes of their teachers from 'outside'. This is because they give very trim, concise, unelaborated précis of the story without producing the expected evaluations.

By the time Athabaskan children are going to school, they have developed an historical body that thinks of itself as having the responsibility to develop in a highly individualistic way and has come to assume that others will adapt themselves to his or her individuality. In our project on the rhythmic integration of talk, as we noted in Chapter 4, we observed an Alaska Native teacher with such students coming to the door of the classroom, quietly listening to the rhythms and watching the movements of the students, and then entering the room on the tempo which had been established by the students. This contrasted with the English teacher from 'outside' who strode into the classroom and, establishing her tempo as the dominant tempo, expected the students to adjust to her.

In Chapter 3 we talked about the differences between the panopticon class and the technologically mediated class. In our professional development seminar, detailed in Chapter 4, we found that teachers who made adjustments to the pace and rhythms set by their students through such means as privatizing their interactions with them on an individual level before starting the full-fledged panopticon class were judged by their students to be more human. Like Smear Face, the professional expert teacher who shows himself to be simple and humble with such students does not lose respect in the process. Athabaskan students carry with them an historical body skilled in seeking out the capabilities of people by watching their actions as they interact with other people.

Moving to a different kind of social interaction, we found in our work with different health service organizations in Alaska that the most common complaint medical professionals such as doctors and nurses had about their Athabaskan patients (as well as other Alaska Native patients) was that they did not comply with their treatments nor with their prescribed medicines. From the Alaska Native point of view, the central complaint was that the doctors don't ever listen to find out what is wrong with them; they only ask an endless series of questions. Since the doctors don't find out what their problems are, why should they comply with the treatment and medication?

We found two factors were operating here: (1) the function of questions in interpersonal interaction and (2) the expectation on whether or not one should directly speak about problems that one has. In the first case, as we have already said, for Athabaskans as for many Alaska Natives, the main function of a question is to suggest that the person questioned think more deeply about their own behavior. It is a form of reprimand or scolding from a person in authority. This works well if it is coupled with the practice we have already noted of learning to carefully observe behavior and to learn from that behavior what lies behind the actions. A person skilled in such interpersonal observation does not need to seek explicit or direct information; such questioning is, in fact, only to show one's lack of proper upbringing and one's immaturity.

The second factor derives from the first; one does not insult others by telling them directly what they should be capable of observing themselves. The greater the respect one has for another, the less one will explicitly tell them about things. So when patients go to the doctor for whom they have both a great respect and also from whom they really require much assistance, they will be very careful not to be insulting and to speak directly about their problems. At the same time they will accept the questioning of the doctor for what it is in their minds, a scolding from an authority to think more deeply about their own actions.

What do patients actually do in such consultations? The most common practice is to begin to tell very specific and concrete stories about events in which the problem they've come to see the doctor about was a relevant factor. These are told in careful, sometimes painfully excruciating detail so that the doctor will be able to draw the correct inferences about not only *what* the problem is but, possibly even more important to the patient, *why* it is a problem.

Unfortunately, medical professionals are mostly trained in practices of direct questioning of the patient and in physical examination of his or her body. They see these extended narratives as distracting and entirely beside the point and so tend to increase their control of the consultation with increasingly direct and pointed questioning. This questioning leads the patient to think more deeply and to tell ever more carefully detailed but unevaluative stories about the circumstances which brought him or her to the hospital or clinic.

An elementary beadwork book

A project that we were asked to do involved helping a small community make elementary bilingual education materials. We met with a group of five Ahtna Athabaskan women to help them plan. They said they wanted to make a little book about 'How to do beadwork'. Athabaskan moccasins nearly invariably have a brightly colored beaded rose on the top of the moccasin tongue as we show in Figure 5.3. They said the purpose of this book was to show children 'how to do beadwork' with this most salient example.

The group decided that each page would consist of a picture. Below the picture would be a description or caption given first in the Ahtna language and then in English. They thought about thirty pages or so would be about right, so we started working our way through first asking what they thought would be the right picture in the sequence and what the Ahtna phrase should be and how that should be translated.

When we started we asked what the first picture should be. Nearly in one voice, almost with a tone of incredulity they said, 'A moose!' They described and roughly sketched out what the drawing should look like for the artist who would do the final drawings, selected the Ahtna phrase and the English translation. Figure 5.4 is the page that was ultimately printed in the book. From there on they then said it should be 'father with a rifle', 'a dead moose', 'father skinning a moose', and 'father with the skin removed from the moose'. Each of these took some extended discussion to get the details right. From time to time we checked and it was confirmed that we were doing a book about 'how to do beadwork'.

5.3

The next sequence begins with 'mother fleshing the moose skin', 'mother cutting the moose hair off', 'mother shaving off the short hair on the skin', and so forth right through page 27 or so with all or most of the steps of tanning a moose hide. We were quite pleased with the book as a book on 'how to tan a moose hide' but at the time when we took our break for lunch we were very puzzled about how this was a book on beadwork.

We remembered the book *Through Navajo eyes* by Sol Worth and John Adair (Worth and Adair 1997) in which they describe a Navajo film-making project. Navajos are classified by linguists and anthropologists as Southern Athabaskans on the basis of the close affinity of their language to the languages of Northern Athabaskan such as Ahtna, Gwich'in, Tanacross, Chipewyan, or Koyukon which we have mentioned already. In their description a Navajo woman made a film 'about rug weaving' in which the bulk of the film showed the woman walking in the woods and gathering things. When the film comes to the point where the woman sets up her loom, the film then jump cuts to a finished rug, and so we began to think this is what we should watch for.

When we resumed after lunch we were to take up the next page which was page 28. The writers of the book wanted 28 to be 'mother untying the smoked

Gaa deniigi nghedzen.
Here stands a moose.

5.4

moose hide', 29 to be 'mother removing the sinew threads' (which she had used in preparing it for smoking), 30 to be 'trimming it around the edges'. That is, trimming it up as workable leather.

Page 31 finally began to get to the beadwork. They wanted this page to be 'mother cutting a pattern out of a piece of paper for a moccasin tongue'. Page 32 was to be 'tracing a pattern on the moose hide', 33 was 'cutting out the moccasin', and 34 was 'putting a pretty design on it' (with a pencil). This page in the finished book is Figure 5.5.

5.5

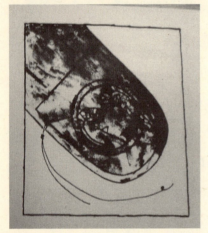

5.6

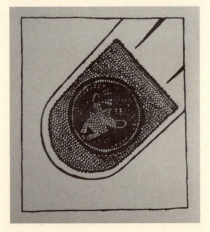

5.7

If we were right that this approach was like that taken by the Navajo film-maker, we were getting to the crux of the matter. The writers then said that page 35 should be 'stitching down the beads with a needle'. They were very explicit that this picture should show the tongue with the drawing on it, the needle with a thread extended with just one or two of the very first beads on it. Figure 5.6 is page 35 as it was printed in the book.

We held our breaths as we waited then for what they would say the next page would be. Perhaps it was not a surprise after all that they said, 'Now she has finished the beading' and that the picture should be a finished beaded moccasin tongue as shown in Figure 5.7. There are only three more pictures showing the assembly of the moccasins, and the last picture was to be 'father wearing the moccasins' much like in Figure 5.3.

Like the medical interview, the actual crucial point is not seen directly; what we see is the context, the reasons for doing beadwork, not the beadwork itself. We were happy enough that this project was consistent with what we had seen in the presentence reports, in medical interviews, in traditional storytelling, in linguistic sessions with a tradition bearer, or school classrooms; we were happy enough that what we were seeing was a careful description of the social contexts in which beadwork would make sense as a regular set of practices for children to learn. But we still needed to ask them if this was a book about 'how to do beadwork' and, if there were no examples of someone actually doing the sewing, how would children learn that. Their answer was an incredulous 'They'd watch their mother sew.'

Mapping the cycles of the historical body: Resemiotization

We could have started mapping this cycle at any point. We started with a pre-sentencing interview with a probation officer in which the Athabaskan participant was quiet in the face of authority, in which he took direct questioning as a reason to be even more taciturn and to reflect on his own remorse. We saw him being careful not to be explicit nor to draw others into the trouble with him. We could have started with a medical consultation in which the same man might have told explicit and carefully constructed stories about the contexts of his actions and of his medical problem, fully expecting the doctor to observe him through these narratives and to comprehend both the sources and the consequences of his illness or medical complaint.

We found in our work throughout Alaska and the Canadian north, but also by comparison with the work of others in the American southwest, that there is a discourse system by which the historical body is constructed out of discourse and action over a period of time. A child is told a story about a character such as Smear Face and begins to think about how to keep from bragging or showing off

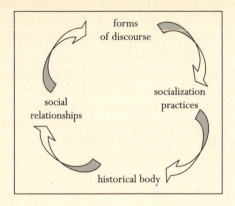

5.8

while at the same time he or she learns to be very capable at doing things. He or she learns to watch others very carefully to do as they do, but also to speak little about it. So the forms of discourse – in this case narratives and questioning – become practices of socialization by which the child comes to inhabit a historical body that observes much and speaks little. This historical body, in turn, is the source of social relationships in social situations which arise. The child or adolescent or adult learns to fill in the details of what others are saying and doing without asking questions or explicitly focusing on their actions in his or her talk. The most important aspect of this is respect for or deference to others. To do this, he or she finds the genres and interaction patterns, the forms of discourse, that have been used by the elders, most useful for his or her own speech. If she or he has learned through stories, it becomes easiest and most natural to explain things to others with stories.

We have adapted this cycle from our earlier writing on the Athabaskan discourse system although here we reproduce it as a general schematic which we believe would apply to any such discourse system which produces a recognizable and reasonably stable identity (Figure 5.8). The historical body that we speak of as 'being Athabaskan' has characteristics which come out of this life history of experience. Together these experiences and characteristics of that experience lead to actions which carry through as one cycle in any semiotic ecosystem in which this person takes part. We hasten to add that these are not the only historical body experiences and practices that a person might have. As we have said in our book *Intercultural communication: A discourse approach* (Scollon and Scollon 2001) each of us has an historical body which is formed within multiple discourse systems. Each of those systems will be formed as a fairly coherent set of forms of discourse, socialization practices, and social relationships. We may be men or women, older generation or younger generation, professionals or laborers or agricultural workers and so forth. Each of these forms of identity is a quite consistent discourse system and consequently there is an ongoing dialectic not just between ourselves and others who are different from us but within our own historical bodies between these different discourse systems.

Each of us is, in fact, a micro-semiotic ecosystem of some commensurate and some incommensurate discourse systems. We may find it difficult when we are in a social situation in which it is most appropriate to select and emphasize one of these discourse systems to suppress or limit the activities of one of the other ones. Our purpose here in this section has not been to suggest that any one discourse system will fully exhaust our understanding of the historical body of any one person. It is a simpler purpose to show how a particular discourse system may be carried within the historical body of a person and that to some extent that discourse system, in turn, carries that person through social situations. One or more of these discourse systems is likely to be a major semiotic cycle within any of the semiotic ecosystems which constitute a nexus of practice. Our goal in a nexus analysis is to try to discover which are the relevant ones and to map as well as we can the sources of those relevant cycles through situations and activities throughout the person's life.

Other cycles: The panopticon and the technologically mediated class

As we have said, our interest in the work we are reporting here was in finding an angle from which to understand institutional discrimination against Alaska Natives in the social institutions of the State of Alaska. We had observed the patterns of communication or the communicative style that we have just described as the Athabaskan discourse system in many different types of social situations. In each case what we had learned in one place shed light on what we were seeing in another. It was important to us to observe not only infants but young adults, not only young adults but elderly tradition bearers. We also felt it was important to know not only how this Athabaskan discourse system worked when it operated within the semiotic ecosystems of more traditional cultural provenience such as when elders were telling stories, but also how it operated or changed in the semiotic ecosystems of the major Cold War discourses of resource development, education within the literacy-dominated schools of the state, and in the political circles in which Athabaskans were needing to work to achieve their political rights within a rapidly changing socio-political and economic world.

These were the concerns that led us to an interest in the asynchronous computer-mediated conference. On the one hand through our Native language documentation work we were seeing how Athabaskan communication worked in traditional settings. In our university classes and in the bilingual education programs we were servicing throughout the state we were seeing interactions with traditional panopticon communicative structures. We were interested in seeing if we could change some of those aspects without changing all of them by implementing our classes as asynchronous and non-centralized communications.

We have described many of the differences between the panopticon class and the technology-mediated class in Chapter 3. In this chapter now we have shown how we mapped just one of the discourse cycles which circulates through many different nexus of practice. Later, in Chapter 7 we will show how our activities, particularly introducing technological mediation to the semiotic ecosystem of the university class, brought us up against the need to examine and map the broad cycles of discourse that circulate through such a nexus of practice. We will examine more closely what cycles of power circulate in such a nexus of practice. If using computers to mediate these interactions for the purpose of achieving asynchronous communications might favor the Athabaskan discourse system, are cycles of literacy being further entrenched at the expense of oral interactive patterns in the historical body? We will also need to examine more closely in Chapter 7 the cycles of administrative and institutional power that our experimental work disrupted as we crossed the lines maintained by institutional credentializing and hiring practices.

In Chapter 6 which follows we will turn directly to the question of discourse analysis. As we suggested when we introduced the idea of an 'Athabaskan' discourse system, our concept of what this system is or whether it is a system at all is tightly linked to our discourse about it. If we speak of what individuals do, that is if we locate our analysis in the autonomous actions of individual social actors, we can ascribe to them powers of agency and intention. At the same time we deny the identity and continuity of the historical body. If we characterize the actions of the probation officer and the offenders as deriving from their 'cultural' background, either we construct them as helpless chips floating along on the rivers of culture or we essentialize social agents as little or nothing but the cultures which have produced them. Equally we might wrongly characterize the changes between the panopticon classroom and the technology-mediated class as deriving directly from the technology itself and thereby engage in a kind of techno-determinism that denies both agency and socio-cultural identity to social actors.

Thus it is important for a nexus analysis to examine its own discourse as well as the discourses of the social actors we are studying. A central thesis of nexus analysis is that discourse, any discourse, is a central agent of change in any semiotic ecosystem. Before turning to that analysis in Chapter 6, now, we will conclude this chapter with a summary of some of the crucial strategies we have used in navigating a nexus of practice.

Mapping semiotic cycles for us has meant that we have come to see the connections among making a beadwork book for an elementary language class-room, the interpersonal behavior of a defendant in a presentencing interview, and a university student taking a computer-mediated class. Perhaps it is obvious that in mapping semiotic cycles we are doing very much the same thing the participants in our beadwork workshop were doing in respect to beadwork. In that case they were making sure that the student understood that the father's activities as a hunter, the mother's activities in tanning a moosehide, and, again, the clothing that people wear are all intersecting in this act of sewing beads for a moccasin tongue. Those other cycles circulate through that beadwork; the bead-work gives them meaning in turn. Likewise, mapping a nexus of practice is the way a researcher sketches out the lines of meaning which circulate through any moment of social action to assist in making the meaning of that moment visible.

It should also be apparent that for ourselves as the writers of this book and as ethnographers who are firmly committed to using the principles of nexus analysis, that beadwork workshop of more than twenty years ago is circulating through our own historical bodies. What first became clear to us in a workshop on an elementary language booklet has now become for us an essential principle of ethnographic analysis.

In this way we can see that the discourses which circulate through any moment of social action including this one of writing a book or your action of reading it may be overt or they may be covert. It is most likely that until we made this latter point explicit most readers would not immediately see the direct line of descent from that workshop to this theoretical position. We can also, then, notice that for this to occur the discourse has gone through multiple resemiotizations. First there were the lengthy discussions of the workshop. These were followed by the printing of the booklet. Following that we have used this as an example of a way of thinking about context *vis-à-vis* focal social action in many workshops, for example in providing consultation for medical personnel in a rural clinic in Alaska. As we have discussed this over the years we have come to realize that we were learning much more than we had thought and that in many ways this was not at all about 'Alaska Natives', it was about gaining a fuller perspective on all human action. Thus these ideas have now been resemiotized here as 'mapping the nexus of practice'.

Many of the discourses present in an action are 'submerged' into practice by long habit. The women in the beadwork workshop were a bit taken aback by our inability to see that they really were on the topic of beadwork when they were talking about skinning a moose or tanning a moosehide. This strategy of indirect contextualizing is deep in their historical bodies. For us it had to be made an explicit, overt discourse before we could then begin to internalize it over more than two decades. So we believe that in mapping the discourses we need to be careful to examine both overt discourses – the things being said – and covert ones – the things which are submerged in practice which nobody needs to spell out.

Overt and covert discourse are simply at different stages in a full cycle of discourse in our view. And, as we have seen, discourse might also be 'precipitated' into material form such as the beadwork booklet or, for that matter, this book which you are reading. Thus we find it important to be certain that we are also taking into account not just spoken discourse and not just written discourse, but also all of the objects which are being used as mediational means in any moment of social action. It was clear to us that the gun used as the first stage in providing the moose skin was as important as beads in the contextualizing of 'doing beadwork'. In each case we want to look for the mediational means being used to carry out an action as each of these means will carry with it anticipations of actions to come. Each is, in turn, an emanation of an earlier cycle.

In the Fieldguide (Appendix) we present a diagram of a hierarchy of timescales that it might be useful to consider in mapping the cycles of discourse which make up a semiotic ecosystem. It would take an expert at sewing beads perhaps several days of work to complete a moccasin tongue. It would take someone quite a bit longer to fully tan a moosehide. Moose are normally hunted for winter meat in late summer and early autumn, the meat dried and put up for the winter and the skin tanned to make clothing. This sequence works on an annual timescale. The beadwork workshop was plugged into a very different annual cycle, the American school calendar. The timescale on which we went from the original understandings in that workshop to our presentation here spans more than two decades. And from a different point of view, the cycles of hunting, tanning, and beadwork are ancient, covering centuries and centuries of cultural practice.

We believe that a nexus analysis needs to be very careful not to get caught up in the time framing that a focus in just one timescale might produce. The team who were preparing the beadwork booklet were working under the time pressures to finish the booklet within just a few weeks so that it could be reproduced and used yet that same school year. Nevertheless, the substance about which they were writing was a matter of ancient cultural heritage. Our own participation had to be geared into the academic and research timescales of busy university teaching, researching, and consultation activities. Each of these timescales came to intersect in our working together in the workshop. We wanted to know more, to examine the repercussions of their view of beadwork for broader social interactions. Within that workshop this was not possible; we had to finish within the two days allocated for the trip to Glenallen. This, in turn, displaced our fuller understanding across times and places so that only gradually were we able to see the links between their thinking and what was happening in medical interviews or presentencing report interviews.

All of these factors from resemiotization of discourses into objects or objects into further discourses to the need to work and think across multiple timescales are part of the mapping of the semiotic ecosystems in which social action occurs. We must reiterate that there is always very much more than any researcher or team of researchers could fully investigate. The important part of mapping is to keep focused on crucial points in the cycles of discourses where changes are occurring and to remain alert to cycles of discourse which may be overt or invisible within the current moment but which, seen in a broader circumference, are active moments in the overall semiotic ecosystem.

6 Navigating the nexus of practice: Discourse analysis and institutional power

Jennifer is not feeling well and the stagnant air of the dormitory is making her feel worse. She survived her first year at the university with pretty good grades, but now that winter has started she can't face another year of this constant life among strangers. There are more strangers living on just her floor of the dorm than all her family, relatives, and friends in her entire home village. She can't do anything without strangers watching her; there are even strangers she has to pass by when she goes to the toilet. Today she is going to go tell her counselor, Susan, in the Rural Education program that she is going to go back to the village and try something else with her life. She is worried that Susan will not let her leave. She thinks, 'It seems like the only thing the university cares about is keeping us here.'

Susan is worried about writing the interim report on her grant for the new Rural Education program. They have instituted many really good activities for students and the College and the University have been very supportive. They've established university visits by families and prospective high school students; they've done potlucks and social occasions for new students; they've had training sessions in cross-cultural communication for their counseling staff and many regular faculty attended because they also wanted to help with the problem of retention. But now one of their best students, Jennifer, says she wants to leave and go back home. How have they failed her and so many other students? How can they eliminate the barriers to participation in university life for such promising students?

Gatekeeping: Access or retention?

In the 1980s we were concerned that Alaska Natives were not achieving educational equity within higher education in the State of Alaska. Since the University of Alaska, as the only publicly supported institution of higher education within the state, bore the burden of examining educational practice and identifying barriers to full participation of Alaska Natives in post-secondary education, we conducted the ethnographic and other studies of the University of Alaska we have described in Chapter 4 with the goal of describing the institutional placement, organization, and functioning of gatekeeping encounters within the university. As we have noted, our other consultation and training responsibilities also gave us opportunities to study the other, private tertiary institutions in the state as well. We hoped that by locating and defining potential organizational barriers to educational equity within the university system, those studies would provide the background by which more pointed research and institutional strategies could be developed for dealing with these barriers. In other words, when we began our research into gatekeeping in public institutions, we took a position much like that of Susan (the counselor) in the vignette above – that the problem was one of providing and facilitating access to the services and resources of public institutions.

Modern bureaucratic and technological institutions such as a university control the flow of people into and through the institution with a series of 'gates'. In the university, gatekeepers such as counselors, teachers, and administrators depend on fair, objective procedures of evaluation to ensure equity in opportunity and mobility. Research which was being conducted at that time such as that by Erickson (Erickson 1976; Erickson and Shultz 1982) had shown, however, that, while gatekeepers try to maintain objectivity, this objectivity is undermined by two kinds of 'leakage' from outside factors. The first of these outside factors that provides 'leakage' is communicative style – the individual discourse practices of participants in the gatekeeping situation. Where the individual and the gatekeeper involved use different discourse practices, there is a strong potential for decisions to be made by the gatekeeper which are discriminatory against the individual.

A second kind of 'leakage' into the objectivity of the gatekeeping encounter is co-membership. Where the gatekeeper and the other individual share some significant particularistic attributes there is a powerful effect of increased advocacy by the gatekeeper on behalf of the individual. That is, common background, interests, or other socio-cultural attributes tend to produce alignment of the gatekeeper and the individual. These two forms of 'leakage' clearly indicate that the gatekeeping encounter is not objectively sealed off but is subject to the effects of other influences, both personal discourse strategies and the broader discourses within which the gatekeeper and the student participate. The structural and organizational properties of the situation only partially determine both the activities within the situation and the outcomes. Particularistic attributes of both the gatekeeper and the other participants also significantly affect both activities within the situation and the outcomes.

While the work of Frederick Erickson and others such as John Gumperz and his students suggested that much might be achieved by careful study of face-to-face discourse in gatekeeping situations, it was also clear that any proposed institutional changes would have to be related to an understanding of institutional and societal organization, that is, the broader discourses which constitute the gatekeeping encounter. Specifically, there were two issues to be faced in proposing changes in the internal dynamics of gatekeeping situations. In discussing the first of these, Erickson and Shultz pointed to a serious policy dilemma raised by their work. While it may be possible to manipulate the variable of communicative style or discourse strategies and co-membership in gatekeeping encounters, it might be specifically prohibited by the 1964 Civil Rights Act to do so. As a result, we felt that addressing the problem of discrimination in gatekeeping situations by looking only at the discourse dynamics of those situations might actually increase the potential for neglecting other serious societal and institutional issues embedded in the broader cycles of discourse we have mentioned such as the increased need to provide educational access to Alaska Natives because of the Alaska Native Claims Settlement Act, the establishment of Alaska Native corporations, or the introduction of state-supported high schools in rural villages throughout the state.

The second issue we had to face was that we felt that organizational changes that might bring about a greater access by students to teachers and counselors of like communicative style might simultaneously place teachers and counselors in an increasingly negative position. Without corresponding organizational changes, some teachers and counselors would have to provide a greater degree of advocacy than they are institutionally capable of doing. Because in many institutions members of ethnic and other minorities are underrepresented (as well as located at less influential institutional positions), this increased load of advocacy for the minority students would make it difficult or impossible for the advocate to accomplish his or her professional goals.

The problem with 'access'

With those considerations in mind we began to think through what we saw as the problem of institutional barriers to educational equity, particularly those barriers which were affecting Alaska Native students. As our research was originally formulated, the 'problem' we saw was one of access. As we originally thought through the problem of how and where Alaska Native students might be finding the university less than responsive to their needs, we phrased this issue as one of institutional barriers to entrance and movement through the institution.

As we began to make our observations and to gather the views of students and faculty, it became apparent that there were very different metaphors of the university informing people's perceptions of the gatekeeping situation. One phrasing was that of the student who said: 'It seems like the only thing the university cares about is keeping us here.' Another student in approaching a teacher about leaving the university voiced the fear that she would not be allowed to do so. This student was particularly afraid to approach her counselor who she felt would be very angry with her and try to prevent her leaving. Other students we interviewed, when talking about withdrawal from the university, preferred wordings such as 'going home' or 'trying something else' to wordings such as 'dropping out'. The faculty-counselor phrasing of the complementary metaphor is seen in the concern with the 'problem of retention'.

Total institutions

Comments of this sort led us to consider Goffman's notion of the total institution as a possible model for viewing the problem of gatekeeping. Goffman (1961) introduced the idea of the total institution, an institution in which the members sleep, play, and work in one sphere under a single authority, where each phase tends to be carried out in the company of others of the same class, all activities are scheduled, and all activities constitute a single, rational institutional plan. Goffman, of course, points out that no one institution displays all of these features and at the same time no single feature of the total institution is not shared by other, non-total institutions. His method is one of 'ideal types'. Among the total institutions one might consider, Goffman mentions prisons, mental hospitals, POW camps, army barracks, work camps, homes for the blind and aged, and monasteries. His own study was of a mental hospital and so we wanted to be careful not to attribute to the university characteristics of such a different social institution. In spite of these cautions, however, we felt it was useful to consider to what extent we could think of the University of Alaska, Fairbanks, campus as a total institution.

It is clear that for some students, especially those who live in the dormitories, the university plays a central role in organizing their sleeping arrangements, their recreational opportunities, and of course their work. Each of these activities except in rare cases is carried out in the presence of others of like class, fellow students of the same age and even class standing in the university. While not all activities are scheduled, the class schedules of students dictate to a great extent when any other activities may be performed. Of course, those taking meals in the

Commons must take their meals within a scheduled period. Finally, all of these activities are viewed by the faculty and the staff as constituting a single, rational institutional plan, a career as a student in pursuit of a college degree.

Goffman points out some further characteristics of a total institution. There is a predominance of surveillance over guidance. There is a clearly defined split between members considered to be 'staff' and those considered to be 'inmates'. This split between the two classes of members is often marked by carefully controlled and limited communication between the two groups and sometimes by narrow and hostile stereotyping of each group by the other. The institutional plant is seen as 'owned by' or belonging to the staff. Work payment is tied to presence rather than to the quality of the work, attendance is more critical than performance. Finally, total institutional membership is basically incompatible with family life.

It is certainly not the case that the University of Alaska or any of the other tertiary institutions in Alaska represents a total institution for all students or faculty. It is suggestive, however, to call attention to some of the comments of students about their presence on the Fairbanks campus. Students point to the apparent concern with keeping them in school. Students often express the feeling that faculty members are unapproachable, that they wish to remain communicatively separated from students. Observationally it is clear that one rarely sees students present at 'open' meetings of the university community. These are regarded as the domain of the faculty. One also sees relatively few faculty members present at 'student' events. As we have seen in Chapter 3, students and teachers are physically differentiated spatially in the panopticon classroom; the space 'owned' by the teacher is large and that 'owned' by the student is tightly constrained.

Perhaps the most frequent student complaint about the nature of their lives on campus is the nearly absolute absence of any sense of privacy or of having their own world. The university is seen as a public place, owned by its faculty and staff. One of the reasons we have used the term 'mapping' in doing a nexus analysis came about simply because in this case we asked people to make maps of their institution. In classes and focus groups we asked students and teachers to make maps of the university and of classrooms. These maps were highly distorted from an objectivist point of view, but clearly revealed the map maker's understanding of physical spaces.

We then asked them to mark several important points on their maps: (1) where they spend most of their time, (2) where their teachers (or students) spend most of their time, and (3) where the university president's offices are located. Students marked their dormitory, the student center, and the main class building but had no clear idea of where to find their teachers and were quite surprised to imagine that the university president might be located on campus as well. Faculty, of course, marked their own office and the classrooms, but rarely knew where the students' dorms were. They were able to mark the president's office quite easily. As to marking the spaces within classrooms, students marked a single desk as their own space and frequently marked the remainder of the room as the teacher's space.

To the extent that attendance is taken as a critical factor in student participation in classes, this also expresses one of the properties suggested by Goffman for a total institution. As we have observed in Chapter 3, in the panopticon classroom, while formal attendance is not often taken, we do frequently see teachers doing the following:

> Teacher (holding up an outline which was distributed at the last class): 'Is there anyone who doesn't have this?'

Or:

> Teacher: 'If you weren't in class last time, would you come up and pick up this handout?'

While the teacher's intent is to make sure each student has the necessary documents for the class discussion, there is an implicit and publically broadcast declaration that there are those who are missing classes. We noticed also that there was an emphasis on attendance and not performance in the continuation of students' fellowships and scholarships. Faculty members are often asked to sign off on a student's attendance for continuing funding but grades in courses do not figure into a student's continued funding at such frequent intervals. Finally, the limited on-campus facilities for married students indicate a basic assumption that students are not expected to have families or at least not expected to bring their families with them to campus.

We do not wish to push Goffman's analysis to an extreme in looking at the University of Alaska. Our concern is with suggesting that for at least some students, their presence on campus was being perceived by them as being housed in a total institution. It should be clear that there are many 'causes', only some of which are within the jurisdiction of the university itself. For example, a great number of scholarships come from organizations that are outside of the university and yet the emphasis of these programs on attendance tends to reinforce the totalizing properties of the on-campus student life. What we wish to emphasize is that if conditions should conspire to give a student the perception of 'inmate' status in a total institution, however incorrect that perception may be, that student may have a very different perception of the university than the one with which we had begun our thinking in this study.

The gate

When we began this study our concern was that a certain class of students (Alaska Native students) was not achieving equal access to the resources of the University of Alaska. From that point of view the gatekeeper was seen as someone who is institutionally invested with the power of making decisions which may grant or deny this access. We saw our central concern being the location of these gatekeepers and the situations in which these gatekeeping decisions were being made as a means of discovering how organizational structure may be influencing these decisions. In this view the gate was seen as either blocking or providing access to the institution. The gate in this case swings inward, it opens into the institution.

If we ask how the gate is viewed in a total institution, we see that it swings outward, it opens onto the world outside of the institution. The role of the gatekeeper is to keep the gate closed against escape and to allow only institutionally approved exit. In this view the role of the institution is to transform the individual and to only allow appropriately transformed individuals to exit. In the total institution the gatekeeper is a guard. In short, in a total institution, retention is the problem.

Retention

When we began this study we conceived of it as an ethnography of communication at the University of Alaska taking the university itself as a speech community and trying to understand the communication between that community and the Alaska Native speech community. The part of this broader ethnography which was supported by the National Institute of Education (NIE) was originally titled 'The Organizational Control of Communicative Differences in a Public University'. After the decision was made to fund the study it was suggested by NIE that the study be retitled, 'Communication Patterns and Retention in a Public University.'

Thus the first discursive move in this project was a negotiation between ourselves as researchers and the funder, NIE. The perspective was significantly altered by this rephrasing. In our perspective the problem we wanted to research assumed that the university was in some ways constructing barriers which were excluding rightful participants in its goods and services; there was something wrong with the institution. In the perspective constructed by NIE the problem was shifted to the students. The institution was fine; what was wrong was the students who somehow fail to remain through to credentialization.

What is striking in retrospect is the way in which the 'retention' model has come to dominate thinking about the issue of the responsiveness of public institutions of higher education to the populations they are mandated to serve. In an address to the university community at that time the Chancellor of the University of Alaska, Fairbanks, Howard A. Cutler, said, 'We, at UAF have reason to be proud of what we have accomplished over the last five years in increasing the retention of our students' (Cutler 1981: 1). In continuing his address he emphasized the factors that have led to higher retentions as well as the factors which characterize drop-outs. It is of interest that this issue of retention was seen fit to be the central topic of his convocation address.

If we trace the trajectory of this discourse backward in time, during the preceding two decades (the 1960s and 1970s) retention had been seen as an issue of major national importance. The concern reflected in the titling of this study by the National Institute of Education, the concern of the Chancellor of the University, and the large number of studies both local and national of the 'problem of retention' reflect a consistent commitment to understanding why students drop out of school. In virtually all of these expressions of concern the wording of the problem appears to reflect the underlying model of the total institution. A widely quoted study had as its title 'Preventing students from dropping out' (Astin 1975).

The guard-like nature of the gatekeeper's role is clearly displayed in the notion of prevention. What is not often mentioned, however, in this discourse of retention is its interaction with another economic discourse. Schreiber more than a decade before had called our attention to the economic base for the concern about school drop-outs (Schreiber 1967). He pointed out that for the preceding two or three decades there had been an improvement in school retention and yet John F. Kennedy made 'retention' a national economic problem when in his 1963 State of the Union message he said, 'The loss of only one year's income due to unemployment is more than the total cost of twelve years of education through high school. Failure to improve educational performance is thus not only poor social policy, it is poor economics' (quoted in Schreiber 1967: 3). In other words, the problem of retention we were facing in the 1980s may have had at its base an economic motive which began with a presidential urge to cut drop-outs from public schools and which had then been extended to institutions of higher education because of recent trends of lowered college-age populations, higher costs of education and of institutional maintenance, and different perceptions among the population at large about the functions of the public university. It was and remains of concern to universities to retain students for purely business reasons.

Given this economic motive, the total institution model provides a convenient model for maintaining institutional security. It is perhaps overly attractive to those entrusted with the care of the institution because of the control over the comings and goings of its clientele it encourages. Without a sophisticated knowledge of the economics of institutions of higher education, we felt students were reacting to this model as they encountered it from day to day in their movement through the university.

Put in terms of a discourse analysis of this nexus of practice, the research problem itself was embedded in these broader discourses of the worlds we were in. We, the researchers, were appropriating from a discourse of discrimination against ethnic minorities in public institutions which was one of the dominant discourses of the 1980s. From the point of view of that discourse, the problem to be addressed was one of rightful and unfettered access to the goods, services, and credentialization of institutions of higher education for Alaska Natives. At the same time faculty members and administration were appropriating from a discourse concerning the economic viability of tertiary educational institutions and of the national economy which had been initiated as early as the 1960s by President John F. Kennedy.

Both of these discourses were constructing their arguments out of very similar materials – the entrance and continued presence of students in the university. From our point of view as researchers, we saw this entrance and successful exit as benefits which were potentially being denied. From the faculty and administrative point of view, they saw this matriculation of Alaska Native students as economic necessities for the university and nation which were potentially being undermined by the non-continuation of students. The students themselves were feeling caught in these competing and incommensurate grinding wheels of different discourses.

Multiple metaphors

There is some reason to believe that the metaphor of the total institution sits in the discursive background of much of our thinking about the nature of the modern university. This metaphor is certainly not the only model in operation, however, and it may be important to consider the outcome of having multiple metaphors informing our activities in the university.

One outcome of the two metaphors we have considered is a differential treatment of those who leave the institution. The total institution model approves of only one kind of exit, institutionally credentialed exit. All other cases are regarded as having failed in some way. Looking through studies of drop-outs one finds a preponderance of negative values attributed to drop-outs. To use an example from our study, Chancellor Cutler, in the address to the university cited above, indicated such factors in the make-up of a drop-out as:

- more lacking in flexibility to deal with changing circumstances
- less emotional commitment to education

- more impulsive
- have unreal expectations
- academically rootless.

In many of our observations we saw that these categories were reiterated in the moment-by-moment discourse of university classes. Teachers also held the same view of students. For example, in one class we observed, as the teacher mentions an article, the title and author of which *he* has forgotten, he says, 'it was rather difficult to understand and so I couldn't assign it to you'. This self-fulfilling prophesy of the poor student was repeated throughout. Students were told that they were not expected to understand. The teacher a bit later asks a strong, direct display question (that is, a question for which there is a painfully obvious answer); there is no response from the students; he says, 'It was in your book'; again, there is no response; the teacher gives a clue; no response; he gives the answer he was seeking. At the end of the class the teacher passes out a test. As he passes it out he says, 'Some of these questions are kind of hard.' There is no response. He resumes the floor rapidly with a steady stream of statements about how difficult the test might be, how much time they may be supposed to have over the weekend to work on it and so forth. Still there is no response. There is really none possible which would not be interactionally insulting to the teacher. Earlier in the class this teacher has shown a short video 'for discussion' and talked without hesitation right over the voice-over narration throughout the video. Finally, as if conceding to considerable pressure from the students, the teacher says, 'Well, maybe we can eliminate one of these questions.' He again tries to get a statement about which question to drop, but allows no time for a response and there is none. He concludes by saying that they can eliminate any one of the questions. After all he knew the test was too hard for them.

On another occasion this same teacher who told us that he feels a strong concern for helping these mostly Alaska Native students which he said he feels are not academically prepared for university life, was trying to teach basic English grammar. We quote the sequence in its entirety. The sentence being discussed was 'Another of his [Gandhi's] symbols was his loin cloth'.

Teacher:	What is the subject of the sentence?
Student:	(whispering) 'Loin cloth'?
Teacher:	Hah? What's the subject?
Student:	(no response)
Teacher:	Is 'loin cloth' the subject?
Student:	(no response)
Teacher:	Can 'loin cloth' be the subject?
Student:	(whispered) no.

> *Teacher*:   (sing-song, great-victory-over-ignorance intonation) No! That can't be the subject, it's not in the subject case. It's in the object case. We have the subject case, the object case and the possessive case. What is in the subject case? What is the subject?
>
> *Student*:   (reading the sentence from the beginning, slowly, diminishing his volume as he goes)
>
> *Teacher*:   (again with cry-of-victory intonation) Right! 'Another'!

In this situation the student's implicit (though incorrect) analysis is ignored. The student has taken the noun phrase with some content ('loin cloth') as the subject. The loin cloth is, in fact, the topic of the rest of the paragraph and in this sentence is being elevated through position as the 'new' element in the sentence as the focused participant in the paragraph. This understanding of the grammatical process of topicalization is destroyed by a teacher who forces guessing as the only possible self-defense. The teacher's explanations explain nothing. Labeling 'loin cloth' as 'object case' is worse than nonsense as linguistic analysis. As labeling it does nothing to help guide the student's understanding of grammatical or sentential relations. Nevertheless, it gives the whole process an aura of knowledge, as if the student only had to be able to label in order to begin to succeed. Thus it directs the cognitive effort in a futile pursuit of the knowledge needed to do the exercise. Simultaneously the only pragmatic means of survival in the face of the embarrassing pressure to perform is to lapse into a fixed attention on the teacher's prosodic cues for guessing.

This fixation on the teacher's prosodic cues rather than sentential analysis is further enhanced by the teacher's own comments. He says, 'This is like music.' First he asks if anyone is interested in music. No one responds, but he continues with his example anyway. He says you only need to practice listening to him in order to be able to punctuate it and to tell what the subject is. It sounds funny when you are wrong, he says. He then goes on to a 'sentence' from the example which makes reference to Gandhi's loin cloth.

> *Teacher*:   'A symbol of poverty'; is that a complete sentence?
>
> *Student*:   (no response)
>
> *Teacher*:   Doesn't sound complete.
>
> *Student*:   (no response)
>
> *Teacher*:   Can't leave it sticking out there by itself.
>
> *Student*:   (no response)

Again, he uses prosodic and intonational cues to 'help' the students guess. When they get it right they get baby talk, when they get it wrong they get 'silly, isn't it?' Here the teacher gives incomplete sentences as instructions and clues about how to not punctuate sentence fragments as complete sentences.

The first message is: Pay close attention to my prosody and my grammar for the only cues that will count. The second message is: Do not do as I do, since I use incomplete sentences, do as you should do on the written exam. Because the teacher assumes that standard written English conventions are internalized by the students, he assumes that student 'failure' is a failure to access knowledge they already have. Their silence confirms his belief in their recalcitrance or lack of emotional commitment to education. To the extent students learn to succeed in this teacher's class and perhaps in the university, they will have made it impossible to pass written tests in standard written English because success in the class is entirely dependent on reading teacher prosody and guessing. There is no other source of knowledge about correct written form than this class, and so there is little hope for students on the coming test. Failure on that test will, of course, further confirm the teacher's assumptions about unreadiness for university academic work.

Transformation or client metaphors

The negative quality of the descriptions of drop-outs may seem a quite natural response, but it is natural only if one works within the discourse of a total institutional metaphor. As a rough analogy we could take the supermarket as the metaphor for the 'access' view of the university as a contrast. In such a model the role of 'gatekeepers' is to provide a service. We would regard it as inappropriate for some supermarket to base its response to customers on a negative evaluation of those who do not shop there. The approach is to entice customers in and to provide services. Where one sees a drop in the number of customers one looks to one's own services and marketing, not to the weaknesses of the population of customers. It is apparently a characteristic of the total institution that, where there is a mismatch between the expectations of the institution and those of its client population, the fault is seen to lie in the client population, not in the institution (Taylor and Bogdan 1980).

As a specific instance we may look at a particular case of a student we interviewed which is typical of the experience of many students at the University of Alaska. This student entered the University of Alaska, Fairbanks, with the intention of deciding whether or not she wanted to pursue a college education. Her plan which she had worked out before coming to the university was to take one year of courses, sampling a few fields in which she had a tentative interest. On the basis of that sampling she planned to apply to another university outside of the state where she intended to pursue a Bachelor's degree. At the end of the first and successful year this student had applied to and been accepted by a university outside of the state. In another view, she had 'dropped out' of college and moved outside the state.

The question we need to ask about such a student is whether or not it is appropriate to say that she is 'lacking in flexibility', has 'less emotional commitment to education', is 'more implusive', has 'unreal expectations', or is 'academically rootless'. Such a student has a clear plan, a definite idea of her educational goals and how to achieve them. In this case one would want to ask if perhaps it wasn't the institution that was lacking in flexibility.

Ambiguity

The possibility of multiple models or metaphors for the nature of the institution and of the multiple discourses circulating through an institution is the source of much ambiguity in interpersonal contacts within the institution. If we think of the 'gate' having two radically different functions depending on whether it is thought of as being guarded against escape or as being held open to allow entrance, we then realize that a gatekeeper is in an ambiguous position because that position sits in the intersection of multiple discourses. Within the economic discourse of full enrollments (and tuitions) or the access-driven discourse of a concern about discrimination, the appropriate response is to block non-credentialed exit. In the client or service model of the institution, the appropriate response is to help qualified individuals to achieve their goals within the institution. Depending on the model, a particular behavior may be viewed as one kind of response or the other.

For a gatekeeper who wants to facilitate the values of the student there is a dilemma. If the student perceives the institution as a total institution and yet wishes to retain a sense of autonomy from the institution, the role of the gatekeeper is one of limiting the control of the institution and ultimately even of providing a convenient exit. The gatekeeper's advocacy of the student's values may well be contra-institutional. Such a student might be encouraged to withdraw and seek another activity in life. On the other hand, if the student perceives the institution as open, then the role of the gatekeeper is one of providing access, of advocating the entrance into and movement through the institution toward credentialization.

The gatekeeping encounter, then, becomes contingent on these perceptions. It is not definable within any simple objective observation of the actions of the participants. It can be interpreted and defined only within the broader discourses which it instantiates for the participants, and these may be very different. If X, then Y; but if P, then Q. In order to work on behalf of the student, the gatekeeper must know whether X or P, that is, he or she must know whether the student perceives the institution as a total institution or as an open institution. But the student may not know this consciously and so the gatekeeper has a work of elicitation to discover for himself or herself and for the student which is the case. The institutional gatekeeper as well as the analyst have a major work of discourse analysis both for the situation itself and for the separate participants in order to see how to interpret the gatekeeping situation within those broader discourses. If the gatekeeper misjudges, actions intended to increase access may be perceived as more closely guarding the gate, or conversely, actions intended to provide convenient exit may be perceived as blocking access to the institution.

In any more complex situation such as a class where there are several participants, the conditions may be mixed. Some participants may be seeking access while others are seeking to avoid the totalizing aspects of the institution. If the gatekeeper responds to one group, he or she behaves inappropriately in regard to the other group. If the gatekeeper tries to remain neutral, this amounts to avoiding the responsibilities of the gatekeeper.

These possibilities may have the effect of immobilizing the gatekeeper. This is at least one account of the way in which institutional considerations impinge on the conduct as well as the construction of the gatekeeping encounter. While the goals of the institution are what determine the gatekeeping encounter, these goals may not be clear, unanimously given or understood. They must be understood in order to carry out the gatekeeping and it must be determined to what extent the other participants share these goals or perceptions of the nature of the institution. In other words, we argue that for any gatekeeping encounter to be effective it must include an understanding of the discursive construction of that encounter that extends considerably beyond the boundaries of that class, interview, or counseling session.

One of the most frequent complaints voiced by students is about the paternalism of faculty members, especially those who are most concerned to provide assistance to Alaska Native students. While this is not likely to be amenable to a simple solution, we believe that one central factor is this difference in perceptions of the nature of the institution and how that affects the conduct of the gatekeeping encounter. In many cases students feel a strong pressure from the totalizing aspects of the university. This pressure is sensed as increasing just at the points where decisions are being made. Here where gatekeepers extend their efforts to 'help' students, students may be perceiving this 'help' as further extension of the totalizing process and resist. In at least a few cases we have known, students have cited this paternalizing pressure from well-meaning teachers and counselors as a reason for 'going home.'

Mapping the institution

In our original conception of the gatekeeping study we planned to prepare 'maps' of the gatekeeping situations of significance to students. As it became clearer that there were different models of the nature of the university being held by different participants it also became clear that there was a different use being made of the more literal 'maps' of the institution which already exist, such as the university catalog. Perhaps the principal difference is that, for the faculty, the 'map' of the institution contained in the catalog is used to determine departmental and jurisdictional boundaries. For students, on the other hand, what is sought is a route through the university. For that purpose the catalog is of relatively little use to a student.

A comparison of faculty and student mappings of the university shows a very different perception of a typical experience. The most common student perception of the university, at least the Fairbanks campus, is that it consists of two quite separate functions. The first function is that of an introduction to college education. For many students the first two years are thought of as for learning about college. Many students, particularly students from rural Alaska, assume that once they learn about how to 'do' college they will go elsewhere to pursue their college educations. It is, in fact, difficult to find students who will express the assumption that they will start a program and four years later graduate from an Alaskan college with a degree. At the same time, we see many students transferring into Alaskan universities from elsewhere. In the talk we cited above, Chancellor Cutler pointed out that at that time the University of Alaska, Fairbanks, regularly enrolled more juniors than previous year sophomores; in 1980 the campus enrolled 16 percent more seniors than there had been juniors the year before.

While the statistics were not as clear as we would have liked them to be, it was clear that there was a very small percentage of students who began their university educations on the Fairbanks campus and graduated on that campus four years later. The most typical use of the Fairbanks campus was either as a two-year preparation for college elsewhere or as a two-year termination of programs begun elsewhere. This perception was shared on the whole among students on the Fairbanks campus.

In a 'State of the University' address in October of 1980, the President of the University was asked if this student perception of the university was supported by any statistics. His answer was that he had no statistics which would tell him whether or not such was the case and further that he had never heard of this. What is significant is that the four-year-program view was the one supported by the university catalog and by the general structure of four-year university programs. These larger discourses sketch out typical pathways to success that require a four-year cycle to complete. While our research showed that it was clear enough that students had little or no expectation of spending any consecutive four years pursuing a degree on the Fairbanks campus, the faculty perception of the typical career was that of the standard, four-year degree program.

What we would emphasize is not the correctness of either view of the typical use of the university, but that there was a strong difference in perceptions and these led to very different discourses about university life and a person's participation in it. As we pointed out earlier, where student and faculty views differed it was not uncommon for negative evaluations to be made of each by the other. Students who were planning to transfer to another college and so were taking a variety of courses to see what their interests and talents might be were labeled 'academically rootless'. Those who intended to go elsewhere, almost certainly to a better school, were labeled 'emotionally uncommitted to education'. On the other hand, faculty members who expressed a concern for developing consistent, coherent, and sustained academic work were sometimes viewed as insensitive to students' needs or as unconcerned about the plans of their students. Or faculty members who expressed a concern for their students were sometimes viewed as paternalistic.

Locating gates

There is a conceptual trap in the idea of gatekeeping. Because it is a metaphor we might attribute to the gate a concreteness that is not appropriate. Our interest in mapping the gates may be a case of overly concretizing the phenomenon. A specific case might help to clarify this point. Some students, like Jennifer in our opening vignette, left the Fairbanks campus to go elsewhere or to return home, citing as a reason for leaving that they felt life in the dorm was unbearable. Among the factors mentioned was the lack of choice and personal control over their living circumstances in the dorm.

This 'problem' may be a very complex issue and not resolve itself into any single 'gate'. Some students expected the university to be an open institution in which they could pursue their own course of study, relatively free from control in their private lives and with a range of options in their educational careers. While in the extreme this expectation might have been unrealistic, for these students the totalizing nature of the university came as a surprise.

For many students the first surprise was that while they had indicated a choice of dormitory accommodations on their applications, they had been arbitrarily assigned to one large dormitory in which every room was like every other one, the furniture was relatively immobile, and they had to live with a roomate who was a complete stranger. While for any student this may be a difficult adjustment, for a student from a rural village with, perhaps, fifty to a hundred people this was often extremely uncomfortable. One student mentioned the enormity of not even being able to go to the bathroom without running into strangers.

This high level of exposure to a public of strangers was most difficult for students from remote rural areas of the state. These were certainly the students who commented most frequently on this experience. It is interesting, then, that quite frequently it was just those students who were arbitrarily assigned to dormitory space without receiving their preferred options. Why?

We found that there was no malicious intent on the part of anyone in this problem. The Housing Office quite reasonably could not assign rooms until after the student had been accepted by the university. University Admissions equally reasonably could not accept students until they had received transcripts from the student's high school. For students whose high schools are in rural areas there was a problem because those schools are often closed during the summer and so they frequently did not get transcripts sent out until late in the summer when they opened up again for the new school year. In rural Alaska, the cost of remaining open even for a few more days to handle these transcripts can be very high. As a result rural students were accepted to the university late in the summer and were too late to receive their preferred dormitory assignments.

The result of this nexus of conditions was that just those students who might most have needed some range of options in their university housing assignments were unable to exercise those options. There was no single point at which we could say a gate was being closed; there was no individual gatekeeper who was either intentionally or unintentionally barring access to the university's resources. The 'gate' consisted of a variety of factors: the student's perception of the university, the need of University Housing to control the distribution of space to accepted students, the need of the university to have transcripts from high schools for admission, and the need of rural schools to release their staff during the summer. The 'gate' was constituted by a set of institutional practices which were distributed in time from the student's first application to the student's withdrawal and were distributed in both physical and institutional space among the University Housing Office, the rural school district, the University Office of Admissions, and the actual dormitory space assigned to the student.

To put this in terms of a semiotic ecosystem, this 'gate' of the dorm room assignment is a distributed gate constituted with four cycles as shown in Figure 6.1:

- university admissions practices and policies
- university housing practices and policies
- rural school district annual cycles of employment and vacation
- the academic life history or career (historical body) of the student.

A university is a complex social institution. Members of the institution do not all share the same view of the nature of that institution. In some cases these differences of view may lead to ambiguity of response and interpretation. Perhaps the most critical conflict is in the degree to which the University of Alaska was perceived as a total institution. There appeared to be a fairly high level of discrepancy between embedded institutional structures and student perceptions of the functions and structure of the university. These differences made it difficult to unambiguously point to a particular situation and argue that that situation was

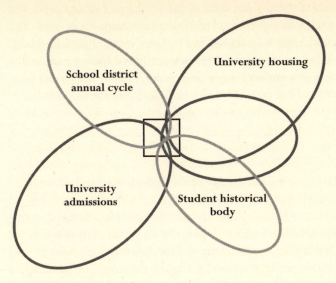

6.1 Dorm selection.

the root of the gatekeeping problem. 'Retention' itself implies a particular view of the university which may be inappropriate if viewed from the vantage point of the client population, the students.

It is clear that our original conception of the problem as one of gaining access to the resources of the university was too simple to be productive. By the same token the notion of retention implies another, contrasting discourse which is also too simple a model of the relationship between a university and its client population to be productive. The idea of gatekeeping, while useful, embodies the trap of undue concreteness. The 'gates' of the institution must be understood as constituted in nexus of institutional practices and values.

A grammar of motives

Kenneth Burke developed a framework for studying the discursive positioning of an argument within a *grammar of motives* in his book of that title (1969 [1945]). Accounts of the reasons people do things can be organized around five distinct lines of argument based on the agent of the action (the social actor), the scene within which the action occurs, the purpose for the action, the means by which the action is accomplished (Burke used 'agency'), or even the action itself (Burke used 'act'). Burke's interest was to provide a discourse analysis (though he himself did not use that term) which could highlight differences among lines of argument or in philosophical positions which could provide a basis for better understanding the points of conflict between different views of human action.

In Burke's *grammar of motives* none of these five positions is given a privileged position, none of them is thought to be a better explanation than any other. The point is that any action might be explained from any one or all of these positions, but *which* position is taken will make a difference in taking subsequent actions.

If we look at a case of a student leaving the university during her second year, we could use any of these five points of view to account for that action as follows.

Scene

The action derives from sources outside of the student. She acts because of the scene she is in whether that is taken as a physical scene or a psychological, cultural, social, or historical one. To take this position one might say she has left the university because the conditions in the dormitory are uncomfortable and not conducive to study. There are too many strangers, too many students are taking drugs or drinking, or the room is a stagnating and stultifying structure of plastic and formica.

Social actor

The action derives from the person's internal will and motivation. She acts because of internal physical or psychological (or even cultural) characteristics. From this position one might say that she has left the university because she feels sick there, because she's not ready for academic work, or she's a rural girl who cannot accommodate to university life. Alternatively, we might also say she left because she has a strong sense of her own worth and feels she is not able to develop herself there.

Mediational means

The action derives from the mediational means (material and psychological) she has for taking action. In this view we might say she had left the university because she didn't have enough money to buy the clothing or books or other material props it takes to present herself as a normal university student. Or we might say that she lacks the academic skills in writing or speaking to perform successfully.

Purpose

The action derives from the expected goals or outcomes of the action. If we took this view we might say that she left the university because she thought going home would make her feel better or, alternatively, that enrolling in a better university in one of the 'Lower 48 States' would be a better option to develop her future.

Mediated action

The action derives from itself in the sense that there is no real external motive or because it is one in a fixed sequence of actions. From this point of view we might say that she has left the university as a straightforward consequence of having had one bad experience after another.

Figure 6.2 shows these five explanatory positions.

If we return, then, to the question of gatekeeping in the university, students placed it as a question of social actors but faculty placed it as a question of the social scene, that is, they discursively constructed it as one of historical and social structures.

And so, in a meeting of students and faculty we found the students on the one hand expressing a sense of the human need for the institution to recognize their interests, feelings, and goals. On the other hand faculty members were asking as one did, 'How does the concept of a total institution apply to small-scale societies?' That is, he was placing that particular problem within a broad, 'scenic' analysis of societal structure. Or another faculty member questioned the usefulness of the gatekeeping concept because in his academic discipline that concept was used in reference to the institutional concern for self-preservation. For him the problem of gatekeeping was placed within the scene of his own

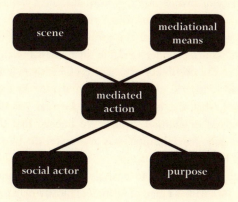

6.2   Burke's pentad of motives.

disciplinary horizon while being wrested out of the human level of the lives of the social actors, the students, there in the same meeting.

In short, faculty response to the preliminary report was to express an academic interest in a problem of the description of structures. Student response was concentrated on human interest in the possibility that there might develop a means of their being able to voice their individual concerns. To the issue of whether or not the university represented a total institution in students' minds, faculty responded by asking if the concept was heuristically fruitful; students responded by asking what could be done about it. Strikingly, both of these views were expressed in the same public, face-to-face meeting.

What constitutes an explanation?

As a further way of highlighting the different discourses of university life used by students and by faculty we can look at what students and faculty tended to offer as explanations of behavior, even such behavior as leaving the university without terminal credentials. Students in such discussions offered highly personal agentive motives, motives which were based on the values and intentions of the social actor. These relied heavily on consciously available rationalizations of their own and of other students' behavior. Alaska Native students were quite skeptical of any generalizations about student withdrawal. In long discussions with Alaska Native students about principles of observation and generalization in courses designed to teach these concepts we found a strong resistance to scenic motivations or generalizations about behavior which will attribute to unknown persons the characteristics of motives of known cases. Students in accounting for behavior relied heavily on personal, human knowledge of circumstances which they take prima facie as sufficient explanation for behavior.

In many cases Alaska Native students go beyond their own reliance on such explanation to question the sincerity of anyone offering more analytical generalized, scenic accounts of behavior. These were most often regarded as attempts to stereotype or generate negative impressions of the group about which the generalization is made. It is, of course, understandable that Alaska Native students would be very sensitive to the possibility of negative ethnic or cultural stereotyping given the widespread existence of just such stereotyping in their experience. We believe, however, that the issue here goes beyond just the hypersensitivity of a particular ethnic or cultural group. We believe that this skepticism in regard to analysis and generalization was characteristic of the worldview held in historical body by these students.

This characterization of skepticism in regard to analysis and generalization was looked upon by faculty members with a range of attitudes, mostly negative. Some treated it as simple naiveté or ingenuousness; some treated it as evidence of stupidity or even ineducability. This unfortunately comes as no surprise since it is very much taken to be a part of the mission of higher education to train students in skills of analysis and generalization, that is, to train students in scenic explanations of human actions. To faculty members on the whole this skepticism was not treated as another and viable perspective on human behavior, but as the problem to be treated by pedagogical means. It is no wonder, then, that students so strongly felt that the university was taking on the restructuring of their worldview. It was.

Another view

If that was all there was to it we could have just got on with the education of students and not been overly concerned with those on whom the education does not 'take'. If the problem, however, is understanding the behavior of individuals, neither perspective is wholly sufficient. Since the early days of experimental psychology it has been clear that the introspective evidence offered by a subject is highly suspect if taken at face value. In virtually every field of the behavioral and social sciences, careful steps are taken to avoid accepting statements of respondents at face value on the evidence that these statements are strongly under the influence of the subject's assumptions about the nature of the situation he or she is in. In this view, faculty members' skepticism about Alaska Native students' reliance on introspective accounts is vindicated.

On the other hand, students' skepticism regarding the use of analytical categories as explanation of behavior shows a sophistication rarely evidenced in the writing of social scientists. It is clear, of course, that the behavior of a category is not the behavior of the individual member of that category. These are behaviors of two different logical types (Bateson 1979). The behavior of a category will allow the statistical prediction of the behavior of a percentage of individual members of that category. It will never allow the prediction of the behavior of any single individual. To borrow Bateson's example, we can predict that a chain will break at its weakest link but we cannot tell which link that will be until a specific link has broken.

What is critical here is that categorical statements about a class can be said to be true of an individual member of the class only *after the fact*. Any statement, however reliably tested, may be proved wrong by the next instance that comes along. The key here is the temporal status of the behavior one is seeking to explain. If one is seeking to explain how we at this moment decide to undertake the next action, categorical statements are of little value. We have no cognitive access to the behavioral categories of the group other than through the roughest of guesses based on our own personal histories and experiences and thus must use other means to move from moment to moment through the sequence of decisions and actions that we call living.

We believed that it was this awareness of the constraints of real-time processing that Alaska Native students were using as the basis of their skepticism of categorical statements. We also felt that it is not naive at all but actually an awareness of a dimension of human behavior that has all but escaped notice in the practical logic of Western behavioral and social sciences. It is also important to note that we ourselves have brought this need for concreteness in real-time into our own work in nexus analysis.

Inference in real time

The process of interpretation in conversation which John Gumperz called 'conversational inference' provides a useful example of this mode of analysis. Conversational inference studies the processes by which people in contact with each other move inferentially from step to step through an interaction. Linguists have been relatively successful in describing the formal structures of a behavioral phenomenon and yet have continued to be relatively cautious about saying anything meaningful about how the structures of a grammar are actually realized in the moment-by-moment production of utterances.

The insight provided by students of conversational inference is that at any point in the stream of interaction speakers and listeners are under the obligation to draw inferences about the meanings being projected by the other and signal both their own projected meanings and their interpretation of the other's meanings. What forces the highly tentative nature of these inferences is the fact that this is carried out under the pressure of real time. People speaking to each other do not have the luxury of the analyst to sit back and carefully study the structure of the utterances heard and spoken but can only draw rather 'quick and dirty' inferences and use these as the basis for the next action they must undertake. It is this 'quick and dirty' aspect of real-time conversational inference that separates it so clearly from the researcher's analytical categories as well as from the communicator's introspection.

As has been frequently demonstrated by linguists, people have virtually no conscious control over their grammar. By years of instruction which many people find tedious people can come to articulate varieties of word classes and even syntactic structures. It is only the specialist in linguistics who can articulate the highly formal nature of these structures. And yet everyone in moving in real time through a conversation relies rapidly and accurately on these structural categories as a basis on which to draw the necessarily 'quick and dirty' conversational inferences.

In this view, such a structural category as grammar can be said neither to cause nor to explain the behavior of speakers in a conversation. At most it is a resource that conversationalists use in drawing rapid inferences. Needless to say, conversationalists move smoothly through an interaction partly on the basis that they share the same, unconsciously held, reservoir of inferences. In this sense then, analytical categories, like grammatical structures, are of only two classes of use: as after-the-fact descriptions of what happened in particular instances or as real-time but unconsciously used bases for inferences about the behavior of other individuals. In the first use they are of a reality that is distinctly removed from the moment-to-moment reality of individuals. They are of a different logical type. In the second use, these structures are at the very best an approximation of behavior that holds good only during the current instance, 'until further notice'.

We would argue then that 'the institutions's knowledge' of such things as gatekeeping is of a logical type that is inherently out of 'real' time. 'Human knowledge', on the other hand, attends to a reality that is based in 'real'-time cognitive processing. They are realities of a different logical type. The conflict between these two realities is not in any sense a competition. It is not a conflict, but a confusion of levels of logical typing that we are considering.

Students may be assumed in most cases not to know a large body of institutional knowledge. That is, students need to learn how to sign up for classes or how to declare and change majors as well as the works of Aristotle or the Alaska Native Claims Settlement Act. The first 'hidden curriculum' is usually picked up from other students rather informally; the second is relatively straightforward and is usually dealt with in ordinary course work. There may be a tendency among faculty, however, to assume knowledge of both classes of knowledge, that is, to assume that students know what a lecture is, what a philosophical treatise is, what a legal act is, or what a written essay exam is. At this level it is clear that this sort of knowledge is not nearly so widely shared in the historical bodies of students. The didactic lecture of the panopticon class on which so much of university instruction relies may be a new interaction order for all entering students except those from a religious background in which the didactic sermon figures prominently. There is at least the possibility that Astin's (1975) finding that Protestant religious affiliation was a good predictor of academic success is based in part on the role the sermon plays in that religious group. It is relatively unusual for students from rural Alaska to have had extended experience with the panopticon class before encountering one in the university.

At an even more subtle level, conventions of expression and interpretation of the spoken and written word may vary considerably in students' experience. In these interpretive conventions may lie considerable cultural differences, as Heath (1983) described in her work. In one of the communities she studied she found that the written word as in a letter or set of instructions for enrolling a child in school was used as the basis for a communal and oral discussion of the 'problem', not as the basis for a formal and literate set of direct responses. And so, students given just the same lectures, videotapes, and exams may be integrating them into very different cycles of discourse.

Tuning in in performance

While these problems of knowledge were found in our work, they did not form the most difficult problem. There were quite successful programs operating which directly addressed the problem of institutional knowledge through special student orientations and the like. A more difficult problem was in the area of performance.

In any performance, the performers must make a mutual adjustment to the performance of the others with whom they are 'en ensemble'. Chapple (1939, 1970, 1980) in a series of studies beginning in the pre-World-War-II period and continuing into the 1980s argued cogently that hierarchies in institutional structure may be viewed as the outcome of relatively minor asymmetries beginning with the two-party face-to-face interaction. In each pair, he argued, there is a 'pacemaker' who sets the rhythm of the encounter. In this pair the 'pacemaker' is the leader. That leader in turn relates in other dyads in which he or she is either the pacemaker or not. Chapple described a kind of pacemaking pecking order in which the leader at the top of the hierarchy sets the pace rhythmically for all who are under him or her.

This work of Chapple provides us with a way of addressing the human/ institutional interface. As the pacemaker represents the institution, the non-pacemaker(s) adjust their interpersonal rhythms to the pacemaker and in doing so, through quite subtle and unconscious behavior, adapt to the institutional rhythm.

In our research we found that an important difference between Alaska Native groups and non-Native groups is in the meaning of leadership or, more specifically, pacemaking. There is no disagreement about who is the leader in the classroom or in fact in the institutional structure. Both groups assume that the teacher is the leader in the classroom as we have noted in Chapter 4. Our evidence suggested that Alaska Natives regard it as being the role of the leader to tune in to the pace set by the one being 'led'. The responsibility for achieving 'ensemble' lies with the leader, not the follower. It is a notion that more closely approaches the Western jazz tradition than the Western symphonic tradition.

One sort of evidence for this concept of leadership comes out of the micro-analysis of rhythmic behavior as recorded on videotape. When people communicate they subtly tune in to each other's rhythms. When speakers exchange turns they come in on the tempo established by the preceding speaker. If they then depart from the former speaker's tempo it is only after the initial confirmation of the preceding speaker's tempo. Thus speakers go through an interaction, speaking at their own tempi, but always initially confirming the tempi of others.

As in music, however, there are moments of ambiguity, moments at which it is possible to take the preceding speaker's tempo as being either two beats to the measure or three (exactly as in the difference between 3/4 time and 6/8 in musical notation, the hemiola). These moments of ambiguity, as in music, become resolved in the subsequent rhythm of the original speaker.

What we have found is a general tendency of Alaska Native teachers to resolve these points of ambiguity in favor of the students' rhythm while non-Native teachers resolve them in favor of the teacher's rhythm. In other words we see Alaska Native teachers tuning in rhythmically to the tempo or pace set by students, while non-Native teachers are 'conducting' their students to the teacher's tempo.

Another sort of evidence is from a very different domain of analysis. Direct questions figure very prominently in many teachers' didactic style as they did in the presentencing reports we discussed in Chapter 5. Alaska Native students very frequently comment on their discomfort with direct questions. When they were asked how one would more appropriately elicit information, the answer given was that in order to elicit more information one needs to provide information. In the reciprocal case students said that if they do not ask questions in class it is because they have not been provided with enough information to form a base for questioning. We interpret these comments in light of Martz's (1981) findings to mean that Alaska Native students expect faculty members to first provide a base of personal or human knowledge about themselves, then to allow students to inform the professor about themselves as a basis for continuing information exchange. As one Alaska Native tradition bearer said, 'I can only speak to you to the extent I know you.'

A test case

Our National Institute of Education study was designed so that it would overlap into the beginning of a second academic year. This was so that hypotheses developed in the first year could be tested during the second year. Thus we had the opportunity to develop in one case a test of some of the principles suggested above. Ron taught the course Alaska Native Studies 120, 'Cultural Differences in Institutional Settings', in the Fall of 1980 and then again in the Fall of 1981. Because it was a course in which students are primarily Alaska Natives it was a strategic site for developing notions relating to the institutional/personal interface. For our purpose here only two ways in which findings of the study were incorporated into instruction will be discussed.

It was our goal to significantly increase the amount of human knowledge given to students about the teacher by himself and to specifically increase one-on-one access of students to the teacher. In the earlier course, in the Fall 1980 course, Ron asked students to fill out a sheet with their names, year in school, major, and home village or city. Students filled out the sheets with just this information and turned them in.

In the later Fall 1981 version, Ron first talked for about twenty or thirty minutes about himself. He told students where he was born, some of the characteristics of the house he grew up in, the surrounding land and how it had been a cranberry patch in his mother's time but he had only known it as a suburban plot with a lawn and squared off with fences. He then gave a personal history of his education giving actual names of important teachers and the places he had done research. He finally gave the quite personal history by which he had come to be teaching that course at that time.

After this personal history, he asked the students to take out a sheet of paper and write down whatever they felt he needed to know to be able to teach them. The response was in every case that students wrote a lengthy and personal view of their own past and how they came to be in that class. Students included not only highly personal information but information directly relevant to the content of the course.

It was not just the amount of information that was surprising. During the Fall of 1980 course Ron had discovered around mid-term that some students had a significant misperception of the content and intent of the course. Ron was able to rectify this during the second half of the semester, but some students had sat through one half of the course not knowing what was going on because of the misperception. In the Fall 1981 version the same misperception showed up in these notes written on the very first day of class. In other words, this format of highly personal knowledge elicited significant information about students' and teacher's perceptions of course content.

The second goal was to increase the one-on-one access of students to the teacher. Ron taught the first version of the course as a traditional panopticon-style class. In the Fall 1981 course, however, he asked all the students to get 'userids' for the University of Alaska Computing Network to get in touch with each other and with him. As an incentive to get students to actually use this system, the course syllabus and reading list were put in a course mailbox in the message system and this was the only access students had to this crucial information.

While we would not want to attribute too much directly to the use of the University of Alaska Computing Network message system, by comparison with the Fall of 1980 course in the first four weeks of class Ron had had more one-on-one communication with students in the class than during the entire Fall 1980 semester. Much but not all of this communication was through the electronic mail system. Even the level of face-to-face meetings in his office was greater than for the former whole semester. In most cases the office visits were preceded by (1) an initial contact during the class period asking if he would be reading the computer mail; (2) a message or two on that system of a highly 'chatty' nature; and (3) a phone call to see if he was in the office.

In summary, it was clear that the establishment of highly personal and human knowledge as well as providing a non-threatening, asynchronous form of access to the instructor that was neither in class nor in the instructor's office led to a much higher sense of involvement with the course for both the students and the instructor. We feel as well that this involvement paid off in an improved grasp of course contents over the course taught in the Fall of 1980.

Discourse in a nexus of practice

In Chapter 2 we outlined our concept of the semiotic ecosystem which consists of a set of cycles of discourse or semiotic cycles which circulate through some particular moment of social life. In Chapter 5 we then followed out just one of those cycles, the historical body of one of the participants in a presentencing interview within the Alaska judicial system. Now here in Chapter 6 we have opened up the circumference of our vision and mapped out a somewhat different, but not wholly different, semiotic ecosystem, the gatekeeping of an institution such as the University of Alaska. In this case we suggested that the crucial cycles are those of the university admissions cycle, the university housing cycle, the rural school district annual cycle and the historical body of a rural student as shown above in Figure 6.1. Of course in a concrete case it could well be the very same person for whom we might map the ecosystem by which he or she was assigned an unsuitable dormitory room at one point in his life cycle and whom we might see later on in the presentencing interview.

A discourse analysis which focuses on such semiotic cycles needs to take into consideration that discourse might be present in any one of six different forms. It might be the speech of the participants in a specific social situation as we saw in the case of the teacher who continually 'dumbs down' his view of his students. It might also occur as an enormous variety of texts from application forms students fill out to the lecture notes used by a teacher. Of course, in addition to texts in writing are the many images and other semiotic systems such as brand names on clothing or the clothing itself as styles of dressing which are a part of our daily expressions of ourselves and our identities. The built environment from the design of dormitories to classrooms as well as other images and semiotic systems materially embed cycles of discourses. Discourses, of course, are submerged in the historical body and practices of all the participants, not just in the buildings and material objects in their environments. Finally, and not insignificantly, there are the discourses of the analysts, both those in which the analyst interacts directly with the members of the nexus of practice and those in which the analyst characterizes the research in which he or she is engaged.

In doing the projects we have described in this book we would have referred to ourselves as anthropological linguists; the newer research frameworks of interactional sociolinguistics and critical discourse analysis had not yet arisen as identifiable theoretical or methodological positions. It should be clear to the reader that much of what we did then flows naturally as tributaries into these three current streams of research. Anthropological linguistics provides us with the comparative ethnographic perspective which we find essential to doing a nexus analysis. Interactional sociolinguistics is most useful in the study of ongoing, real-time, face-to-face social interaction which is at the center of any nexus analysis. The critical analysis of discourse provides a theoretical framework for the study of the circulation of power within the semiotic ecosystems with which we are concerned.

In sum, we have found it important to remember four things in conducting a discourse analysis and a motive analysis:

1   Anything which can be said one way can be said another and there are consequences of the choice of the way in which it was said. A student may be 'exploring educational opportunities' or a student may be a 'drop-out'.

2   In order to understand those consequences of an alternative discourse, it is best to try to rephrase or rethink how something might have been said differently. A student might be described as 'unmotivated' or the university might be described as 'unresponsive to the student's needs'.

3   Much discourse is 'silent' or 'submerged' through resemiotization into objects, forms, the historical bodies of participants in a nexus of practice, or the built environment in which actions take place. We have found it important to stay alert to the many ways in which discourse(s) are present at any particular moment that are outside of the clear courses of spoken language and written texts.

4   We ourselves as researchers are engaging in discourses about the nexus of practice we are engaged in and which we are studying. Our own 'special' privilege in this is that our training may allow us to conceive of alternative discourses or of discourses that are submerged or hidden to participants. Even in this we need to remember that we are also operating from the position of having discourses submerged in our own historical bodies of which we may not be aware but which are active in the actions we are taking in our research project.

It is this latter concern with the ways in which our own discourses, historical bodies, and actions as researchers are producing social change to which we turn in Chapter 7.

7 Changing the nexus of practice: Technology, social change, and activist discourse analysis

The university president's Computer Advisory Committee begins its meeting with the charge to resolve the bottleneck which is being produced by the rapidly increasing numbers of users of the university's central computers and the very limited number of ports allowing access to the computers. This is drastically increasing computer response times for all users. A fixed amount of money is allocated and the committee is encouraged to think of any workable solution. Within fifty or sixty minutes the discussion arrives at the obvious solution of setting up two large microcomputer laboratories on the two main campuses, one in Fairbanks and one in Anchorage, to take the immediate pressure off the central mainframe. The committee chair calls a coffee break.

When the committee reconvenes some twenty minutes later, the committee is joined by the vice-president for finance who suggests that the committee find some other solution that doesn't involve microcomputers. During the break, word that the committee was considering such a recommendation had gotten out of the meeting, back to the company on the East Coast that leases and manages the university's computing services, back to one of the Regents of the university, then to at least one university office and back to the meeting. When microcomputers nevertheless were proposed by the committee as its strong and clear recommendation, the president disbanded his advisory committee and went about solving the problem on his own with the help of consultants from the leasing company in Pennsylvania.

Ray is a teacher inTununak, 630 miles from Fairbanks on Nelson Island on the Bering Sea. He is taking a course called 'Microcomputers for Teachers', via audio conference and email from the Graduate School of Education out of the university in Fairbanks. Sally is in her second year on campus taking an Alaska Native Studies course, 'Cultural Differences in Institutional Settings'. Their class is hooked up for discussions on the University of Alaska Computer Network. One day she discovers that Ray's on the system. He was her teacher two years ago in Tununak and so they start up a conversation and pretty soon her younger brother gets into it – he's a student of Ray's – and then most amazing, her mom and dad start to send her messages. It's the best Sally's felt about being away in Fairbanks in over a year and she's encouraging her brother to study hard and apply for university in another two years too.

Ron, who is teaching both classes, gets a message from Ray that says he not only has to drop out of the course but to break off the computer communications. The school district has refused to pay the telephone costs for him to take the class. They had approved it for him only for his own personal participation in the university class. They will not support the rest of this 'frivolous' messaging of school kids and parents with students in Fairbanks and are angry about his misappropriation of school district funds. The university will not budget any money for costs of students participating in its classes beyond the normal support of providing classrooms. Textbooks, lab fees, and all other costs are to be borne by the students. The Rural Education program which is designed to facilitate the entry of rural students into the university in Fairbanks will not pick up the costs; they have no jurisdiction to pay telephone charges for families and school children in rural Alaska.

Discourse, communication technologies, and power

In the month before we began our use of computer conferencing to conduct classes at the University of Alaska in 1980, there were fifty-seven messages sent on the UACN email system, as we noted in Chapter 3. By 1983 or so we had introduced several hundred university students and faculty to the use of email messaging as a medium of instruction. Beyond those users we had introduced the use of email messaging to the functioning of several administrative offices of the university such as the University of Alaska Instructional Telecommunications Consortium. Outside of the university we had begun regular email use among members of the Alaska Humanities Forum as well as within the National Endowment for the Humanities state-based programs division.

In this sense we were certainly active agents in the rapidly developing use of email communications in academic, administrative, and management functions. It would be a mistake, however, to imagine that we were alone in this burgeoning use of email during this period. It was happening everywhere, as a quick Internet search of the history of the Internet itself will tell you. The first commercial email systems were being implemented at this same time and we had very low numbered accounts in two of them. One day Ron was doing what has become a very common activity in our world today. He was sitting in his office scanning the three networks to which he had access to see who was currently available to chat. He started a conversation with a user he found and, though we have only memory to go by in this case, the conversation went something like this:

Ron:	I see you're online now.
Other:	Yep, what's the weather where you are?
Ron:	About 45 below with ice fog.
Other:	Jeez, WHERE are you?
Ron:	Fairbanks, where are you?
Other:	Denver; what kind of games do you play?
Ron:	The Prisoner, mostly, but you should ask my son about other games.
Other:	Oh, I see; I'm thirteen – using my dad's computer. Bye.

No single account of discourse in the development of the emerging Internet could grasp even the simple outlines of the complicated changes in social interactions that were beginning to develop in these new media. University professors were beginning to chat with teenagers, colleagues throughout a nationwide business were beginning to skirt around the formal structures of memos and meetings to talk to each other about things happening in their businesses. Business and play were becoming so fully integrated in these multi-threaded discourses that in many cases it became difficult to know what was play and what was business and what was the work of managing the conversation itself as we've noted in Chapter 3.

The focus in this final chapter is not on the question of how social change occurs in general, but more specifically about how discourse analysis in the form of nexus analysis is relevant in bringing about social change. In our work in Alaska during the years 1978 to 1983 or so, we tried to change things within the semiotic ecosystems of the university class, medical consultation, court deposition, probation presentencing interview, and other moments in which we believed discrimination was being constructed in the actions of members of bureaucratic public institutions. In many cases these changes worked very well, in some cases they went seriously awry, but in all cases, the changes that took place were largely not predictable.

When we worked with the State of Alaska Judicial Council we argued that the pressures on Alaska Native people both in courts and in such interviews as the presentencing reports were such that they almost inevitably led to negative attributions of Alaska Natives by the non-Native judges or probation officers. As we were not lawyers nor much informed about the actual moment-by-moment workings of either the courts or presentencing interviews, we could not make concrete, specific recommendations about how to alter these events to produce less discriminatory outcomes. What we could do, however, was to describe typical characteristics of face-to-face interactions, expectations on how one should present oneself, particularly in the presence of authorities, and how processes of attribution worked where differences in communicative style were coupled with differences in authority. That is, we could trace the lineages of the historical bodies present to these encounters as well as analyze the discourses in place and how these come together in the interaction order to enable certain kinds of actions and to inhibit other kinds of actions.

At the annual bilingual education conference in Anchorage one year as Ron was having breakfast a man came up to him and introduced himself as a judge who had been at the Judicial Conference the year before. The judge said that because of what he had heard in Ron's lecture at the Judicial Conference he had gone through his roster of activities and examined them. Only some of them required a formal hearing in court. Only some of the formal hearings in court required him to be dressed in formal robes. All he had done was to not wear his robes whenever it was allowed and to hold hearings in his chambers whenever it was allowed, and he felt his perception of the cases involving Alaska Natives had completely changed. He had begun to hear things he'd never heard before and to get a vastly richer view of cases from the Alaska Native point of view.

At a workshop with doctors in the Health Service hospital in Bethel we had the task of trying to assist the doctors in arriving at more sensitive understandings of their patients' needs while remaining within the very difficult time constraints imposed by chronic understaffing and the consequent excessive case loads. We presented the materials which we have discussed in Chapter 5 on the production of the Ahtna beadwork book. We asked the doctors if they might not be having a similar problem. That is, in the case of the beadwork book what was shown was everything but the beadwork – all of the contextual knowledge it takes to understand *why* beadwork is important. We learned later that these doctors began to see their patients from this point of view. They began to hear patients telling them the reasons they felt their illness or injury was of significance and leaving it to the doctors to use their professional expertise to analyze the injury itself. As their discourse in the medical consultation shifted away from direct

questioning about symptoms and medical history to listening to the contextualiza-
tions on the one hand and direct physical observation of the patient on the other,
they said that their problem was being solved. They felt they had much greater
confidence in their diagnoses and, in a complementary way, the problem of
patient non-compliance with their treatment was also evaporating as patients
began to feel that the medical staff were carefully listening to them.

We have already examined in some detail how our own use of computer-
mediated communication redistributed participation frameworks among students
and teachers in university classrooms in ways which were very comfortable for
students for whom the panopticon class felt like pressure to conform and to perform under pressure. These changes which we brought about through our work
were quite successful though they were changes that we could not have predicted
at the outset.

Nevertheless, we must be clear that the changes we were bringing about
were not always and universally welcomed within the institutions in which we
were working nor even by the individuals who were most affected by them. The
more we used the university computer network for teaching, the greater was
the pressure on us to stop using these resources for such 'frivolous' uses. As
the opening vignette suggests, computing resources had entered the university
not for educational or pedagogical purposes. Those resources were constructed
as administrative and management resources and their owners resented the
intrusions by faculty in the social sciences and the humanities who were using
computers only to talk. They would certainly have resented it more if they had
observed us chatting with teenagers in Denver from our offices in Fairbanks.

As this example of Ron's abbreviated chat about games with the teenager in
Denver shows, one of the lines that was beginning to be blurred had to do with
our social identities as adults and kids, as university professors and students, as
parents and children. During one of our classes, the teenaged son of one of the
university directors joined in for a week or so of conversation with the other
students who in that case were all graduate students. He used his father's email
account and conveniently failed to make clear that it was the son, not the father
engaged in the conversation. Things went very well until one of the graduate
students in the class discovered the real identity of the person she had been
chatting with. Not only was it not the director, and not only was it a teenaged
boy, this boy was one of her own students in her junior high school class. She was
shocked to find that a person she regarded as young and immature during school
hours was an able computer conversationalist when the context was a university
graduate seminar.

In another case a male colleague joined the class to experience the nature of
the electronic discussions about which he'd heard a good bit from other people
who were involved in it. After several somewhat bombastic proclamations about

the nature of communication, students in the class began sending us private messages which said they'd suspected Ron had invented this false character as a way of playing with various identity features of this nearly identity-less medium. One student, for example, said that she couldn't continue responding to this 'person' until she knew whether it was a male or a female.

Of course now we know that among the most striking features of Internet chatrooms are these ways in which identity is played with by participants. Then it was striking and sometimes shocking to discover just how much of our perceptions of *what* others were saying had to do with *who* we thought they were.

Perhaps more important in the long run than these questions of personal identity were the problems which occurred when the use of electronic mail messaging crossed major institutional boundaries as suggested by the second vignette. This produced major complexities for the funding, management, and credentializing structures of the university. To give just two cases, we can elaborate first on the one mentioned in the vignette. The program we mentioned in Chapter 6 was established with external grant money on the university campus, the purpose of which was to try to 'solve' the drop-out problem of rural students. They had money to fly parents into campus from villages, to fly potential high school students to campus as part of their pre-enrollment preparations, and to fly currently enrolled students home at vacations so that they would not lose their sense of belonging to the community. It was a good and well-intentioned program.

When our students in the university class began using our class computer conferencing to do these same things – to send messages among campus students, village high school students, parents and teachers – all of this very positive and enthusiastic traffic was stopped by the interested institutional parties – the school district and the university. It was crossing funding and management jurisdictions and no funds were allowed to cross over jurisdictions in the name of 'fiscal responsibility'. The school district did not want to be accused of spending district money on university responsibilities; the university did not want to spend money on secondary school responsibilities.

A second case involved our course 'The Social Impact of Instructional Telecommunications'. While the university was a statewide entity, each campus was jurisdictionally independent. Within that broad system were two main classes of institutions – university campuses and community colleges. The faculty of the community colleges were organized as union bargaining units, the university campuses were not. As it was a graduate course, the bulk of our students were not only graduate, they were employees of the university. Those who were bargaining unit members would have their tuitions paid as part of their negotiated agreement; those who were not organized within a union would not. We were first told that we could not teach such a course until it was worked out whether or not all would pay fees or none. Secondly we were told that, since it was a Fairbanks course, all students would have to apply for and receive admission to that campus in order to take the course, even if they were senior administrators within the same university but on a different campus. We tried to solve that by suggesting that Fairbanks students could be enrolled through that campus, those from other units could be enrolled through their own units, but that was stopped by the requirement that, in that case, we teachers would have to apply for teaching positions in each of the colleges and campuses where students would be enrolled and, incidentally, most did not have positions open at that time. We ultimately received the go-ahead two or three weeks into the semester to do the course on a one-time-only basis. The course was never done again as far as we know.

Interrogation

It is a near truism in contemporary thought that the power to define is the power to control social action. The work we have discussed in this book argues that more fundamental than the power to define – the power to make statements – is the power to interrogate. Grammatically, the difference between the statement and the question – the indicative and the interrogative – is that while the statement requires no response, the question requires a response from the person questioned. As Esther Goody pointed out in her research the statement has an information function; the question has both an information and a control function.

As we did these projects we began with statements based on our research over the preceding years as well as our ongoing research projects. As the several nexus of practice began to change, these statements began to change into interrogatives. The judge we have mentioned began to ask himself: Why must I hold depositions in court? Why must I wear judicial robes in every case? The teacher in our class asked: Why can't I just let my students here in town talk to the university the same way I am doing? It's good for me, why wouldn't it be good for them? The committee considering changes to computing resources began to ask: Why are we working with just a single mainframe in Fairbanks when much of the actual uses of computers is learning to program in BASIC which can be done with a small, independent machine? We asked: Why shouldn't students and faculty and administrators talk to each other via the central computer network since we all have email accounts allocated to us?

As we began to find out, there were very real but entirely unstated answers to these questions having to do with organizational structure and power. Nexus analysis, in this view, takes the question, not the statement, as its representative anecdote. The outcome of a good nexus analysis is not a clear statement upon which further action may be taken. The outcome of a good nexus analysis is the process of questioning which is carried on throughout the project.

Toward an ethnography of motives: Why did we do this work?

In Chapter 6 we introduced Kenneth Burke's grammar of motives. We did not introduce the analysis of motives earlier for two reasons. The first reason is that there is a plethora of candidates as motives for human action and the stated choice of motives is always a strategic, positioning choice. The second reason is that, whatever motives we might attribute, we believe we will have to consider them to be rather widely distributed across people, times, places, and actions – that is across broad ecosemiotic cycles.

All of us have some friends who are closer than others and our families are normally closer than our friends. We ourselves have many friends who are Alaska Natives and, as an interethnic couple with children of 'mixed' ethnic heritage, the problems of discrimination in public institutions and between people from different ethnic groups in the US are deeply personal, family questions for us. It could easily be argued that we engaged in these various research projects because we liked some people more than others or that we at least felt some deep sympathy for the problems they encountered because these were problems we ourselves were intimately involved in in our own lives. Thus we might consider this category of motive for our work under the rubric of *affect*.

Burke began in the 1930s to open up the topic of motives for human action to linguistic analysis.

> Speech in its essence is not neutral . . . It is intensely moral – its names for objects contain the emotional overtones which give us the cues as to how we should act toward those objects. Even a word like 'automobile' will usually contain a concealed choice (it designates not merely an *object*, but a *desirable object*). Spontaneous speech is not a naming at all, but a system of attitudes, of implicit exhortations.
>
> (1965 [1935]: 177)

If we extrapolate just slightly, it is clear that not only all speech and all discourse, but also all action is inherently a system of attitudes. Any action implies value, attitude, affect, emotion. In this point Burke's rhetorical analysis shares much with the social semiotics of Hallidayan linguistics and with critical discourse analysis. We say and do things to show our values and attitudes, our positionings and placements of ourselves and of others. This is as much true of researchers who are engaged in their research projects as it is for any other humans going about their day-to-day lives.

To make the notion of motive a bit more complex before moving on, it is fair to say that on the whole linguists and many discourse analysts have assumed or asserted that the primary motive for communication is not affect but the representation of the world and of the speaker's attempts to take action within the world. From this point of view it could be said that the motive which has propelled our work was a desire to clearly describe and represent the inter-actional dynamics brought to social situations by members of different socio-cultural groups. There would be a good amount of accuracy in that argument.

With Burke's work and later with Goffman's, social scientists became conscious of identity production as a primary motive for human action. And sociolinguists and critical discourse analysts have taken it that the production of social positions of power and relationship are significant motives of our utter-ances. Throughout our work we have been made conscious of the power and identity-making aspects of discourse analysis.

A painful irony of this work in its earliest period – in the late 1970s and early 1980s – was that, because of its catchiness in using the newest electronic media, we became rather popular as people to 'speak for' Alaska Native people. One of the reasons we were able to find places within the variety of organizations and projects which we outlined in Chapter 4 was that we were credentialed within the institutions of power with academic degrees (PhDs). From this point of view, then, we could say that our own work in ethnography and in discourse analysis produced highly salient and marketable identities for ourselves within an academic and governmental world.

At that time there were very few Alaska Natives with such degrees, and state and national governmental agencies were as yet unwilling to seek advice outside of a very narrow range of credentializations. A number of the projects in which we were involved were directed precisely at this problem – to achieve such credentialization for Alaska Natives – and as these projects began to succeed we felt it essential that we ourselves withdraw from taking on this identity as representatives for groups of which we were not members.

Of course the work of Piaget and that of many other cognitively oriented psychologists implies that the primary motive of actions in the world, including language actions, is cognitive structuring. As we have argued in Chapter 6, students and university faculty and administrators act within the institutional structure in ways that resonate with how they think about it. When the metaphor guiding a person's conception of the university is that of a socialization model – students are in the institution to become like their teachers – they regard any other use of the institution as a failure. The institution becomes a total institution bent on reform and the metaphor produces the notion that retention of students is the problem. When the metaphor guiding a person's conception of the university is that of a client service such as a supermarket – students are in the institution to receive services and goods that may be used outside for other purposes – they regard the socialization and totalizing aspects of the university to be traps to be carefully avoided. To put this a bit extremely, it would be as if you feared in going to the supermarket that, instead of emerging with your milk and eggs, you might be trapped into a life of working as a cashier.

Looked at from the point of view of cognitive structuring, you might argue that our motive in doing these research projects was to use our actions as researchers and as participants in the nexus of practice to try to rethink and to re-enact the institution. There would be a good bit of accuracy in that characterization as well.

In contrast to these motives located in affect, representation, identity, or cognitive structuring, many theorists working within the frameworks of economics or political science, for example, take the primary motive of human action to be a utilitarianist greatest good for the greatest number beginning, obviously, with the greatest good for the ego. That is, they take self-interest as the primary and presupposed motive for human action. We would be falsifying our position to say that these activities did not serve our own interests very well. During this period we found it relatively easy to achieve research grants and publication of our results. We were frequently invited to meetings and conferences. The stars of our careers rose. We do not believe on introspection that we were ever primarily motivated by these personal advantages, but it would certainly be false to say that we did not benefit from these projects. It would be even more accurate to say that it was our success in some of the projects which led to our ability to conduct others of them. Thus our own self-interest, it might be said, served the general good we were pursuing across this range of projects.

And then, of course, there is the narrator of Dostoyevsky's *Notes from underground* who believed that the highest motive a human could possess was the power to will one's own disadvantage; he believed that only by doing something that was clearly *not* in his own self-interest could he prove he had free will. Again, we do not believe that we were motivated to undermine our own self-interest, but we did come to feel that by 1982 or 1983 the time had come when our original motives were becoming transmuted into a constellation that could only really be viewed as self-serving if not in direct conflict with our concern to provide support and assistance in the restructuring of the nexus of practice standing at the heart of institutional discrimination in public institutions in Alaska.

At that stage we felt that the central difficulty in our ability to develop our work within this nexus of practice was our academic positions of power and credentialization. We began to feel that this was disabling our capacity to work within other zones of identification. We left the university so that we could independently develop our work with technological interventions on the one hand and Ron ran for and was elected to public office where he began to learn the ecosemiotic system of state and municipal politics from the inside of an elected position.

Thus we might have an array of at least six possible reasons we did the work we have discussed here in this book:

- affect
- representation
- identity
- cognitive structuring
- self-interest
- self-disadvantage (to prove free volition).

So why did we do it? This boils down to the question, 'Who gets to say?'

We are all more likely to produce good motives for the actions we take and less charitably produce baser motives for the actions of others. And there is the subsidiary question, 'What motives might someone have in claiming they know the motive for our action?' The search for a motive for a human action rather quickly shifts into a search for a motive for claiming a motive.

Entire disciplines are arguing over this question and, obviously, we are not able to solve this question at a fundamental level in this book. In that case, then, is it important to think about this at all? We believe it is not just important but central to any form of discourse analysis. Henri Bergson in his 1910 book *Time and free will* argued that human motives should not and theoretically could not be laid on a Newtonian time-line of directional causality. His argument was that whatever motives might be adduced by ourselves or by any analyst of our actions in doing these research projects were *outcomes* of doing the research, not the *causes*. Put in more contemporary terms – perhaps those used by discursive psychologists – the causes of the actions of these research projects are discursive constructions, not behavioral primes, though they might well have been constructed 'in advance' as anticipations. That is immaterial to the case. In this view of human motives, whether they are post-action narratives or pre-action anticipations, we believe that any and all motives are matters of discourse, not psychological or material primes.

If this view is right, and we believe a very good case has been made for it, then the motives of human action are a rich and essential territory for discourse analysis. We would go so far as to say that we will learn little about human motives and human actions without discourse analysis if this view is at all correct. Of course, then, it is a major task confronting discourse analysis to investigate just how much validity we want to ascribe to this Bergsonian view, not simply to set aside the question of motives as lying outside of our line of work as discourse analysts have done so often in the past.

And that is only the first problem that arises in trying to account for our motives in doing this work. The second problem arises from everything we had said up to that point before getting to the problem of motives. If we are serious about seeing actions as ecosemiotic systems from multiple points of view, across multiple timescales, involving not just multiple social actors but with each social actor having different levels and kinds of involvement in the action, and if we see then that many different kinds of material and semiotic mediational means are involved in those widely distributed actions, where do we even begin to ascribe motives? Whatever motives we might want to ascribe to doing this work, we would also have to take into consideration some discursive construction – not only our own but those of all of the other participants in these nexus of practice. There would not and could not be any single motive, any single narrative history of motive that would very usefully account for how this work got done. We will need some theory of complex interactions among multiple motives of multiple participants across time and place.

Nexus analysis

This book is an attempt to begin to organize such a theory of complex social actions among multiple motives, multiple participants, and across cycles of varying timescales. At the time we conducted the projects we have discussed in this book we tried to get at this by talking about non-focused research as a dialogue or a conversation. Now we think we would refer to this as organic research – a kind of research that grows and develops and changes structure as it progresses. Back then, however, beyond sketching the outlines of how this might work, we don't think we really were able to integrate a theoretical position that would give us the basis for a theory of social action. Part of that problem, it now seems to us, was that we were still working with the model of the indicative, declarative statement as the fundamental model of research. Perhaps we felt that dialogue would ultimately lead us to those nice, finalized declarative sentences about action. Clearly a major pressure to do this continues to be exerted by the dominant view of research within at least Western canons of science. Our university's website on the use of human subjects in research defines research as follows:

> 'Research means a systematic investigation, including research development, testing and evaluation designed to develop or contribute to generalizable knowledge.' A human subject is a living individual about whom an investigator, (whether professional or student) obtains data through an interaction with the individual or obtains identifiable private information.
>
> (Overview of Research with Human Subjects in the Social and Behavioral Sciences. Georgetown [University] IRB [Institutional

Review Board]-c Website Social and Behavioral Sciences Committee,
http://www.georgetown.edu/grad/IRB/irb-overview.html.
Accessed, July 11, 2002, 9:05am)

What is crucial here and what sets research apart from a conversation with a friend, for example, are the phrases 'systematic investigation' and 'generalizable knowledge' and the structural relationship between them. Research produces generalizable knowledge with systematic investigation. X using Y does Z. An agent (research or the researcher) with a mediational means (systematic investigation) produces an outcome (knowledge).

Some years ago we also took a stab at sorting this out in an unpublished talk 'Gutenberg, Babbage, and Woz: Will Pac-Man Gobble up the Humanities' that Ron presented at the Washington Linguistics Club. We were trying to think through what might make the difference between a project we'd call humanist and one we would call scientific. At that time he said,

> It would be easy to say that the hallmark of the humanist stance is critical inquiry but that is also, I believe, the essence of the scientific stance. What seems to differentiate the two enterprises I'd like to phrase as the difference between being driven toward questions as opposed to being driven toward answers. It seems characteristic of the activity of the humanist to reach such stages of rest as are achieved when one has gotten to the phrasing of what feels like a significant question. I think, in my experience, the stance of the scientist at this point is one of considerable agitation to get on with doing the answering.

We would want to stick with this notion now, with what he set out in that old paper. We believe we could now argue in agreement with Harvey (1996) but also with Glansdorff and Prigogine (1971) that practice and social change are driven by inquiry, by the questions, by the instability of processes of change in our social systems and in our systems of thought that arise from questions and which, ultimately, settle down (but only temporarily at that) in places we cannot possibly predict or control.

From this point of view, then, we see nexus analysis as an 'intervention', but it is one that does not purport to have a positivist solution. We would argue that inquiry is a fundamental human characteristic and a fundamental source of social change. We might go further to argue that inquiry is a human right which constitutes the balancing mechanism to the false security of authoritative knowledge, whether that authoritative knowledge is derived from tradition or from the procedures of science. In short, inquiry is social activism. We now think it is the only effective form of social activism. What is incompatible with social activism is an attempt at a positivist knowledge of the outcomes of inquiry. The analytical model is not to begin with inquiry to arrive at the declarative transitive sentence but, on the contrary, to begin with the simple declaratives and to move toward the interrogative, in particular the interrogative of motive: Why? Hence our subhead above, 'Toward an ethnography of motives'.

Theoretical actions

Here we can now summarize the three main stages and actions of a nexus analysis:

- Engaging the nexus of practice: Recognition of the crucial moments of mediated action and of establishing oneself within a zone of identification.
- Navigating the nexus of practice: Discovering the key semiotic cycles which circulate through the nexus of practice, mapping those cycles for anticipations and emanations and points of transformation and resemiotization, and establishing their timescales and linkages.
- Changing the nexus of practice: Conducting a discourse analysis and a motive analysis of accounts given for actions by the multiple participants of a nexus of practice.

Unfinalizability

In keeping with this fundamentally unfinalizable quality of the theoretical framework, we close by posing what we believe are important questions we must use to query contemporary uses of technology and their consequences for social change. Even if consumer technologies are good for business and the economy, do they have unfortunate or undesirable consequences for discourse and social organization? Is the ever shorter timescale upon which technological change is introduced into society producing breaks in linkages or blockages of potential linkages with other social practices and forms of social organization? Is the restructuring of organizations such as universities, businesses, and government agencies through and *for* the information technologies we now have also a catalyst for changes in academic, business, or governmental discourse that lead to us saying, doing, and thinking things in ways that we never imagined before, and do we want this as an outcome?

We close with a plea to continue to open up the processes of discussion, debate, and interrogation which will ultimately lead to social changes in the discourses within which we live. It is a charge to discourse analysts to locate ourselves within meaningful zones of identification and to continue to pursue our active interrogations of the discourses of our lives.

Undoing the rubber bands

When our daughter was very young we found ourselves in a continuing actional dialogue with her over a set of picture cards. This was a set of cards which had a picture of a bird on one side along with the Chinese name of the bird. On the other side was the pronounciation of the Chinese word and an English word translation. These were very pedagogical playthings. The dialogue with Rachel arose because whenever we saw this set of cards strewn across the floor we would tidy up by putting them all neatly together in a stack and putting a rubber band around them. Rachel didn't show very much interest in the cards on the whole, but it seems that every time she saw them stacked up with a rubber band around them, she enjoyed taking off the rubber band and spreading them around on the floor. It was an endless cycle of order and entropy.

We think this is much like the problem we have been facing in our thinking about human action. It could be a reflection of the necessary ebb and flow of dialogue between science and the humanities, between the declarative sentence and the question, between theory and practice. What we think has caused confusion for us is that we had been reversing the terms at least in some cases. At first we thought of inquiry – the interrogative, or question – as a preliminary stage to the declarative and we thought of the declarative as the basis for action. While we have had an interest in human action and social change, we had rather mistakenly (now as we see it) thought that to be able to achieve meaningful action what would be required would be clear, declarative statements about the nature of human action. Now we believe that the situation is just the reverse of this. Human action arises not from the declarative transitive statements of science and of theory but from the interrogatives of the humanities and of practice. We have been working at tidying up the cards to get them in order with a rubber band around them so that we could see how to take action. Now we would argue that the way to precipitate action is to do just the opposite: Snap off the rubber band, spread out the cards, and let the entropy flow.

Appendix: A practical fieldguide for nexus analysis

Overview

This fieldguide has been designed to guide researchers using *nexus analysis* as the basis for their field research. While it is designed to guide a full nexus analysis, you may find it useful as a guide for any ethnographic study of discourse.

The fieldguide consists of three central tasks or activities – engagement, navigation, and change – and their time scheduling over a one-year field period as a typical field research project. You will want to adjust the proposed scheduling according to your own research needs. The fieldguide may also be used in short-term studies (in classes or pilot research projects) by focusing on just one or several aspects of a full analysis. The longer timespan of one year will give you an idea of how to place a shorter study within the framework.

The sequencing of tasks begins by engaging the researcher in the key mediated actions that are relevant to the social issue under study, and then moves to navigating and mapping the cycles of discourse, of people, and of mediational means which are at the heart of the significant actions being studied. Although we discuss changing the nexus of practice as the third stage, a *nexus analysis* recognizes throughout the analysis that the processes of change are the results of the activities of the researcher in recording the actions, engaging in discourses with the participants, and constructing new courses of action.

A *nexus analysis* of the kind which is organized by this fieldguide is based on concepts which have been developed by many scholars over several fields. While this fieldguide assumes a certain familiarity with mediated discourse analysis, it should be useful for any fieldwork projects in activity and practice theory, multimodal discourse analysis, interactional sociolinguistics, critical discourse analysis, and linguistic anthropology.

Figure A.1 shows the three activities of a nexus analysis.

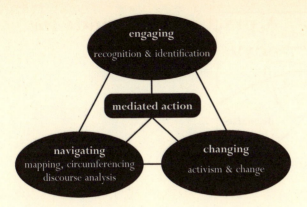

A.1 Activities of nexus analysis.

1 Engaging the nexus of practice

January–February: The first as well as the final problem of a nexus analysis is to discover the social actions and social actors which are crucial in the production of a social issue and bringing about social change. The opening task is to look for those actions and participants. In many cases this is a matter of recognition and selection. The tasks in the first section of the fieldguide provide heuristic ways of narrowing down to a clear focus on very specific actions as the center-point of a nexus analysis. It is important in this process for the researcher to enter into a *zone of identification* with those key participants. There is no study from afar in nexus analysis. Identification in a nexus analysis means that the researcher himself or herself must be recognized by other participants as a participant in the nexus of practice under analysis.

We schedule this activity as the first two months of a twelve-month nexus analysis. Of course this would also make a very effective short-term project in itself in a course on ethnographic field methods.

Recognition and identification of the nexus of practice

Social action occurs at the intersection of three factors: the historical bodies of the participants in that action, the interaction order which they mutually produce among themselves, and the discourses in place which enable that action or are used by the participants as mediational means in their action. Figure A.2 shows these three main factors. Your recognition of the nexus of practice and your ability to create a zone of identification can be seen as five main activities:

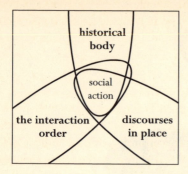

A.2

- Establish the social issue you will study.
- Find the crucial social actors.
- Observe the interaction order.
- Determine the most significant cycles of discourse.
- Establish your zone of identification.

Establish the social issue you will study

Whatever issue you study, you will become deeply involved with it. The first place to look for that issue is in your own life, your own actions, and your own value system. What do you wish somebody would do something about? What do you think ought to be changed in the world in which you regularly live? What gets you upset when you see the news or hear what is going on in your city or country or the world?

It is important to begin your study as soon as possible. You cannot know at the outset what all of the consequences and ramifications of your study will be nor can you know at the beginning what you will think is the main issue itself later on in the study. So by all means do not spend too much time on this stage.

Find the crucial social actors

Who are the the primary social actors in the mediated action in which you are interested? In this case 'who' means both who they are in the sense of their identities and social roles and what are their individual histories. You want to know what social identities they are producing or claiming through the actions you are analyzing, what social statuses do they bring into the site of engagement in which this action occurs as well as how they are producing them. You also want to know their histories or historical body with this action, with the discourses which are circulating through this action, and with the other participants in the situation. Basically you want to know who are they to do this and how they became enabled to take this action. The main point is to make every attempt to identify the key figures who will justify deeper study as you move into the second stage, navigating the nexus of practice.

Observe the interaction order

In trying to identify the crucial moments to study for your nexus analysis, then, you will need to discover what are the typical interaction orders within which the actions occur. Are people usually alone or in small 'withs'? Do these actions occur in task groups or teams? Do they occur as performances before audiences?

Of course we cannot easily separate our interest in the historical bodies of individual participants and the interaction order, so we will want to know what is the history of this interaction order for these participants. Do they often go shopping together or is this the first time? Is this a class which is meeting right at the beginning of the semester or near the end of the semester when people know each other very well?

Determine the most significant cycles of discourse

Your question about discourses is twofold: Given a particular scene, you want to know what discourses are circulating through that scene and in particular through the actions you are interested in analyzing. Looked at the other way around, as we shall discuss below when we talk about making a scene survey, you want to know about any discourse what scenes and actions are the means or sites of its circulation.

Be sure to think about whether or not the discourses you are observing are overt or covert, spoken or written. Are these discourses 'precipitated' in the form of the 'crystalized' design and form of material objects such as the design discourse that has produced the desk we are using or the software in this word processor? Are these discourses anticipatory of actions to come?

While the main task of answering these and other questions is taken up later in navigating the nexus of practice, here for the moment the goal is to locate the central and crucial discourses which are intersecting with the interaction order and the historical bodies of the participants to produce the focal mediated actions of your study.

Establish your zone of identification

The activities of establishing a social issue to research, finding the most significant social actors, observing the interaction order, and determining the cycles of discourse are concerned with the *recognition* of a significant nexus of practice; they have been directed toward finding or recognizing the main mediated action (or actions) which sit at the center of the nexus of practice you will study. Along with this recognition you are also locating yourself in a zone of identification with the participants in this nexus of practice.

As you conduct your preliminary studies of the scene, participants, events, discourses, and actions you are finding, you will almost inevitably be drawn into closer participation with the participants in those nexus of practice. You should not seek to stay aloof from the nexus of practice. On the contrary, it is your goal to become a full-fledged participant so that your 'research' activities merge with your 'participation' activities. Aristotle supposedly said that if you want to convince an Athenian it is better to be an Athenian. If you want to change a mediated action (and consequently a nexus of practice) it is necessary to be a participant in that nexus of practice.

Above all, it should be remembered that this first stage, engaging the nexus of practice, is really preliminary to a nexus analysis. The nexus analysis consists of navigating the cycles of discourse and the histories of the historical bodies which constitute a mediated action and of the discourse analysis and motive analysis of how that navigation is done by both the analyst and the participants. Where it is abundantly clear what the key mediated actions are, the only really indispensable aspect of engaging the nexus of practice is to establish the researcher within a zone of identification.

Strategies for getting the answers

If you are not immediately or obviously already involved in a nexus of practice which you are interested in studying, the recognition of a significant mediated action might consist of a combination of the following elements which are taken up in turn below (these elements are based on R. Scollon 1998; see bibliography for full citation). Also any of the several books on the ethnography of communication (e.g. Saville-Troike 2002) will give you very useful suggestions from the comparative research literature. You may also want to develop your own concept of the issue you want to study by making a survey of the public discourses on social issues, by conducting scene surveys or focus groups as we suggest below.

Discourses survey

There are two very effective types of survey which can help to ensure that you are working within cycles of discourse that are germane to an important issue as well as the crucial points at which mediated actions occur – media content surveys and public opinion (or 'What's in the news?') surveys. The first of these can be done relatively easily by collecting current newspapers and magazines, visiting news websites, and watching television news broadcasts. While 'hot' issues tend to change rapidly in these media, a careful analysis can show which issues continually return for attention. You can also check the websites of governmental, non-governmental, and corporate grant-making organizations to see which issues they have currently identified as needing research.

Scene surveys

Scene surveys can make your study more concrete by locating the people, places, and actions within those places which are keeping the cycles of discourse in flow. The idea is to find where the mediated actions in which you are interested take place, who the central participants are and in what forms of the interaction order, and what discourses are circulating through those scenes. We have organized these scene surveys around three kinds of questions:

> *Historical body questions*: Where do the people you have identified as the main participants spend their time? Which ones are important for the issue you are studying? One of the surest ways of locating the crucial scenes is simply to follow the main participants through their daily and weekly cycles of activity.

> *Interaction order questions*: What is the place of the participants within the interaction orders you observe throughout their days? Our actions not only arise from our own personal histories and values but are also constrained or enabled by the people we are together with at a particular moment of action. You need to know not only what are the scenes within which people take action, but how they organize themselves for social interaction within those scenes.

> *Discourses in place questions*: The crucial scenes you will study can also be found by following the cycles of discourse. Of course you will be asking these questions about social actors, the interaction order, and discourses concurrently in any attempt to locate the crucial scenes for your study. As you follow a person's daily round of habitual places and scenes, you will be asking what are the interaction orders dominant within those scenes and what discourses are cycling through them. Your main purpose at this stage is simply to narrow down to a few scenes in which you find there is an intersection of the people on whom you want to focus, the interaction order that is most germane to your study, and in which the discourses you are concerned about are significant factors.

Focus groups

Once you have identified the most crucial scenes, participants, and mediated actions relevant to the social issue you are studying, you need to check these selections with the participants in your nexus of practice. In our experience you can achieve a more robust analysis if you actually step outside this primary group to conduct focus groups whose participants are demographically like the ones you are studying or working with but not the same ones or even not known to them. If you have been careful in your preceding work, these focus groups will mostly confirm your thinking. Pay particular attention to divergences, however, as these will indicate that you are still not directly on center in your recognition of mediated actions to study.

Getting the answers

A well triangulated and carefully comparative study should cover four types of data (Ruesch and Bateson 1968 [1951]; but also see S. Scollon 1998; R. Scollon 1998, 2001a, 2001b; R. Scollon and S. Scollon 2001).

- *Members' generalizations*: What do participants say they do (normatively)? This is often at variance both with objective observation and with that member's own individual experience.
- *Neutral (objective) observations*: What does a neutral observer see? Often at variance with the generalizations made about the group or the self.
- *Individual experience*: What does an individual describe as his or her experience? Often characterized as being different from one's own group.
- *Interactions with members*: How do participants account for your analysis? This will mostly focus on the resolution of contradictions among the first three types of data.

As much as possible your research throughout your nexus analysis project should include all four of these kinds of data. You should try to discover if there are normative expectations held by the participants in your nexus of practice. You want to find out how they are expressed, how they are encoded, how they are learned, and how they are enforced. Much of this aspect of your project will be done as your discourse and motive analysis which we discuss later in this fieldguide. But, of course, it is not enough to know what people say they do. You need to observe directly to see to what extent members' generalizations about the nexus of practice meet with the 'reality' you observe. People often act very differently from their own descriptions of their actions or the actions of members of their group.

   Therefore, the third kind of material you need to get is how individual members experience their nexus of practice as individuals. While they might describe generalized behavior of 'people' in that nexus, they might also claim that their own actions are quite divergent. Perhaps for one it is a scene they've participated in once and for others it is something they do frequently. Each of these different experiences would give a different understanding of the nexus of practice. Finally, you should talk about your analysis with members to see to what extent they agree or disagree with what you have observed. This latter step often comes somewhat later; we think that focus groups are a good place to seek this kind of data if it does not arise naturally elsewhere in your study.

Collecting data, then, should be based on trying to get all four types of data. You should use as much objective recording as you can (video and audio recording; photographs; artifacts such as magazines, newspapers, CDs, tickets, posters, handbills; fieldnotes taken in the scene; interviews of participants). Sometimes you will get all four types of data in one batch of material. An interview or a conversation, for example, might give you quite a range of data, as when a person says, 'Everybody says we should X' (members' generalization), 'but I usually do Y' (individual experience). Then you observe that while this person is saying X and Y, he is doing Z (objective observation). You say, 'But I just noticed that you are doing Z' (interactions with members).

A necessary but not sufficient step

These activities may be useful to you in locating a specific action to study in a specific site of engagement, but you should not become either distracted by these activities or satisfied that you have really done a nexus analysis. This is all really preliminary to the main tasks which are navigating the nexus of practice and changing the nexus of practice through your own actions in conducting your discourse analysis and motive analysis.

2 Navigating the nexus of practice

March–October: The main work of a nexus analysis is navigating the nexus of practice as you do your discourse and motive analysis. A nexus of practice is the point at which historical trajectories of people, places, discourses, ideas, and objects come together to enable some action which in itself alters those historical trajectories in some way as those trajectories emanate from this moment of social action.

In the first task, engaging the nexus of practice, you have established the social issue you will study, found the crucial social actors, observed the interaction order, and determined the most significant cycles of discourse. This has given you your zone of identification and helped to identify the crucial mediated action (or actions) where that social issue is being produced, ratified, or contested. Now the task is to map the cycles of the people, places, discourses, objects, and concepts which circulate through this micro-semiotic ecosystem looking for anticipations and emanations, links and transformations, their inherent timescales, and to place a circumference of relevance around the nexus of practice. Conceptually these may be separate tasks but in practice it is very difficult and largely pointless to try to keep them separated. Here we take up the cycles first and then look at the mapping concerns following that.

Semiotic cycles

If we think of an action as a moment in time and space in which the historical bodies and the interaction order of people and the discourses in place intersect, then each of these can be thought of as having a history that leads into that moment and a future that leads away from it in arcs of semiotic cycles of change and transformation. In some cases the action itself may give further impetus to the cycle like a pumping station along an oil pipeline or it may deflect or alter the cycle like an electron passing through a magnetic field. To some extent the cycles or life histories of people, places, discourses, and objects can be seen only through these moments of freshened impulse or directional change and transformation.

In thinking of these cycles do not try to map all the semiotic cycles of every person, discourse, or object that occurs within the place where the action is occurring. The purpose of your activities in engaging the nexus of practice (Section 1) was precisely to make a selection so that you can focus your inquiry. Concentrate now on mapping the cycles into and away from the mediated action you have selected and set aside other considerations at least until they can be demonstrated to be important to consider.

Persons — Historical body

First, your concern is not with a full life history of each of the social actors involved in the nexus of practice. Instead, your interest is to understand how the action-practice and the mediational means you are studying came into the historical body of each of the participants. Secondly, there are often many hidden participants in an action, especially when a mediating technology is involved. The computer technicians mediating an email chat, the finance company employee monitoring a credit card transaction, the chef in a restaurant, or the driver of a bus may each have a role that can be invisible at first as we are accustomed to just setting aside as non-relevant these participants who are in a 'supporting role' to our actions. So the goal here is to try to be certain you have included all of the relevant participants, but at the same time try to keep focused on those aspects of the historical body which are relevant to the action in which you have an interest.

The guiding question here is: *How did these participants all come to be placed at this moment and in this way to enable or carry out this action?* This question may be developed with the following more specific questions we suggest that you keep in mind:

- How habitual or innovative is the action-practice for that person? That is, to what extent is this a 'practice'?
- How intentional (agentive) or accidental? How do you know? (To think about this see *discourse analysis* below.) According to whom is this intentional? (For more on this see *motive analysis* below.)
- When and where is the last prior 'like' action? That is, is there a link between this action and this type of place or these other participants? For example, a person might not normally drink coffee or smoke cigarettes but always makes an exception with a particular friend.
- To what other practices is this linked for this person? Does he or she always do something else at the same time? Anyone who has tried to quit smoking gradually comes to realize the myriad practices that are linked to having a cigarette. Also ask this for other people, mediational means, places, discourse, concepts.
- How much is this action keyed to the uniqueness of the person, or, alternatively, how dispensable is the person? Could it be anybody who does the action, just so long as it gets done? A president can sign a bill into law; a municipal worker can paint the traffic lines on the street. Neither can simply switch and accomplish the other action.
- What is the emotional valence or the emotional impact on the participant of this action? Is it exciting, routine, or boring to do this; is the action sought or avoided? Is it so much part of the historical body that the person sometimes wonders why it isn't as enjoyable as it used to be or as anticipated?
- What discourses are transformed, resemiotized, or internalized in this action? A doctor giving an exam plays out in action many years of the formal study of medical discourses from physiology to patient care. A dentist replacing a filling plays out commercial discourses and teacher–student evaluational discourses as well as nurturing dependent discourses and discourses of oral health care. A camper lighting a camp stove plays out in action the reading of the instructions for that stove.

Discourses in place – Semiotic aggregates

There are very few 'pure' places in our worlds where everything in that place serves a single purpose and where there is nothing extraneous. When we cross the street at a street corner we pay attention to (foreground) not only approaching cars but the design of the walkways, the roadway, the pedestrian crosswalks, and the traffic lights that regulate the vehicles and pedestrians. We ignore (background) the markings of the infrastructure from gas and water access plates on the ground to municipal numbers identifying the light and traffic signal poles. When we have a cup of coffee in a coffee shop we foreground such things as the type of coffee we want to order and we background conversations that might be going on at tables around the shop. On the other hand, a person working for the company might be interested in maintaining a good conversational ambience and so be keeping those conversations in a kind of middle ground while waiting on a customer.

Concerning the places where actions occur the guiding question is: *What aspects of this place are central or foregrounded as crucial to the action on which you are focusing and what aspects are backgrounded?* Further questions to have in mind would include the following:

- What 'place' supports are available for this action such as furniture of particular kinds or the ambience or lack of it?
- Is this a customary or unusual place for this action? That is, does this design, including structures and objects, support or undermine the action being taken?
- What co-occurrences with other actions by other people are part of the 'background'?
- What is the historical trajectory of this place; in what cycles does it function? What's embedded in its history – ancient, new, special purpose design? Is it on the rise or decadent? Is it being transformed by this action?
- Are the linkages among those parts selected to be foregrounded typical (historical) or occasional? That is, for example, how long has coffee been 'traditionally' taken with (or without) milk in this place?

Discourses in place – Overt discourse

A place is constituted not only by the built structures, furniture and decorative objects but also by the discourses present in that place. A coffee shop might be constituted by a combination of many private conversational discourses, the semi-public service discourses involved in placing and receiving orders, the backstage discourse of the servers, commercial discourses of the products on sale and many others.

It is only an analytical heuristic to try to separate discourses from other aspects of the built environment of places. Is the brand-name coffee machine in a coffee shop part of the built environment or one of the discourses? Of course it is both, depending on the focus of our analysis. What is important is that for the server the coffee machine is foregrounded in her or his action of making the coffee but backgrounded for the people having a conversation at a table just a few feet away even though both the machine and its brand name remain clearly visible.

As we noted with the built structures and other design aspects of the place the guiding question is: *What discourses in this place are central or foregrounded as crucial to the action on which you are focusing and what discourses are backgrounded?* Specific questions might include the following:

- What kinds of overt discourse are present? These might be expected to include:

  o The interaction order; that is, the talk, writing, gesturing or image making of the people who are there as singles, as conversational pairs, as customer and server, and all of the other combinations by which people organize their social gatherings.

  o Signs, images, graphics, texts, music; most public places at least in the urban worlds we inhabit are full of signs, advertisements, the brand names and logos on our clothing and other objects and often enough background music.

  o Place discourses (see *places* above); street corners can be distinguished from parks and meeting or seminar rooms, coffee shops, living rooms, and kitchens. How are these semiotic aggregates in themselves discourses that contribute to the action under examination?

- How 'noisy' or quiet is this place (from the point of view of the number and kinds of discourse present)? Shopping malls and urban business districts tend to be 'noisy' in the sense that there are many different and often unrelated discourses calling out for our attention. Parks and residential areas are often much quieter in presenting many fewer discourses. How are these differences useful to the participants in constructing their actions?
- Is the action polyfocal or monofocal? That is, does this action focus on a single discourse with high intensity or does it play among multiple discourses simultaneously?
- Whether there are many or few discourses, there is always the question of how the selection to focus on one or several is made. Is this done gesturally or by 'cleaning' away unwanted background discourses?

Discourses – Internalized as practice

Many of the discourses present in an action have been 'submerged' into practice by long habit. The first time you cook a particular dish you might use a recipe and follow it carefully. After a few times you only need to glance at the recipe to remind yourself of the main ingredients and the sequence. Finally, you just 'spontaneously' cook this dish. As a child a parent or teacher might carefully rehearse with you that 'the red light means stop; the green light means go'.

Ultimately, you come to just stop or proceed when you see the light with no memory of the steps by which you internalized this discourse.

Not all of our actions are internalized this way from what were once very explicit and external discourses, but in mapping the cycles of discourse within a nexus of practice, especially when we set a larger circumference (see *timescales* and *circumferences* below), we want to know how discourses become transformed into practices and objects and then how those practices and objects are, in turn, transformed into new discourses.

Here the guiding question is: *What discourses are 'invisible' in this action because they have become submerged in practice?* This is a complex question to address as it's difficult to see 'invisible' discourses in the present event; these discourses tend to be visible only by mapping semiotic or discourse cycles backward (or forward) around the arc of their circumference away from the event on which you are focused. But that is, in fact, the goal in a nexus analysis. Particularly important actions are ones in which the process of transformation itself is visible, and so this is a good place to begin the study with the following questions:

- What discourses are being foregrounded *for the purpose of becoming habitual?*
- Are any of the participants 'teaching' any of the others?
- What actions or practices (or objects or built structures) are being fore- grounded as part of the discourse of participants?
- Are any of the participants calling attention to objects or structures so that they can be talked about?
- Overall how 'automatic' are the actions here? (Automatic actions are likely to embed submerged discourses.)
- Conversely, how new or unpracticed are the actions you are studying?
- If the action is new or unpracticed, are there anticipations of future arcs of the cycle where this action is expected to become practice?

Objects – Cultural tools (mediational means)

In mediated discourse analysis (or activity theory or mediated action theory) there is no meaningful distinction between objects and concepts as mediational means (cultural tools). Here we treat them separately just as we did discourses and practices above, even though what begins as an external object such as a musical instrument for a musician, a spatula for a cook, or a car for a driver becomes 'submerged' as it is internalized in action as a concept 'the music', 'cooking', or 'driving'.

The guiding question about objects as mediational means is: *What is the history of this object as a mediational means for this action?* This can be opened up a bit through the following questions:

- To what degree is the object (mediational means) designed for the action or is it an 'opportunity' object? Pounding in a tent stake with a handy rock uses an opportunity object as a mediational means. Conversely, a Phillips-head screwdriver is designed for a very specific kind of screw and other tools are very difficult to use for the action of turning in one of these screws.
- How is the object which is the mediational means for this action altered in – or through – the action?
- How did this object come to be present for this action; i.e. through whose agency?
- What is the state or degree of repair or attrition?
- How thoroughly internalized is this mediational means and by which social actors? How old (or new) is it in the historical body?
- Is this object the result of a resemiotization? (see *transformation* below). The agenda of a meeting, for example, is normally a printed text which has resemiotized discussions among a few key administrators or managers which is then used as a mediational means for the conduct of the meeting by all participants.

Concepts – Cultural tools (mediational means)

While the questions are the same basic questions as you have just considered, where the mediational means are concepts, it is likely that that is the result of a much longer *timescale* of internalization.

The guiding question about concepts, like objects as mediational means, is: *What is the history of this concept as a mediational means for this action?* The following questions may help to fill out your understanding of the trajectories involved in these mediational means:

- What conceptual or psychological tools are used (language, semiotic codes, number systems, knowledge of how to fill out forms or to order 'designer' coffee, social codes for behavior)?
- How widely are these shared among the participants?
- How long or fully internalized are these concepts?
- Are they internalized about the same or equally for all participants?
- Where, when, or with whom were these concepts internalized?
- To what extent are these psychological or conceptual mediational means the result of some 'resemiotization'? A word such as 'learning-disabled' or 'non-compliant' may be used as a concept to resemiotize a long history of social interactions and tests.
- How are these mediational means transformed in and through the action? (See *transformation* below.)

Mapping

You should have identified the crucial actions in which you are interested and this will have defined your focus on specific people, places, discourses, and mediational means (both concrete objects and concepts). Now the goal is to examine the semiotic cycles of each of these from the point of view of the considerations below.

Anticipations and emanations

Much of our lives are taken up in either anticipating actions which are yet to come or reflecting on actions now past. Many of the actions we take are themselves anticipations of actions yet to come or the result of earlier actions. Grocery shopping may be enjoyable in itself but is largely a matter of anticipating the meals which we will cook and eat later on. Cleaning up the kitchen after a meal is an emanation of the actions of cooking and eating a meal. It is also, of course an anticipation of wanting to have a clean kitchen in which to plan and cook the next meal.

As a way to plot the place of an action on the arc of a cycle over a longer *timescale* the following questions might be useful:

- To what extent is this action anticipatory of a following action or an emanation from a preceding action? And which actions? How are these determined (see *discourse analysis* and *motive analysis* below)?
- How is this action anticipated in the historical body of the persons involved?
- Do they dress before leaving home so as to be able to accomplish this action later in the day?
- Or was this action anticipated much earlier such as in taking a training course or planning a vacation or making plane, hotel, or other reservations, or booking a room for a meeting?
- Is this action talked about as an anticipation or an emanation (see *discourse analysis* below) or perhaps as both?
- Design is a major form of anticipation, cleaning and waste disposal are major forms of emanations from actions and events. How are anticipation and emanation 'built in' in the mediational means used?

Points and intervals

Actions are points along the circumference of the semiotic cycles of people, discourses, places, and mediational means, and some of them are of major importance (see *transformations* below). While it is unlikely that we could imagine states of complete inaction, between major actions are intervals of lesser activity. In mapping the cycles it seems most useful to concentrate first on the points of action in these cycles and return to a study of the intervals only when it seems that is necessary for a fuller understanding of a particular action.

The guiding question concerning points and intervals is: *What are the key points in the cycle of this person, discourse, etc. where there is a change or a transformation (resemiotization)?* A subsidiary question is: *What is happening in the intervals between these points as anticipations of (or reflections upon) these changes?* Further questions:

- How often does this action occur in the life cycle of this (these) person(s), or mediational means, or discourses? Is it very frequent, very rare?
- What are the immediately preceding and following intervals like or is this action a point in a tight series of actions? (A driver on a long stretch of cross-continental highway may 'act' so little that sleep sets in; a driver in a crowded city is constantly stopping, starting, passing, and checking for the presence and actions of other vehicles.)
- Are the objects used as mediational means used frequently for this or for other actions or are they specially used and only rarely?
- Is this place a place of action (i.e. frequent and varied actions as in a train station or shopping mall) or a 'quiet' place where little is expected to happen?

Timescales

People have normal life expectancies as do some semiotic cycles of discourses, actions, and objects. A person might live sixty or seventy years but the discourse surrounding a new technology might last only a few years. (How much longer will anyone remember what a 'floppy disk' is?) We have developed Table 1 based on Lemke's work (Lemke 2000a, 2000b, 2002). Much discourse analysis is limited to studies within the Circadian timescale. The questions you are interested in when you do a nexus analysis are often located on a much longer timescale such as the lunar or even solar timescale. Sometimes it is years between the first encounter with a discourse and its subsequent internalization as habitual action in practice. Furthermore, each of the elements for which you are mapping a cycle – participants, the interaction order, mediational means, discourses, and places – is likely to be based on a different timescale: for example, a musician of fifty years of age who plays a concert of two hours on a violin that is hundreds of years old in a concert hall that was just completed two weeks ago including works from the eighteenth century and others newly commissioned for that performance. The timescale may be inherent in the element you are concerned

Table 1   Timescales

Biorythm	Semiotic process	Duration	Semiotic unit
Cardiac-respiratory	Vocal articulation	Fraction of a second	Edge of awareness; the phoneme
	Utterance	Fraction of a second	Single action, a step in walking, holophrase, short monologue, in context
Circadian	Exchange	Seconds to minutes	Dialogue, interpersonal relations, developing situation, utterance, sentence, crossing a city street, ordering fast food item
	Episode	~15 minutes	Thematic, functional unit; speech genre; conversation, work break, fast food purchase, intermission in games & concerts
	Event	~Hour	Curriculum genre, informal meal (lunch), conversation, grocery shopping, meeting (short)
	Event sequence, ritual	~2–3 hours	Business meeting, shopping trip, formal meal, movie, ball game, concert
	Business day	~Day	Work day, school day, open hours for a business
Lunar	Project unit or unit sequence, sale	~14 days	Project deadline, pay period
Solar	Advertising campaign, sale, roadwork,	~4 months	Organizational level; unit in next scale
	Urban planning, public works projects; personnel rotation	~3–4 years	Organizational level; limit of institutional planning; length of time in job
Human life cycle	Urban development, company lifespan	~30 years	Biographical timescale; identity change
Historical-cultural	National, cultural, social change	~300 years	Historical timescale; new institutions

with – a human lifespan has a 'normal' expectancy and so you may regard a participant as early, middle, or late in that 'normal' timescale. At the same time, the significance of an action (or activity or activity system) is partly a question of how the participants place it on such a timescale. A person in her twenties might be relatively early on that 'normal' timescale in calendar years but as a patient in a consultation with a doctor concerning the possibility of a terminal disease might feel herself very late on that timescale. The idea of timescale should never be thought of as a simple matter of 'objective' calendar time or expectancy. This is a question for *discourse analysis*: How are the timescales constructed by the participants in the action under consideration?

Thus the basic timescale guiding question is: *What are the material-physical timescales on which these cycles operate and how are those constructed discursively by the participants?* Follow-up questions would be these:

- What is a typical timescale for the people, discourses, places, and mediational means that are crucial to the action you are studying?
- How are these timescales constructed discursively and by whom?
- How much agreement is there about these constructions?
- Where in the cycle does this action occur? A person might apply for an immigration visa at the time when the local economy is lagging but the foreign economy is booming, but when the visa is issued a decade later those relationships might be reversed.
- Is this the first time this new object is used as a mediational means or is it comfortably adjusted to the person who is using it?
- What relationships or linkages are there among or across timescales? You might wear a new pair of shoes that are still not adjusted to your feet for a short social event but not for a long walk in the country.

Links and interactions among semiotic cycles

The original meaning of 'nexus' is a link between two different ideas or objects. In mapping the semiotic cycles of the people, discourses in place, and interaction order involved in the action you are studying, it is important to study not just the separate cycles but the links and interactions among them.

The central question is: *How have just these elements come together at just this moment to produce this particular action?* Questions by which to expand this basic question are the following:

- Do some of these elements (or all of them) seem completely inevitable or completely accidental? Why are the inevitable ones so *linked* to this action?
- Are two practices always linked or only accidentally and sporadically? (Do you listen to a certain kind of music when you read a certain kind of magazine?)
- Do all participants see these linkages the same way?
- Does this person always use exactly this object as a mediational means in taking this action? (For example, a favorite pen for writing, a 'good luck' pair of socks for playing baseball.)

- Are the links simply arbitrary and associational – you've just always done it that way (a particular kind of music that you want when you're cooking dinner) or are they necessarily linked as part of a larger activity (you must pay with cash in this kind of store)?
- Are there incommensurabilities as well? That is, are there prohibited or impossible elements or linkages?
- How are these 'present' in the situation? Are they just absent or is there explicit discourse concerning their absence?

Transformations and resemiotizations

Actions often transform a cycle from one kind of action/object or discourse into another. An agenda written on paper may become a sequence of topics that are discussed orally at a meeting. That oral discussion then becomes a decision that is recorded in written minutes of the meeting. Those minutes are then the basis of discussion among an executive group which makes a written policy statement. That policy statement then becomes a mediational means by which following actions are taken. In each case the semiotic cycle is transformed (or resemiotized) from one semiotic mode to another, from text to speech and back to text, and then into objects, for example.

Re-examine each of the points you have mapped on each cycle to see if there are places in which the actions accomplish a transformation or resemiotization from action to mediational means to further action. Do not get stuck on just following physical objects or concepts, discourses, or just people and their actions. Be alert to changes of state in these semiotic cycles. Many important aspects of nexus analysis are tied up in this point. A car is, in this sense, the resemiotization of an enormous complex of engineer's discourses, resource extraction and manufacturing actions and discourses, and a world-wide system of trade and financial exchange. As a mediational means for the action of driving to the store, a car carries along with it a very complex and multiply resemiotized set of discourses and actions.

From the point of view of transformation and resemiotization the most important question is this: *Is the action under examination a point at which resemiotization or semiotic transformation occurs?* Questions preliminary to asking this question are:

- What anticipations on the part of which key social actors lead up to this action?
- What emanates from this action?
- To what extent is the action embedded in historical body in different ways for the participants involved? And do these differences provide a source for transformation and resemiotization?

Circumferences

Actions are part of larger activities and activity systems, and those are part of even larger entitites we call life histories or histories or eras. Each of the semiotic cycles that constitute a nexus of practice may work on a different timescale. The idea of 'circumferencing' the action you are studying is to try to follow the circumference for each cycle far enough that you can include the most important elements that give meaning to the action as well as to see the points at which semiotic transformations or resemiotizations are happening.

The guiding circumferencing question is: *What are the narrowest and widest timescales on which this action depends?* In thinking about how to follow these circumferences, keep in mind the following questions:

* Is the action limited in some way by the circumference set by participants, discourses, objects, places, etc.? A physician's examination that must be completed within twelve to fifteen minutes may be extremely limited in its ability to take note of processes that cannot be observed within the cardiac-respiratory timescale. For wider circumferencing the doctor is dependent on discourse – largely the questions and answers of the medical history.
* Do all participants agree on the most relevant timescale or circumference?
* How are conflicts resolved and by whom?

How to proceed

We have just outlined a set of questions that we know are difficult to investigate or to try to answer in any complete way. We suggest that you should make broad-stroke maps of the nexus of practice to begin with. Then select some cycles to follow out along their circumferences – the historical body of a person, a practice, a sequence of actions in an activity, a discourse that looks promising. Your purpose is to open up the circumference beyond the narrow circadian limits of much discourse analysis over the course from March to October through wider studies.

Sketch out the history of the participants, the mediational means, the discourses, and the place and set an approximate circumference. You probably do not need to know the history of medicine back to Hippocrates to decide that a fifteen-minute doctor–patient medical exam is probably too short to grasp the full trajectories of the actions involved. But you probably also do not need a full analysis of contemporary economic conditions and practices to see that it would be difficult to very quickly alter that particular nexus of practice.

Once you have sketched out the main lines and cycles which constitute the mediated action in which you are interested, the most effective way to proceed is to start with what you can learn from the participants about their own cycles (with observations, interviews, focus groups) as a guide to where to look earlier in the process. Be particularly attentive to anticipations (see *discourse analysis* and *motive analysis*):

- How do they talk about *why* they have come to take this action?
- Of what history do they see it as the outcome; what future is it projected toward? Compare: 'I always have coffee at this time of day' and 'I need a cup of coffee because I have a big meeting coming up in twenty minutes'. The first locates the *motive* for the action within the agent and his or her historical body, the second locates the *motive* as an anticipation of what is yet to come.

In any event it is important to study some sequence of actions or some participants longitudinally over the eight months from March to October. You are looking for repeated sequences of actions, the transformations of discourse to action or from action to discourse. The easiest and most effective way to do this is to simply become committed to working within the nexus of practice toward the achievement of some definite outcome and then carefully map the life history of that action.

This will inevitably lead to the discovery of other crucial points in the circumference of the semiotic cycles you are studying. Each of those is a new nexus of practice that you might study with its own semiotic cycles circulating through it. In each case then you will need to decide whether it is more fruitful to follow out those new cycles or to return to your focus on your original semiotic ecosystem, your original nexus of practice. There is no certain answer to which direction you should take. This is a judgment you will have to make as part of your own participation in this nexus of practice. What is clear is that whether you follow out a new cycle or continue back to the original nexus of practice, that choice in itself will transform what you will learn and how you will participate in the nexus of practice.

Probably the most important points to be alert for are those moments along any one of the cycles (persons, places, interaction order, mediational means, practices, discourses) in which a transformation or resemiotization occurs. There tends to be a certain irreversibility about those moments which make it easier for actions to go forward rather than to return to reconsider. Those are also the moments in the cycles of a nexus analysis at which it is most likely that you could bring about social change because those are the moments at which changes are already occurring.

Discourse analysis

In the broadest sense of discourse analysis everything we have suggested up to now is a discourse analysis. Getting the answers to the questions suggested above entails interviewing and observing and then analyzing the results. Here in this section we focus on the somewhat narrow concept of discourse as language (or other semiotic system) in use. Discourse is present throughout a nexus analysis in at least six forms:

- speech of the participants in mediated actions (whether foregrounded or backgrounded);
- texts used as mediational means (whether foregrounded or backgrounded) such as books, magazines, train schedules, street signs, logos and brand names, directions for use on packages and other objects);
- images and other semiotic systems used as mediational means (pictures, gestures, manner of dressing, design of buildings and other places, works of art as focal points or as decorations);
- submerged in the historical body of the participants and in the practices in which they engage;
- submerged in the design of the built environment and objects;
- speech or writing or images of the analysts in conducting the nexus analysis (either within or apart from the moment of the mediated action).

The discourse analysis you will want to conduct on these six types of discourse will vary as widely as these types of discourse, of course. It may be useful to organize a discourse analysis around three main types of interrogation of the data as these are derived from critical discourse analysis, interactional sociolinguistics, and linguistic anthropology.

Critical discourse analysis is primarily concerned with questions of power between social interests in society and so critical discourse analysts most frequently work from the point of view of a social semiotic analysis of texts, speech, and images as reflexes of power interests. From this point of view the main question you would want to bring to each of these six forms of discourse is: *How are social power interests produced in this discourse?* Thus from this point of view you would want to ask of all of the material in the six different forms of discourse noted above:

- What are the big 'D' discourses present in this discourse? For example, the academic discourse of discourse analysis is inevitably present in any nexus analysis and so power relations between academics and other social groups within that society are also present.
- How are those discourses 'present' as overt (texts, talk, logos, signs, books, objects, technologies, people, etc.) and how are they submerged (as practice or historical body)? What power is implied in some participants (like the analyst) keeping notes and making recordings?

- What hidden discourses and dialogicalities are there? That is, what's not being said, being evaded, or so obvious that it's virtually invisible but nevertheless governing the entire action or activity?
- Where the discourses are overtly present, how are they designed and produced both in the sense of the material design and the sense of the social interests invested in their design?
- What are the systemic and power relations among the modes in which discourses are present?

Interactional sociolinguistics is primarily focused on interpersonal relationships, participation structure, positioning, alignments and identities. Although this work is often based mostly on talk, it is clear that participants in speech events also take up positions and alignments in relationship to the places they are in and the objects they are using in those places.

From this point of view the governing question is: *What positions and alignments are participants taking up in relationship to each other, to the discourses in which they are involved, the places in which these discourses occur, and to the mediational means they are using, and the mediated actions which they are taking?* Questions which will suggest lines of discourse analysis to follow are:

- How are cohesion, reference, topical relevance, etc. managed (i.e. single-topic classroom discourse as opposed to multi-threaded computer-mediated discourse)?
- How are alignments achieved in taking actions, particularly in moments of resemiotization?
- How are the participants in the nexus analysis positioned in respect to the analyst conducting the discourse analysis? This is particularly important in the opening stage of a nexus analysis (engaging the nexus of practice).
- What participation frameworks within what interaction orders are used to achieve consensual alignments at points of transformation? What genres such as narrative or conversation, or what styles and registers?

Linguistic anthropology has carried forward the interest in examining the relationships between language and culture on the one hand and between those and thought on the other. The primary strategy in examining these perennial questions consists of a very close analysis of the structures of the language used (grammatical, lexical, morphological, semantic, and genre) and through a broad comparative-contrastive analysis.

For a nexus analysis the central question here is: *How are socio-cultural or historical thought or cultural patterns in the language (or other semiotic systems such as images or gestures) and its genres and registers providing a template for the actions of participants in the nexus of practice?* Many of the most stimulating questions can be developed out of the traditional questions of the ethnography of communication such as:

- What genres, registers, keys are used by participants in taking this action?
- What kinds of speech events and speech situations are taken for granted or presupposed by the participants (including the analyst)? For example, is it common experience or rare for the participants to be tape recorded or video recorded as they act?
- How is this 'same' action carried out by other people in other social groups and at other times and places? Can the action be said to be playing out of cultural or social scripts?
- If there is reason to believe that there are social or cultural scripts, how have these been internalized as mediational means for taking this action?
- *Most obviously*, what languages are used in taking an action; are they the same or different from the language of analysis; does that make a difference in the templates being developed to analyze the action?

All of these discourse analysis questions should be asked of each of the six forms of discourse you find through your nexus analysis.

Motive analysis

Kenneth Burke's *Grammar of motives* (1969 [1945]) proposes that any action can be imagined and therefore talked about from any one of five points of view: The scene, the social actor (Burke's 'agent'), the mediational means (Burke's 'agency'), the mediated action (Burke's 'act'), and the purpose. Each of these points of view forms an explanatory position or a discursive motive for the action. Figure A.3 shows these five explanatory positions. A person who uses new media technology in conducting his business might explain this in terms of scene (what lies outside or prior to him or his interests) by saying he uses this technology because this is how people are doing things now. Or he might ascribe his motive to the social actor (himself, in this case) by saying that he is using this new technology because he wants to develop his own ability in this area. He could also explain his actions from the point of view of the mediational means by saying that it's the only means he has at his disposal for accomplishing his task. A motive that was located in the purpose would be to say something like: 'Even though I don't much like these new technologies, it's the most efficient way to get business done.' Perhaps more rarely, an action is explained in terms of the action itself, or an action sequence: 'It just seems like one thing led to another.'

A motive analysis is an aspect of discourse analysis which seeks to understand how participants, including the analyst, are positioning themselves in

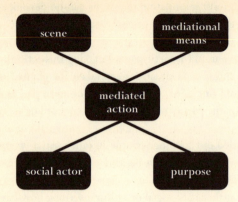

A.3 Burke's pentad of motives.

giving explanations for actions – are they taking on full responsibility, are they displacing responsibility to society or 'people', or perhaps to technology, or are they giving a purely goal-driven (purpose) explanation? Or are they, as in the last case, just claiming that things have just happened?

The goal of a motive analysis is *not to try to establish any fundamental underlying or 'true' motive.* The purpose of a motive analysis is twofold: (1) You want to establish how participants characterize actions and their explanations, and (2) You want to engage in those characterizations to see if taking a different perspective may change the nature of the actions themselves.

From this we can derive the basic question that should govern your motive analysis: *How do participants ascribe and allocate motives for their actions among the elements of a nexus analysis?*

- For each trajectory, person, object, etc. how is the grammar of motives exploited to account for or explain actions?
- How might it have been otherwise? It is a useful strategy simply to rephrase an explanation that is given as having an alternative motive.
- How much agreement is there among participants in ascribing or imputing these motives and explanations?
- What representative anecdotes, metaphors drive these actions?
- It is particularly important to look for shifts in the motive schemes being used. 'I wanted to do X because of Y (scene), but as it turned out, I really hated it (agent).'

Of course a motive analysis should be fully integrated within your discourse analysis from the start of the project. When you set out to initially identify your significant mediated action(s) upon which to focus, it is very likely that public discourse sources will consider that an action is motivated in very different ways from the ways individual social actors might motivate it. A public discourse source which is critical of international fast food chains might say that the action of eating a hamburger in Hong Kong is motivated by worldwide globalizing economics (scene); a source favorable to such economic entities might also attribute it to a scenic motive by saying it is because it is economical and nutritious food. A person buying and eating a hamburger in Hong Kong might say it reminds her of home (social actor motive). The point for a nexus analysis is that none of these is the *true* motive but the ascription of motive itself is a discursive strategy by which social actors position themselves in relationship to the actions which they take.

3 Changing the nexus of practice

November–December: In engaging the nexus of practice you located yourself as a participant in the nexus of practice which you are trying to understand and change. From the beginning your activities are part of the common activities of that nexus of practice. And you have begun to navigate the cycles of the nexus of practice through your work of documentation and analysis. These activities are actions such as recording, talking, writing, and acting through making documents, images, and other mediational means and through doing your discourse analysis. A nexus analysis departs from traditional ethnographic research by making these communications become actions which occur within the nexus of practice. A nexus analysis not only positions the analyst within the nexus of practice, it brings the other participants into the nexus analysis.

The final two months of a twelve-month nexus analysis are given over to analyzing change in the nexus of practice through re-engagement. This may occur through direct actions which are motivated by the nexus analysis or through engaging in the negotiations with that nexus of practice to bring your analysis and understanding back into the semiotic ecosystem. Figure A.1 which we presented at the outset of this fieldguide sketches out these ongoing relationships. We have located these activities here in the final two months only because it is at this time that you will have available the widest range of materials with which to do this re-engagement.

To put this in the terms we have discussed as navigating the nexus of practice, a nexus analysis begins by identifying crucial mediated actions and then begins to resemiotize or to bring about a semiotic transformation of those actions through the discursive activities of mapping the trajectories of people and places, mediational means and discourses, which constitute the mediated action. Those new mapping and analytical discourses are then further resemiotized as actions and mediational means which in the end become part of the historical body, inter-action order, and discourses in place of the nexus of practice itself.

Actions

One of the major ways in which the discourse analyst engages a nexus of practice and navigates within it is through the study of the discursive construction of motives and through negotiating a re-analysis of those motives.

This leads to the crucial final (and of course the first) question of a nexus analysis: *What actions can you take as a participant-analyst in this nexus of practice that will transform discourses into actions and actions into new discourses and practices?* This may be elaborated by asking:

* How does the discourse of nexus analysis enter into your nexus as one of the semiotic cycles?
* How is this cycle shifted or given further impetus?
* How is it transformed or resemiotized from discourse into action into mediational means that participants may use as the basis for further actions?

It is important to remember that in doing a nexus analysis you are not in any privileged position to bring about unilateral social change. What you have to contribute as an ethnographer or nexus analyst is the time and skills in analysis to open up and make visible links and connections among the many trajectories of historical bodies, discourses in place, and interaction order which constitute our social life. By your actions of analysis you are altering trajectories for yourself and for the others in the nexus of practice and that in itself is producing social change. What these changes are will always remain to be seen as the nexus of practice is transformed over the time of the nexus analysis.

References

The research and the theoretical framework we set out in this book rest upon a foundation in the academic literatures of several fields including anthropological linguistics, sociolinguistics, psychology, and literary criticism. In order to avoid excessive footnoting and citation in the main text of the book, notes and general comments on our sources are provided here in the first section. The second section gives the full publication citations for all sources used in the main text as well as in these notes.

Notes on references used

Preface

Dating the start of the Internet is difficult. While the forerunner of the World Wide Web was initiated in 1973, it is generally felt that the true Internet began with the establishment of the US National Science Foundation's NSFNET in 1986 (Cerf 2002). The projects we describe here took place about five years before this latter date.

Throughout this book we use the terms 'Alaska Native(s)' and 'Alaska Native people'. These are the terms which have been adopted by the first inhabitants of the place now known as Alaska as part of a larger project of building political unity among many different language and cultural entities throughout the State of Alaska. The establishment of the Alaska Federation of Natives so as to produce a single political block for negotiations between themselves and both the State of Alaska and the US Federal Government lent a certain legal weight to the adoption of this term as well. In Canada very similar political processes have led to the use of the term 'First Nations' or 'First Nations people'. In any event the term 'native' does not have derogatory meanings within the context of the Alaska Native socio-political activities we discuss here.

The bibliography for the course 'Language, Literacy, and Learning' was published as R. Scollon (1985b). Our working papers on dissipative structures are R. Scollon (1977) and S. Scollon (1977). In those papers we make reference to Prigogine (1976) and Glansdorff and Prigogine (1971). Prigogine's more influential 1984 book had not yet, of course, been published. Other publications of ours which are based on these projects are R. Scollon (1981a, 1981b, 1981c, 1982, 1983, 1985a), and R. Scollon and S. Scollon (1980a, 1980b, 1981, 1983, 1984a, 1984b, S. Scollon and R. Scollon 1984, 1988).

Chapter 1: Discourse analysis and social action

Bourdieu (1977, 1998) uses the term 'genesis amnesia'. Elias (2000 [1994]) used the term 'sociogenesis' in the 1940s in approximately the meaning we are suggesting for 'phylogenesis'. Vygotsky's (1978) term 'internalization' also captures the idea that we tend to lose our memory for the ways and circumstances under which discourses, texts, and technologies become part of our daily lives. We make use of this important concept in discussing cycles of discourse (Chapter 2).

Elsewhere (Scollon and Scollon 2003) we have presented idea that technologies of many kinds underpin social interaction from social technologies such as the formal interview (Fairclough 1996) to the built environment. The concept of the 'panopticon' which originated with Jeremy Bentham in the nineteenth century was brought into contemporary social theory by Foucault (1977).

Discourse analysis is, in a sense, a flowing together of many separate streams of origin including social theory, linguistics, literary criticism, anthropological linguistics, and sociolinguistics. Our use of the term (R. Scollon 1999, 2001a, 2001b; Scollon and Scollon 2001) is closest to the definitions put forward by Gee (Gee 1989, 1990; Gee, Hull, and Lankshear 1996; Gee 1999) and by Blommaert (Forthcoming).

The Federalist Papers (Hamilton, Madison, and Jay 1961 [1788]) are prescient in their anticipation of the consequences for socio-political life brought about by changing means of communication and transportation as the government of the US spread across the continent of North America.

Kenneth Burke's *Rhetoric of motives* (1950) as well as his *Grammar of motives* (1969 [1945]) were major influences in the thinking of Hymes (1966, 1972, 1974) and consequently in the development of the field now known as the ethnography of communication, although Burke's terms have been somewhat recast as well as shifted in their functions within the theory from a concern with motives of human action to descriptors. We prefer to remain with Burke's original intent to focus on questions of motive analysis. The terms 'circumference', 'circumferencing', 'motive analysis', and 'zone of identification' are developed from Burke.

We have developed our use of the terms 'mediational means' and 'cultural tools' primarily from the writings of James V. Wertsch (e.g. 1991, 1998) as we also have used 'mediated action' though these concepts are Wertsch's explication of the work primarily of Vygotsky (1978) and the terms are used widely by other researchers within a socio-cultural framework (e.g. Cole 1995; Cole and Griffin 1980; Cole and Wertsch 1996; Lantolf 1999).

Our use of the terms 'social action', 'site of engagement', 'nexus of practice', and 'social practice' are theoretically elaborated in R. Scollon (2001a, 2001b). The term 'historical body' is from Nishida (1958) and we prefer to use it over the more current term 'habitus' (Bourdieu 1977, 1998). The term 'discourses in place' is from Scollon and Scollon (2003). 'Interaction order' is Goffman's (1983) and we owe much to his career-long development of the sociological understanding of how people interact in face-to-face situations.

Dittmar and Bredel (1999) use the term 'radical social change' (RSC) for periods in history such as the relatively rapid change in Germany which was signaled by the collapse of the Berlin Wall.

Chapter 2: Cycles of discourse

The perspective we take on social action as an intersection of the interaction order (Goffman 1983), the historical body (Nishida 1958), and the discourses in place is more fully developed in Scollon and Scollon (2003). Nexus analysis is extended from the analysis of a nexus of practice (R. Scollon 2001a) and we have written about it also in R. Scollon (2002) and Scollon and Scollon (2002).

Conceptualizing discourse across longer timescales and through cycles of change and transformation derives from several sources. Our first reading about ecosystems was Holling (1976) and the other papers in that edited volume. Details about the fir-spruce-birch budworm ecosystem are from Holling (1976). Holling cites the following as his sources: Baskerville (1971), Wellington (1952), Morris (1963). Further details on the trees of Canada are from (Hosie 1969) and a general discussion of this ecosystem is in *Encyclopedia Britannica* 14: 1029.

The Swedish geographer Torsten Hägerstrand (1975, 1978; Carlstein, Parkes, and Thrift 1978) first suggested that it was important in the study of social phenomena to see a place as the coming together and linkage of multiple and separate trajectories of people and objects. Gu (1999, 2001) called our attention to this important work. We have also found Lemke (2000a, 2000b, 2002) and Star and Griesemer (1989) important in developing our thinking about timescaling of the trajectories of different cycles of discourse.

Iedema (2003), Mehan (1993), and Latour (1996) have all argued that there are cycles of transformation from discourse to objects to new discourses to new objects for which Iedema uses the term 'resemiotization'. Bernstein (1990) uses 'recontextualization' for what is a very similar concept, and the papers in Silverstein and Urban (1996) use 'entextualization' as does Blommaert (forthcoming). We have tried to integrate these various concepts into the idea of cycles of discourse and of ecosemiotic systems here and in the following chapters.

Chapter 3: From the essay to email: New media technology and social change

Papers in Bruce (2003) cover a wide range of topics from the relationships between new and old media technologies to critical commentaries on the nature of the World Wide Web, all from the point of view of examining literacy in our contemporary period. The idea of focusing on social action is set out theoretically and methodologically under the rubric of mediated discourse analysis (R. Scollon 1998, 2001a, b). Jones (2004 cf. p. 187) is an elegant statement of the problem of 'context' when communications are redistributed across both virtual and material spaces.

The platform event as one form of the interaction order is from Goffman (1983) and the panopticon is from Foucault (1977). Rogers and Agarwala-Rogers (1976) present a variety of models including the 'hub-and-wheel' structure for the organization of group communication which were useful in our first thinking about how classrooms were altered with the introduction of media technologies.

On the process of selection among discourses in place see Norris (2002, 2004, cf. p. 188, in press). The latter one of these citations provides a useful theoretical and methodological framework for analyzing these multiple discourses being carried out simultaneously in an elaborate weave of foregrounded and backgrounded communications. For our use of 'essayist literacy' see Scollon and Scollon (1981).

Halliday (1978, 1985) gives an explication of the three unified functions of language within the framework of systemic-functional grammar.

Edward T. Hall (1959, 1969) introduced the idea that how we communicate with others is tightly linked to the distances we stand or sit apart as we communicate under the general rubric of proxemics. More recently the term multimodal discourse analysis is used to cover some of the same territory (de Saint-Georges, 2004; Kress and van Leeuwen 1996, 2001; Kress, Jewitt, Ogborn, and Tsatsarelis 2001; Norris 2002, 2004 in press); Scollon and Scollon 2003.

Chapter 4: Engaging the nexus of practice: Oil, the Cold War, and social change in Alaska in the 1980s

Telephone calls and email requests to both the Russian Embassy in Washington, DC, and to various departments of the US government were answered politely but did not result in providing us with the length of the Russia/US border. First responses were that the answerer didn't know but would find out. This was followed by saying that, apparently, it wasn't possible to get that information. Our statement here is based on the often stated 'fact' about Alaska. It remains, alas, an undocumented, perhaps undocumentable, fact.

Alaska population numbers for 1981/2 are from the Alaska Population Overview, 1999 estimate, May 2000. Juneau: AK: Alaska Department of Labor and Workforce Development, Research and Analysis Section, Demographics Unit.

The development of studies of gatekeeping encounters was strongly stimulated by the work of Frederick Erickson (Erickson 1976, Erickson and Shultz 1982) and John Gumperz (Gumperz, Jupp, and Roberts 1979), both of whom visited our projects in Alaska on several occasions. The videotape (with Eliza Jones: *Interethnic communication*, Number Five in the Series of videotapes on language in Alaska, *Talking Alaska*. Fairbanks, Alaska: Alaska Native Language Center, 1979) was modeled on the Gumperz, Jupp, and Roberts *Crosstalk* video.

Chapter 5: Navigating the nexus of practice: Mapping the circumferences and timescales of human action

The study of their child by William and Teresa Labov was published as Labov and Labov (1978). The stories of Gaither Paul were first printed by the Alaska Native Language Center (Paul 1980). Other sources on Chipewyan stories are Scollon and Scollon (1979) and Li and Scollon (1976).

Chapter 6: Navigating the nexus of practice: Discourse analysis and institutional power

Conversational inference was introduced by John Gumperz (1977a, 1977b, 1978) and his students, notably Tannen (Gumperz and Tannen 1979; Tannen 1984). Levinson extended this idea to include what he calls 'interactive intelligence', the process by which one makes inferences about another's behavior on the basis of one's own introspection about action.

Chapter 7: Changing the nexus of practice: Technology, social change, and activist discourse analysis

An important paper by Goody (1978) is our source on the two functions (information and control) of questions and, therefore, of the role of questions in regulating social interaction.

In our reading of their work the discursive psychologists (e.g., Edwards and Potter 1992; Harré 1994, 1998; Harré and Gillett 1994; Wetherell, Taylor, and Yates 2001) share much with Burke's interest in developing a rhetoric of motives though to our knowledge they have not been directly influenced by his writing.

References cited

Astin, Alexander W. (1975) *Preventing students from dropping out*. San Francisco: Jossey-Bass Publishers.

Baskerville, G. L. (1971) *The fir-spruce-birch forest and the budworm*. Report, Forestry Service, Fredericton, NB: Canada Department of Environment.

Bateson, Gregory (1979) *Mind and nature: A necessary unity*. New York: E. P. Dutton.

Berger, Peter, Brigitte Berger, and Hansfried Kellner (1973) *The homeless mind: Modernization and consciousness*. New York: Random House.

Bergson, Henri (1910) *Time and free will: An essay on the immediate data of consciousness*. F. L. Pogson (tr.). London: George Allen and Unwin, Ltd.

Bernstein, Basil (1990) *The structure of pedagogic discourse: Class, codes and control, Vol. VI*. London: Routledge.

Blommaert, Jan (forthcoming) *Discourse: A critical introduction*. Cambridge: Cambridge University Press.

Bourdieu, Pierre (1977) *Outline of a theory of practice*. Richard Nice (tr.) Cambridge: Cambridge University Press.

Bourdieu, Pierre (1998) *Practical reason: On the theory of action*. Stanford: Stanford University Press.

Bruce, Bertram C. (2003) *Literacy in the information age: Inquiries into meaning making with new technologies*. Newark, DE: International Reading Association.

Burke, Kenneth (1950) *A rhetoric of motives*. Englewood Cliffs, NJ: Prentice-Hall.

Burke, Kenneth. 1965 [1935]. *Permanence and change: An anatomy of purpose*. Indianapolis: The Bobbs-Merrill Company, Inc.

Burke, Kenneth (1969 [1945]) *A grammar of motives*. Englewood Cliffs, NJ: Prentice-Hall.

Carlstein, Tommy, Don Parkes, and Nigel Thrift (1978) The Lund school: Introduction. In Tommy Carlstein, Don Parkes, and Nigel Thrift (eds) *Human activity and time geography*. New York: John Wiley and Sons. 117–121.

Cerf, Vint (2002) A brief history of the internet and related networks. http://www.isoc.org/internet/history/cerf.shtml. Accessed on October 26, 2003. Last updated November 18, 2001.

Chapple, Eliot D. (1939) Quantitative analysis of the interaction of individuals. *Proceedings of the national Academy of Sciences* 25: 58–76.

Chapple, Eliot D. (1970) *Cultural and biological man*. New York: Holt, Rinehart and Winston, Inc.

Chapple, Eliot D. (1980) The unbounded reaches of anthropology as a research science, and some working hypotheses. Distinguished Lecture for 1979. *American Anthropologist* 82.4: 741–58.

Cole, Michael (1995) The supra-individual envelope of development: Activity and practice, situation and context. *New Directions for Child Development* 67, Spring: 105–18.

Cole, Michael and Peg Griffin (1980) Cultural amplifiers reconsidered. In David R. Olson (ed.) *The social foundations of language and thought: Essays in honor of Jerome S. Bruner*. New York: W. W. Norton and Company.

Cole, Michael and James V. Wertsch (1996) *Contemporary implications of Vygotsky and Luria*. Worcester, MA: Clark University Press.

Cutler, Howard A. (1981) Convocation speech. University of Alaska, Fairbanks. January 22, 1981.

De Saint-Georges, Ingrid (2004) Materiality in discourse: The influence of space and layout in making meaning. In Philip LeVine and Ron Scollon (eds) *Discourse analysis and technology: Multimodal discourse analysis. Georgetown University Round Table on Languages and Linguistics 2002*. Washington, DC: Georgetown University Press. 71–87.

Dittmar, Norbert and Ursula Bredel (1999) *Die Sprachmauer*. Berlin: Weidler Verlag.

Edwards, Derek and Jonathan Potter (1992) *Discursive psychology*. London: Sage.

Elias, Norbert (2000 [1994]) *The civilizing process: Sociogenetic and psychogenetic investigations*. Edmund Jephcott (tr.) with some notes and corrections by the author. Revised edition ed. Eric Dunning, Johan Goudsblom, and Stephen Mennell. Oxford: Blackwell.

Encyclopedia *Britannica* (1992) *The New Encyclopedia Britannica*, 15th edition. Chicago: Encyclopedia Britannica.

Erickson, Frederick (1976) Gatekeeping encounters: A social selection process. In P. R. Sanday (ed.) *Anthropology and the public interest: Fieldwork and theory*. New York: Academic Press.

Erickson, Frederick (1980) Timing and context in everyday discourse: Implications for the study of referential and social meaning. *Sociolinguistic Working Paper Number 67*. Austin, TX: Southwest Educational Development Laboratory.

Erickson, Frederick and Jeffrey Shultz (1982) *The counselor as gatekeeper: Social interaction in interviews*. New York: Academic Press.

Fairclough, Norman (1996) Technologization of discourse. In Carmen Rosa Caldas-Coulthard and Malcolm Coulthard (eds) *Texts and practices: Readings in critical discourse analysis*. London: Routledge.

Foucault, Michel (1977) *Discipline and punish*. New York: Pantheon Books.

Gee, James Paul (1989) Literacy, discourse, and linguistics: Essays by James Paul Gee. *Journal of Education* 171.1.

Gee, James Paul (1990) *Social linguistics and literacies*. London: The Falmer Press.

Gee, James Paul (1999) *An introduction to discourse analysis: Theory and method*. London: Routledge.

Gee, James Paul, Glynda Hull, and Colin Lankshear (1996) *The new work order: Behind the language of the new capitalism*. Boulder, CO: Westview Press.

Glansdorff, P. and Ilya Prigogine (1971) *Thermodynamic theory of structure, stability and fluctuations*. New York: Wiley-Interscience.

Goffman, Erving (1961) *Asylums*. Garden City: Anchor Books.

Goffman, Erving (1983) The interaction ritual. *American Sociological Review* 48: 1–19.

Goody, Esther N. (1978) Towards a theory of questions. In Ester N. Goody (ed.) *Questions and politeness: Strategies in social interaction*. New York: Cambridge University Press.

Gu, Yueguo (1999) Towards a model of situated discourse analysis. In Ken Turner (ed.) *The semantics/pragmatics interface from different points of view*. Oxford: Elsevier Science.

Gu, Yueguo (2001) Towards an understanding of workplace discourse. In Christopher Candlin (ed.) *Theory and practice in professional discourse*. Hong Kong: The City University of Hong Kong Press.

Gumperz, John (1977a) Sociocultural knowledge in confersational inference. In Muriel Saville-Troike (ed.) *28th Annual Roundtable on Language and Linguistics*. Washington, DC: Georgetown University Press. Revised version published in John J. Gumperz (1982) *Discourse strategies*. New York: Cambridge University Press.

Gumperz, John (1977b) The conversational analysis of interethnic communication. In E. Lamar Ross (ed.) *Interethnic communication. Proceedings of the Southern Anthropological Society*, University of Georgia, Athens: University of Georgia Press.

Gumperz, John (1978) The retrieval of sociocultural knowledge in conversation. Paper presented at the American Anthropological Association, November 1978. Revised version published in John J. Gumperz (1982) *Discourse strategies*. New York: Cambridge University Press.

Gumperz, John, Tom C. Jupp, and Celia Roberts (1979) *Crosstalk: A study of cross-cultural communication*. Southall: National Center for Industrial Language Training.

Gumperz, John and Deborah Tannen (1979) Individual and social differences in language use. In Charles J. Fillmore, Daniel Kempler, and William S.-Y. Wang (eds) *Individual differences in language ability and language behavior*. New York: Academic Press. Revised version published in John J. Gumperz (1982) *Discourse strategies*. New York: Cambridge University Press.

Hägerstrand, Torsten (1975) Space, time and human conditions. In A. Karlqvist, L. Lundqvist, and F. Snickars (eds) *Dynamic allocation of urban space*. Farnborough: Saxon House.

Hägerstrand, Torsten (1978) Survival and arena. In Tommy Carlstein, Don Parkes, and Nigel Thrift (eds) *Human activity and time geography*. New York: John Wiley and Sons. 122–45.

Hall, Edward T. (1959) *The silent language*. Garden City: Doubleday.

Hall, Edward T. (1969) *The hidden dimension*. Garden City: Doubleday.

Halliday, M. A. K. (1978) *Language as social semiotic*. London: Edward Arnold.

Halliday, M. A. K. (1985) *An introduction to functional grammar*. London: Edward Arnold.

Hamilton, Alexander, James Madison, and John Jay (1961 [1788]) *The federalist papers*. New York: Mentor.

Harré, Rom (1994) Is there still a problem about the self? *Communication Yearbook* 17: 55–73.

Harré, Rom (1998) *The singular self: An introduction to the psychology of personhood*. London: Sage.

Harré, Rom and Grant Gillett (1994) *The discursive mind*. Thousand Oaks, CA: Sage.

Harvey, David (1996) *Justice, nature and the geography of difference*. Oxford: Blackwell.

Heath, Shirley Brice (1983) *Ways with words*. New York: Cambridge University Press.

Hiltz, Starr Roxanne and Murray Turoff (1978) *The network nation: Human communication via computer*. Reading, MA: Addison-Wesley Publishing Company, Inc.

Holling, C. S. (1976) Resilience and stability of ecosystems. In Erich Jantsch and Conrad H. Waddington (eds) *Evolution and consciousness: Human systems in transition*. Reading, MA: Addison-Wesley Publishing Company.

Hosie, R. C. (1969) *Native trees of Canada*. Ottawa: Queen's Printer for Canada.

Hymes, Dell (1966) Two types of linguistic relativity. In William Bright (ed.) *Sociolinguistics: proceedings of the UCLA Sociolinguistics Conference, 1964*. The Hague: Mouton. 114–67.

Hymes, Dell (1972) Models of the interaction of language and social life. In John J. Gumperz and Dell Hymes (eds) *Directions in sociolinguistics: The ethnography of communication*. New York: Holt, Rinehart, and Winston.

Hymes, Dell (1974) *Foundations in sociolinguistics: An ethnographic approach*. Philadelphia: University of Pennsylvania Press.

Iedema, Rick (2003) Multimodality, resemiotisation: Extending the analysis of discourse as multi-semiotic practice. *Visual Communication* 2.1: 29–57.

Johansen, Robert, Jacques Vallee, and Kathleen Spangler (1979) *Electronic meetings: Technical alternatives and social choices*. Reading, MA: Addison-Wesley Publishing Company.

Jones, Rodney Hale (2004) The problem of context in computer-mediated communication. In Philip LeVine and Ron Scollon (eds) *Discourse analysis and technology: Multimodal discourse analysis. Georgetown University Round Table on Languages and Linguistics 2002*. Washington, DC: Georgetown University Press. 20–33.

Kress, Gunther, Carey Jewitt, Jon Ogborn, and Charalampos Tsatsarelis (2001) *Multimodal teaching and learning*. London: Continuum.

Kress, Gunther and Theo van Leeuwen (1996) *Reading images: The grammar of visual design*. London: Routledge.

Kress, Gunther and Theo van Leeuwen (2001) *Multimodality*. London: Edward Arnold.

Labov, William and Labov, Teresa (1978) The phonetics of 'cat' and 'mama'. *Language* 54.4: 816–52.

Lanham, Richard (1983) *Literacy and the survival of humanism*. New Haven: Yale University Press.

Lantolf, James P. (1999) Second culture acquisition: Cognitive considerations. In Eli Hinkel (ed.), *Culture in second language teaching and learning*. Cambridge: Cambridge University Press. 28–46.

Latour, Bruno (1996) On interobjectivity. *Mind, Culture, and Activity* 3.4: 228–45.

Lemke, Jay L. (2000a) Across the scales of time: Artifacts, activities, and meanings in ecosocial systems. *Mind, Culture, and Activity*, 7.4: 273–90.

Lemke, Jay L. (2000b) Opening up closure: Semiotics across scales. In Jerry L. R. Chandler and Gertrudis Van de Vijver (eds) *Closure: Emergent organizations and their dynamics*. New York: The New York Academy of Sciences.

Lemke, Jay L. (2002) Travels in hypermodality. *Visual Communication* 1.3: 299–325.

Levinson, Steven C. (1990) *Interactional biases in human thinking*. Working Paper No. 3, Project Group Cognitive Anthropology, Max Planck Gesellschaft, Berlin.

Li, Fang-Kuei and Ron Scollon (1976) *Chipewyan texts*. Institute of History and Philology, Academia Sinica, Special Publications No. 71. Nankang, Taipei, Taiwan.

Martz, Cecilia U. (1981) You are welcome: A study of cross-cultural sensitivity in four university classrooms. Master's Project, Center for Cross-cultural Studies, University of Alaska, Fairbanks.

Mehan, Hugh (1993) Beneath the skin and between the ears: A case study in the politics of representation. In Seth Chaiklin and Jean Lave (eds) *Understanding practice: Perspectives on activity and context*. Cambridge: Cambridge University Press. 241–68.

Morris, R. F. (1963) The dynamics of epidemic spruce budworm populations. *Mem. Entomological society of Canada* 31: 1–332.

Nishida, Kitaroo (1958) *Intelligibility and the philosophy of nothingness*. Tokyo: Maruzen Co. Ltd.

Norris, Sigrid (2002) The orchestration of identities through multiple modes. Paper presented at the Sociolinguistics Symposium 14, Gent, April 4–6.

Norris, Sigrid (in press) *Analyzing multimodal interaction: A methodological framework*. London: Routledge.

Norris, Sigrid (2004) Multimodal discourse analysis: A conceptual framework. In Philip LeVine and Ron Scollon (eds) *Discourse analysis and technology: Multimodal discourse analysis. Georgetown University Round Table on Languages and Linguistics 2002*. Washington, DC: Georgetown University Press. 101–15.

Paul, Gaither (1980) *Stories for my grandchildren*. Fairbanks: Alaska Native Language Center.

Prigogine, Ilya (1976) Order through fluctuation: self-organization and social system. In Erich Jantsch and Conrad H. Waddington (eds), *Evolution and consciousness: Human systems in transition*. Reading, MA: Addison-Wesley Publishing Company. 93–133.

Prigogine, Ilya (1984) *Order out of chaos: Man's new dialogue with nature*. New York: Bantam Books.

Rogers, Everett M. and Rehka Agarwala-Rogers (1976) *Communication in organizations*. New York: The Free Press.

Ruesch, Jurgen and Gregory Bateson (1968 [1951]) *Communication: The social matrix of psychiatry*. New York: W. W. Norton & Company.

Ruppert, James and John W. Bernet (2001) *Our voices: Native stories of Alaska and the Yukon*. Lincoln, NE: University of Nebraska Press.

Saville-Troike, Muriel (2002) *The ethnography of communication*. Third edition. Oxford: Basil Blackwell.

Schreiber, Daniel (1967) *Profile of the school dropout*. New York: Random House.

Scollon, Ron (1976) *Conversations with a one year old: A case study of the developmental foundation of syntax*. Honolulu: University Press of Hawaii.

Scollon, Ron (1977) Dissipative structures, Chipewyan consonants, and the modern consciousness. *Department of Linguistics, University of Hawaii: Working Papers in Linguistics*, 9.3: 43–64.

Scollon, Ron (1981a) Human knowledge and the institution's knowledge. Final report to the National Institute of Education on grant No. G-80-0185 'Communication Patterns and Retention in a Public University'.

Scollon, Ron (1981b) Computers and linear thinking. *The Computing Teacher* 9.4: 59–60.

Scollon, Ron (1981c) The rhythmic integration of ordinary talk. In Deborah Tannen (ed.) *Georgetown University Roundtable on Languages and linguistics 1981*. Washington, DC: Georgetown University Press. 335–49.

Scollon, Ron (1982) Gatekeeping: Access or retention. Southwest Educational Development Laboratory, *Working Papers in Sociolinguistics* 96.

Scollon, Ron (1983) Computer conferencing: A medium for appropriate time. *Quarterly Newsletter of the Laboratory of Comparative Human Cognition* 5.3: 67–8.

Scollon, Ron (1985a) The land, always our motive: A report on the Alaska Humanities Forum computer network. *Federation Reports* 8.1: 17–22.

Scollon, Ron (1985b) Language, literacy, and learning: An annotated bibliography. In David R. Olson, Nancy Torrance, and Angela Hildyard (eds) *Literacy, language, and learning: The nature and consequences of reading and writing*. New York: Cambridge University Press.

Scollon, Ron (1998) *Mediated discourse as social interaction: A study of news discourse*. New York: Longman.

Scollon, Ron (1999) Mediated discourse and social interaction. *Research on Language and Social Interaction* 32.1&2: 149–54.

Scollon, Ron (2001a) *Mediated discourse: The nexus of practice*. London: Routledge.

Scollon, Ron (2001b) Action and text: Toward an integrated understanding of the place of text in social (inter)action. In Ruth Wodak and Michael Meyer (eds) *Methods in critical discourse analysis*. London: Sage, 139–83.

Scollon, Ron (2002) Intercultural communication as nexus analysis. *Logos and Language: Journal of General Linguistics and Language Theory* III.2: 1–17.

Scollon, Ron and Suzanne B. K. Scollon (1979) *Linguistic convergence: An ethnography of speaking at Fort Chipewyan, Alberta*. New York: Academic Press.

Scollon, Ron and Suzanne Wong Scollon (1980a) Ethnic stereotyping: Some problems in Athabaskan–English interethnic communication. *Method: Alaska perspectives* 2.2: 15–17.

Scollon, Ron and Suzanne Scollon (1980b) Literacy as focused interaction. *Quarterly Newsletter of the Laboratory of Comparative Human Cognition* 2.2: 26–9.

Scollon, Ron and Suzanne Scollon (1981) *Narrative, literacy and face in interethnic communication*. Norwood, NJ: Ablex Publishing Corporation.

Scollon, Ron and Suzanne B. K. Scollon (1983) Face in interethnic communication. In Jack Richards and Richard Schmidt (eds) *Language and communication*. London: Longman.

Scollon, Ron and Suzanne B. K. Scollon (1984a) Language dilemmas in Alaska. *Society* 24.4: 77–81.

Scollon, Ron and Suzanne Wong Scollon (1984b) Cooking it up and boiling it down: Abstracts in Athabaskan children's story retellings. In Deborah Tannen (ed.) *Coherence in spoken and written discourse*. Norwood, NJ: Ablex Publishing Corporation.

Scollon, Ron and Suzanne Wong Scollon (2001) *Intercultural communication: A discourse approach*. Second edition. Oxford: Basil Blackwell.

Scollon, Ron and Suzie Wong Scollon (2002) Nexus analysis: Expanding the circumference of discourse analysis. PARC Forum, Dec. 12, 2002. Palo Alto Research Center.

Scollon, Ron and Suzie Wong Scollon (2003) *Discourses in place: Language in the material world*. London: Routledge.

Scollon, Suzanne (1977) Langue, idiolect, and speech community: Three views of the language at Fort Chipewyan, Alberta. *Department of Linguistics, University of Hawaii: Working Papers in Linguistics*, 9.3: 65–76.

Scollon, Suzanne (1981) Professional development seminar: a model for making higher education more culturally sensitive. Presented at annual meeting of the National Association for Asian and Pacific American Education, Honolulu, Hawaii. Available on the Internet as: http://www.eric.gov.Acquisition number ED238662.

Scollon, Suzanne B. K. (1982) Reality set, socialization and linguistic convergence. Doctoral dissertation. Department of Linguistics, University of Hawaii.

Scollon, Suzanne (1998) Methodological assumptions in intercultural communication. In Bates L. Hoffer and John H. Koo (eds) *Cross-cultural communication: East and West*, San Antonio, TX: Institute for Cross-cultural Research, Trinity University. 104–9.

Scollon, Suzanne and Ron Scollon (1984) Run trilogy: Can Tommy read? In Hillel Goelmen, Antoinette Oberg, and Frank Smith (eds) *Awakening to literacy*. Exeter, NH: Heinemann Educational Books.

Scollon, Suzanne and Ron Scollon (1988) Face in interethnic telecommunications at the University of Alaska: Computer conferencing as non-focused interaction. In Regna Darnell and Michael K. Foster (eds) *Native North American Interaction Patterns*. Hull, Quebec: Canadian Museum of Civilization, National Museums Canada.

Silverstein, Michael and Greg Urban (1996) *Natural histories of discourse*. Chicago: University of Chicago Press.

Star, Susan Leigh and James R. Griesemer (1989) Institutional ecology, 'translations' and boundary objects: Amateurs and professionals in Berkeley's Museum of Vertebrate Zoology, 1907–39. *Social Studies of Science* 19: 387–420.

Tannen, Deborah (1984) *Conversational style*. Norwood, NJ: Ablex Publishing Corporation.

Taylor, Steven J. and Robert Bogdan (1980) Defending illusions: The institution's struggle for survival. *Human Organization*, 39.3: 209–18.

Vygotsky, L. S. (1978) *Mind in society: The development of higher psychological processes*. Cambridge, MA: Harvard University Press.

Wellington, W. G. (1952) Air mass climatology of Ontario north of Lake Huron and Lake Superior before outbreaks of the spruce budworm and the forest tree caterpillar, *Canadian Journal of Zoology* 30: 114–27.

Wertsch, James V. (1991) *Voices of the mind: A sociocultural approach to mediated action*. Cambridge, MA: Harvard University Press.

Wertsch, James V. (1998) *Mind as action*. New York: Oxford University Press.

Wetherell, Margaret, S. Taylor, and S. J. Yates (2001) *Discourse theory and practice: A reader*. London: Sage.

Wittgenstein, Ludwig (1980) *Remarks on the Philosophy of Psychology*, 1.78, cited in John Shotter, *Cultural politics of everyday life: Social constructionism, rhetoric and knowing of the third kind*. Toronto and Buffalo: University of Toronto Press (1993). 83.

Worth, Sol and John Adair (1997) *Through Navajo eyes*. Albuquerque: University of New Mexico Press.

Index

academic discourse 5, 6, 7
action: and attitudes 144; identity
   production 145; mediated action 11,
   12, 127, 181; semiotic cycles 166–7;
   and social change 62–5, 63*f*, 92, 178
Adair, John 98
affect 144
Agarwala-Rogers, Rehka 182
agent motives 11
Alaska: in the 1980s 16, 69–71; border
   with Russia ix, 70, 182–3; discourse
   problems 59; literacy 36–7;
   organizations xi, 71–3; population
   72, 81, 183; socio-political life 7–8,
   70–1; technology 7–8, 69–70; *see also*
   Alaska Natives
Alaska Federation of Natives 179
Alaska Humanities Forum 138
Alaska Native Claims Settlement Act ix,
   70
Alaska Native Corporations 88
Alaska Native Language Center (ANLC)
   ix, xii–xiii, 70, 71, 76, 82, 93, 183
Alaska Native Studies Program (ANS)
   xii–xiii
Alaska Natives 81, 179; discrimination
   against 74, 75, 81, 82, 110–11,
   116, 117–18, 140; language use 82;
   leadership/pacemaking 132–3; social
   interaction 76, 85–7, 95–6, 132–3;
   students 75, 110–11, 117–18, 128–9,
   130, 133; University of Alaska 81;
   see also Athabaskan communication
Alaska Purchase 70

Alaska State Judicial Council 88, 140
amnesia 3, 180
ANLC *see* Alaska Native Language Center
ANS (Alaska Native Studies Program)
   xii–xiii
Aristotle 156
Astin, Alexander W. 115, 131
Athabaskan communication 71, 79, 80;
   beadwork booklet 72, 97–101, 98*f*,
   99*f*, 100*f*, 140; discourse system
   92–102, 102*f*, 103–4; language
   acquisition 79, 92–3; social interaction
   95, 96; socialization practices 102;
   storytelling 93–5, 102; terminology
   91–2
attitudes and values 144–5
audio conferences 1–2, 6, 56

Barnhardt, Carol xiv, 76, 77
Bateson, Gregory 129
beadwork booklet 72, 97–101, 98*f*, 99*f*,
   100*f*, 140
behavior: explanations of 129–30; human
   vs. institutional 74; students 128–9
Bentham, Jeremy 180
Berger, Brigitte 80
Berger, Peter 80
Bergson, Henri 147
Bernet, John W. 93
Bernstein, Basil 181–2
bilingual education ix, 71, 140; *see also*
   beadwork booklet
Bless-Boenish, Bonnie xiv
Blommaert, Jan 5, 90, 182